MIMESIS
INTERNATIONAL

HISTORY
n. 9

Silvia Vacirca

FASHIONING SUBMISSION

Documenting Fashion, Taste and Identity in WWII Italy through
Bellezza Mensile dell'alta moda e della vita italiana

This volume is published with the support of the Department of History, Anthropology, Religions, Art, Media and Performing Arts (SARAS), Università La Sapienza, Rome.

© 2023 – MIMESIS INTERNATIONAL
www.mimesisinternational.com
e-mail: info@mimesisinternational.com

Isbn: 9788869774218
Book series: *History*, n. 9

© MIM Edizioni Srl
P.I. C.F. 02419370305

Cover image: Models, Italrayon Fashion Show, Milan Trade Fair 1934, Historical Archive, Fondazione Fiera Milano.

TABLE OF CONTENTS

INTRODUCTION	7
1 TOWARDS A TOTALITARIAN FASHION	21
1.1 *Ente nazionale della moda*	24
1.2 "*Marca di garanzia*" and "*Marca d'oro*"	34
2 DRESSING ITALIAN	39
2.1 Fashioning Fascism	42
2.2 There's a War Raging... But You Wouldn't Know It	56
2.2 The Clothing Card	70
3 ALL THAT IS AIRY TURNS INTO STONE: *BELLEZZA*'S CODE OF ELEGANCE	99
3.1 The Birth of *Bellezza*	99
3.2 Costuming Fashion	122
3.3 "Behind Closed Shutters"	149
4 "WILL ALL WOMEN WEAR LACE COLLARS?": FILM FASHIONS	167
4.1 The Cinematic Venus	167
4.2 Desiring Fascism: The Garment as Spectacle	175
BIBLIOGRAPHY	189
INDEX	215
ACKNOWLEDGEMENTS	221

INTRODUCTION

A little more than six months after Italy declared war on France and England on the 10th of June 1940, the *Ente nazionale della moda* ("National Fashion Agency")[1] launched *Bellezza Mensile dell'alta moda e della vita italiana* ("Beauty, A Monthly Fashion Magazine of Haute Couture and Italian Life"), the first Italian fashion magazine aiming to position itself at the level of *Vogue* and *Harper's Bazaar*, which on the eve of the Second World War were the two most important international fashion magazines. Inside *Bellezza*'s pages, the protagonists of contemporary Italian culture helped sculpt the myth of Italian fascist *alta moda* ("high fashion").

Fashion, along with plastic surgery, gymnastics and mastery of the body, was called upon to participate in the creation of the "new humanity" that fascism aimed to shape. A sartorial fascism "of stone":[2]

> Barely hidden by the black bathing suit, her figure blossoming into graceful curves like a beautiful drawing, on an elastic frame that feels ready to leap, jump, dive. [...] The nose, the whole face clearly defined, without blemishes and without allusions, was the only thing that recalled the flesh.[3]

---

1   Fascism constituted the *Ente nazionale della moda* in 1935, establishing its offices in Turin.
2   Gentile, E., *Fascismo di pietra*, Laterza, Bari 2007.
3   Ferro, M., *Ritratto di donna*, Turin 1933, cit. in Di Castro, F., (edited by), *L'alta moda capitale 1900-1960. Torino e le sartorie torinesi*, Fabbri, Turin 1991, p. 31.

Nothing should be further from stone than fashion and in 1944, architect Gio Ponti and cosmopolitan countess Elena Celani – nicknamed "Bichette" – had in fact debated from the pages of *Stile*[4] and *Bellezza* whether with the advent of fascism, fashion had not fallen out of fashion and whether it should petrify into "costume."

Despite the cultural relevance and prestige of *Bellezza*, the involvement of the *crème de la crème* of the Italian intellectual, cosmopolitan and artistic elite of the time and the enthusiasm and fond memories of those who actively participated in it, *Bellezza* has never been – with some notable exceptions – the focus of much attention. Furthermore, the meaning of fashion under fascism has for the most been misunderstood, variously interpreted as a legacy of the bourgeois patriarchal state opposed by the regime, a display of empty rhetoric or a continuation of the artistic and decorative culture of the Italian Renaissance.

In this book I will outline some aspects of the mythology of fashion created by fascism during the Second World War through the pages of *Bellezza* and other previously unexamined sources. I will look at fashion photographs as documents that record both the existence in Italy of *alta moda* garments and the emergence of fashion photography itself.[5] The study of the history of fashion admits of a range of possible approaches,[6] each one casting a different light upon its subject: journals are often used as ancillary historical sources, consulted to support a broader and more complex theoretical construction or history, while this book puts the fashion magazine itself in the spotlight, considering *Bellezza* both as container and vehicle for representations of high fashion,

---

4   A journal "of ideas, of life, of events and above all of art" created and directed by Gio Ponti for publisher Garzanti in January 1941.

5   For a comparison between the photographic culture of Parisian and Italian fashion, see Quintavalle, A. C., "Moda: le tre culture", in Bianchino, G., et al., (edited by), *La moda italiana. Le origini dell'alta moda e la maglieria*, Electa, Milan 1985, pp. 11-57.

6   Riello, G., "Per una storia della moda. Concetti, oggetti e cultura materiale", *Venezia arti*, 25, December 2016. For a critical guide to the use of historical sources, see Muzzarelli, M. G., Riello, G., Brandi, E. T., (edited by), *Moda. Storia e storie*, Bruno Mondadori, Milan 2010.

as a material artefact with its own history and as an object of individual cultural consumption.

Many historians, as well as much of the media, believe that an ongoing love affair exists between fashion and Italian identity. The Made in Italy brand is considered as synonymous with "sophisticated taste, elegance and attention to detail".[7] But understanding fashion during the fascist period as the manifestation of a centuries-old natural link between Italian identity and the realm of the aesthetic would neglect the specific character of the culture and experience of the dictatorship which, while depriving Italians of their freedom, mobilised national and local cultures, the arts and fashion at the service of the totalitarian state and the construction of a "new humanity."[8]

The very evocation of the Renaissance in the culture of fascism had a political function. Jacqueline Musacchio has decoded the deeper meaning of the revival of the Renaissance technique of majolica (a form of lead-glazed pottery) in the gifts given to new mothers for their contribution to the demographic campaign,[9] and Claudia Lazzaro has revealed how the rebirth of the Italian Renaissance garden under Mussolini should be seen as a manifestation of the cult of Italian identity, a symptom of the fascist search for a new national identity based on the reconstruction of a mythologised past.[10]

Historian Victoria De Grazia has seen the regime's attitude towards women as a reflection of a patriarchal and capitalist culture "which adds nothing original to the notions that have always been widespread regarding women and which have been

---

7   Ivi, p. 1.
8   Gentile, E., "L'italiano nuovo per la nuova civiltà", in *Il culto del littorio*, Laterza, Rome-Bari 1993, pp. 16-174; Berezin., M., *Making the Fascist Self: The Political Culture of Interwar Italy*, Cornell UP, Ithaca-New York 1997.
9   Musacchio, J. M., "Mussolini, Mothers and Maiolica," pp. 145-156, in Lazzaro, C., Crum, Roger J., (edited by), *Donatello among the Blackshirts. History and Modernity in the Visual Culture of Fascist Italy*, Cornell UP, Ithaca-London 2005.
10 Lazzaro, C., "Politicizing a National Garden Tradition: The Italianness of the Italian Garden", in ivi, pp. 157-172.

absorbed by women themselves."[11] According to this point of view, Italian female culture in the years between the two world wars was stretched between an emerging modern cosmopolitan mass-commercial culture embodied by fashion and the leisure industry and the Catholic cultural tradition to which fascism, in essence, added nothing new.

De Grazia states that although "the Duce's regime relied on the traditional authority of family and religion to enforce biologically determined roles as mother and caretakers,"[12] its attempt to consolidate the nation's economic power ended up bringing about those very changes it had set out to avoid. What this perspective seems to ignore – besides the fact the fascist regime destroyed the Italian economy – is that fascism had proclaimed itself a revolutionary movement[13] which did not intend to preserve or restore the old: an avant-garde which would

---

11 Addis Aba, M., "Littoriali al femminile", in Grimaldi, U. A., (edited by), *Cultura a passo romano. Storia e strategie dei littoriali della cultura e dell'arte*, Feltrinelli, Milan 1983, p. 144-164; cit. in Tarquini, A., *Storia della cultura fascista*, Il Mulino, Bologna 2016, p. 159.
12 De Grazia, V., *How Fascism Ruled Women. Italy, 1922-45*, University of California Press, Los Angeles 1992, p. XI. In respect to the numerous and important works on women in the Resistance, there is little literature on the role played by women in the fascist dictatorship. See Detragiache, D., "Le fascisme féminin, de San Sepolcro à l'affaire Matteotti (1919-1925)", *Revue d'histoire moderne et contemporaine*, 30, n. 3, 1983, p. 367; Fraddosio, M., "The Fallen Hero. The Myth of Mussolini and Fascist Women in the Italian Social Republic (1943-45)", *Journal of Contemporary History*, 31, n. 1, 1996, pp. 99-124; Willson, P., *Italiane. Biografia del Novecento*, Laterza, Rome-Bari 2011; Bartoloni, S., *Il fascismo e le donne nella "Rassegna femminile italiana" 1925-30*, Biblink, Rome 2012; Willson, P., "Fasciste della prima e della seconda ora", in Mori, M. T., Pescarolo, A., Scattigno, A., Soldani, S., (edited by), *Di generazione in generazione. Le italiane dall'Unità a oggi*, Viella, Rome 2014, pp. 183-206; Benadusi, L., "Storia del fascismo e questioni di genere", *Studi storici*, 55, n. 1, 2014, pp. 183-196.
13 Nine feminists, already active in the feminist movement of the time, attended the meeting in Piazza San Sepolcro in March 1919. Many had political backgrounds: old party companions of Mussolini like interventionist Regina Terruzzi; Red Cross nurse and interventionist Elisa Majer Rizzioli, founder of the Female Fasces and volunteer from Fiume and a highly active propagandist; and Ines Donati, who had participated in the squadrist raids.

erect a new civilization.[14] The belief that the fascist regime's attitude towards women was a mere prosecution to that of liberal Italy – if not better – is inadmissible because the totalitarian state was "assigned a primary pedagogical function with the aim of transforming the mentality, character and customs of Italians to generate a new man – a believer in and practitioner of the cult of the *littorio*."[15] And this also applied to women.

Fashion and its control by the regime were not incompatible with the relationship between women and the fascist dictatorship – as the model of the "exemplary wife and mother" opposed to the "crisis woman"[16] has it – but were an integral part of the totalitarian character of the regime. Fascism, after all, was built upon elements of modern rationality:

> The organisation of the party, the mobilisation of the masses, the sacralised ideology in the form of a new secular religion, the use of technology for propaganda and collective indoctrination, the impulse to modernisation, subordinating it to the achievement of higher objectives of power and expansion on a continental or even planetary scale.[17]

---

14 Gentile, E., *Le origini dell'ideologia fascista 1918-1925*, Il Mulino, Bologna 2011; Tarquini, A., *op cit.*, p. 160.
15 Gentile, E., *Il culto del littorio, op. cit.*, p. VII.
16 Cfr. De Grazia, V., *op. cit.*; De Grazia, V., "Nationalizing Women: The Competition between Fascist and Commercial Cultural Models in Mussolini's Italy," in De Grazia, V., Furlough, E., (edited by), *The Sex of Things: Gender and Consumption in Historical Perspective*, University of California Press, Berkley 1996, pp. 337-358; De Grazia, V., "Il patriarcato fascista: come Mussolini governò le donne italiane (1922-1940)", in Duby, G., Perrot, M., *Storia delle donne. Il Novecento*, Laterza, Rome-Bari 1992, pp. 141-175; Chang, N. V., *The Crisis-Woman: Body Politics and the Modern Woman in Fascist Italy*, University of Toronto Press, Toronto 2015, for an in-depth study of the discursive role of the expression "woman-crisis" in fascist culture; De Giorgio, M., *Le italiane dall'Unità a oggi*, Laterza, Rome-Bari 1992; Gundle, S., *Figure del desiderio. Storia della bellezza femminile italiana*, Laterza, Rome-Bari 2007; Pickering-Iazzi, R., *Mothers of Invention: Women, Italian Fascism, and Culture*, University of Minnesota Press, Minneapolis-London 1995.
17 Gentile, E., (edited by), *Modernità totalitaria. Il fascismo italiano*, Laterza, Rome-Bari 2008, p. IX.

These elements were reflected in the efforts the regime put – starting from the second half of the 1930s – into the totalitarian organization of the national fashion industry.

In this regard, fashion scholar Eugenia Paulicelli's reading[18] of an essay by De Grazia is instructive. In it, the author examines an account of the *Grande adunata delle forze femminili* ("Great Gathering of Women's Forces") on the 28th of May, 1939 written by Stefani, the regime's official press agency: it was the first national female event in which the conventional signs of class and individual distinction were replaced by organisation into homogeneous groups: the rural housewives, the workers, the leisure and sports groups, the professionals, the artists, the "speed cohorts" of cyclists, cars, motorcycles and ambulances and the Red Cross nurses, the latter captured in the moment of turning their heads in unison to salute the *duce*, the climax of an event charged with echoes of the Great War.

According to Paulicelli,[19] the coexistence of women in uniform and women in folkloric costume would confirm the fundamental ambiguity of the regime towards modernity, aspiring to include both the modern type in fascist uniform and the traditional type in regional costume. For her part, De Grazia underlines how Stefani's description was uncertain of the nature of what it was describing, whether it was a fashion show or a military parade, and with a help from Georg Simmel[20] she concludes that this indecision is yet more proof "of the fundamental tension between mass collectivist imagery and the pursuit of individuality and exclusivity typical of the modern fashion industry"[21] which runs through every regime, both liberal and fascist.

But if the parade is looked at as a fashion show – as it was perceived and promoted by the Stefani agency – it loses any trace

---

18 Paulicelli, E., *Fashion Under Fascism: Beyond the Black Shirt*, Berg, Oxford-New York 2004, pp. 17-20.
19 Paulicelli analyses De Grazia's words, making reference also to a newsreel of the event archived with the Archivio Luce.
20 De Grazia, V., "Nationalizing Women," *op. cit.*, pp. 337-58, cit. in Paulicelli, E., *op. cit.*, p. 19. The Georg Simmel's essay referred to is *La moda*, Mondadori, Milan 1998.
21 De Grazia, "Nationalizing Women," *op. cit.*, p. 352.

of ambiguity, becoming a picturesque, sumptuous and theatrical display of the regime's "totalitarian modernity" which now included the female masses. From the point of view of the agency's text, the uniforms of the groups painted a fashionable view. Rightly, De Grazia notes that Stefani adopted the vocabulary, tone and performativity typical of a fashion review. In addition to separating and uniting the social body, as well as instilling fear and awe, the uniform created a visible hierarchy and seduced with the shape of a modern form. Furthermore, uniforms were the symbol of the new political ambitions of rebirth, whereby any Italian woman could become a "new woman" – an athletic, beautiful, healthy and dynamic member of the mystical body of the nation, ready for sacrifice.

The uniform itself and its presence on the public stage were subject to varying interpretations by contemporaries. For the Piedmontese Marquise Irene di Targiani Giunti – General Inspector of the Italian Red Cross from 1921 to 1937 – the uniform was an instrument of discipline that aimed to "bury individual selfishness in the common cause."[22] Young Ida Cagossi from Emilia, who later became a partisan, remembered how

> at the age of eleven, her lively black and white uniform nourished her sense of being at the centre of things: "Walking along the road that took me to and from school, I was anxious to keep the black cloak open over my uniform, letting it fall over my shoulders to show off the various accolades attached to my white blouse. I walked chest out, with a firm step, and every time I crossed someone's path I would peek at my reflection in the mirrors of the shops, to check the effect produced."[23]

Through the uniform, women become aware of their *newness* with respect to the past and of their common identity as "Italian women."

On September the 7th, 1943 journalist Camilla Cederna published an article entitled *Moda nera*[24] ("Black Fashion," black

---

22 Targiani, I. G., *La donna nella famiglia, nel lavoro, nella vita sociale*, Course for visiting female fascists, Federation of Fascist Fighting Leagues of Rome, Rome 1935, cit. in De Grazia, V., "Nationalizing Women," *op. cit.*, p. 353.
23 *Ibidem.* Cf. also De Grazia, V., *Le donne nel regime*, *op. cit.*, p. 159.
24 Camilla Cederna published it in *Il pomeriggio*, the afternoon edition of the *Corriere della Sera* of the 7th of September 1943. Taking up the text of the

being the colour chosen by the regime to symbolise fascism), where fascist fashion was identified with the uniform *tout court* and the political direction of the day was narrated through the symbolic figure of the woman wearing a fascist uniform:

> If certain official photographs are kept in family albums it may be that one day, while they leaf through them, the children wonder why their grandmother or mother dressed in mourning in those days, and why they had put on their father's tie, and wore on their heads an odd little boat-shaped hat that truly made them look rather ugly. Was it possible then that they were the same women intent in other photos upon swaddling a newborn or watering round beds of roses with vague gestures and light-coloured clothes?...Who knows! Sometimes children are satisfied with evasive answers, and on the other hand they would not know what a small-town fascist commander was; so they will turn the page, in search of images of waves and games or more pleasant family groups.[25]

Cederna compared women in uniform to "cockroaches," underlining how the uniform transformed their meekness into vanity:

> The dark photographs belong to a time that is not theirs, to a time when the building's concierge, seeing the grandmother in question leave the house, used to compare her, with all due respect, to a cockroach, saying in dialect, "she looks like beetle," and it was strange, she thought, since she was still an attractive lady; It was also a pity that, usually so mild, when she was in uniform she put on a lot of airs! Seen from a distance, they in fact did resemble large insects, the women dressed in this dark fascist uniform which, with its long jacket, absurd desert model in black wool and

---

article from *Giornalismo italiano, vol. 3: 1939-1968*, edited by and with an introductory essay by Frano Contorbia, Mondadori, Milan 2009, pp. 195-199. Cederna recalled that article many years later in the volume *Milano in guerra*, Feltrinelli, Milan 1979. After the 25th of July, the regime seemed finished; ways of dressing and gestures that, until recently, had seemed – perhaps not to everyone – ordinary and typical of everyday life, now become the object of jokes in public. Cederna's sarcasm is aimed above all to women who agreed to dress in "an absurd and somewhat inhuman style," imitating "their superiors and party officials." Writing in those days, uniforms and badges seemed destined to end up in landfills along with the rubble of bombed cities.

25 *Ibid.*

belt made of rough fabric, had above all the task of appearing austere, but often succeeded in arousing smiles from onlookers.[26]

The uniform cast a spell on female members of the party, especially those who held a certain rank. In fact, it was a garment that not only embodied modernity from a sartorial point of view, but which also expressed a hierarchy and conferred upon the wearer a certain degree of authority:

> But great was the fascination exercised by this uniform on most of the women enrolled in the party, and especially upon those who possessed a rank. In short, they took it extraordinarily seriously, as a certain symbol of prestige and authority, and when they wore it, a radical change took place in them as if by magic: in fact, many good ladies needed only to button up their jackets and tie their ties for them to immediately change personality and expression. Their eyes, strange to say, lost their usual appearance and took on a false one, proud and without kindness, the eyebrows beetled and frowned, while a curtness characterised all their movements. And the air of importance! Almost none had it inborn, but for those specific official ceremonies they borrowed a pompous manner that perhaps the orbace wool and the shoulder pads communicated to them and which then resulted in scornful little glances at the crowd around them dressed in civilian clothes or in flowery fabrics.[27]

Cederna refers to the cultic aspect of the uniform and its superiority over Catholic worship when she writes that these women were "priestesses of a sect without a smile, they walked as if martial fanfares were playing only for them, and in church, stiff, during the blessing of a banner, they did not even pray, because their uniform was certainly not made for praying."[28] After the 25th of July, 1943 however, the uniform became a dangerous object and had to be carefully hidden from the view of passers-by, perhaps beneath "a large flowery dress,"[29] as Camilla Cederna noted, not unironically. Perry Wilson has shown how during the 1920s, uniforms were an essential component of the

---

26 *Ibid.*
27 *Ibid.*
28 *Ibid.*
29 *Ibid.* Ironically, the "large flowery dress," as Cederna seems to acknowledge, was only another fascist "uniform," since flower prints were so widespread they had become one of the symbols of autarkic fashion.

"theatricality of politics,"[30] rituals that aimed to instil a mystical belief in the state. In uniform, "members of the oceanic crowd lost their individuality by merging into a disciplined army of the faithful."[31]

In reality, the individual sentiment was not lost in the fascist rally, rather it was amplified. The individual found himself in the pulsating oceanic crowd, trampling on in military parades. The crowd of the totalitarian state was not the literary one described by Edgar Allan Poe[32] in his short story *The Man of the Crowd*, but the organized mass of Gustave Le Bon,[33] who described the collective soul and the primitiveness of the masses, and whom Freud called "brilliant."[34] The fascist crowd was framed, uniformed, aligned in harmonic and geometric or "oceanic" formations embodying the power, unity and discipline of the nation. It did not admit of empty spaces[35] or an "off-screen," while the photographs and the silver screens could barely contain it. It represented an alternative view to the anonymous, alienated and disordered chaos of the modern metropolitan crowd.

In this sense, fashion – as a discourse – was not opposed to tradition. Fascism never tried to impose folkloric costume on

---

30 Willson, P., "The Nation in Uniform? Fascist Italy 1919-1943," *Past & Present*, 221, November 2013, pp. 239-272; see also Gentile, E., "Theatre of Politics in Fascist Italy," in Gentile, E., *The Struggle for Modernity. Nationalism, Futurism and Fascism*, Preger, Westport-London 2003, pp. 109-126.
31 Willson, P., *op. cit.*, p. 239.
32 Poe, E. A., "The Man of the Crowd," in *The Portable Edgar Allan Poe*, edited by J. Gerald Kennedy, Penguin Classics, New York 2006; for an examination of the relationship between metropolis, order and chaos, see Rubeo, U., «Tra alienazione e mercato: la città moderna secondo Edgar Allan Poe», *Fictions. Studi sulla narratività*, 5, June 2007, pp. 63-74.
33 Le Bon, G., *Psicologia delle folle*, Tea, Milan 2004.
34 Freud, L., *Psicologia delle masse e analisi dell'Io*, Bollati Boringhieri, Turin 1975, p. 22.
35 In 1931 Gaetano Polverelli, head of Mussolini's press office, issued directives for the press. Among these we read: "Photographs of Italian events and landscapes must always be examined from the point of view of their political effects. In the case of crowds, discard photographs showing blank spaces; in the case of new roads, monumental areas, etc., discard those that do not give a positive impression of the work, traffic, etc.," in Castronovo, V., Tranfaglia, N., *Storia della stampa italiana*, Vol. IV, Laterza, Rome-Bari 1976, p. 142.

Italian women but it did express a peculiar fashion culture which, at times, brought it into conflict with the Church.[36] National and regional photographic archives testify to the presence of women, even rural housewives, flaunting seductive modern clothes – however cheap – and attitudes, or in uniform striking severe poses in public spaces. These images received little visibility either during the fascist period or after the war, when the mass media and intellectuals were busy building new myths.

In this context, architect and "anti-rationalist" intellectual Gio Ponti appeared as a prophet of the Italian *alta moda* destined to emerge from the war and dominate Europe. Among other places, it was inside the pages of *Bellezza* that the process of the "politicisation of aesthetics" identified by historian Emilio Gentile[37] took shape. It should be emphasized that under the regime, the appearance of women was a political issue, since beauty was promoted as a spiritual duty of the "Italian woman": "Everything, absolutely everything, has been put at the service of the cult of beauty by the power of men. Men? This is the first time we have spoken of them in this long discourse. Yet for whom if not for them do we 'live in beauty'?"[38] According to critic Raffaele Calzini, the Italic feminine type possessed "innumerable and seductive varieties and nuances, which reflect the changing and always picturesque physical face of the shared homeland,"[39] while in 1938, the year of racial laws, the *Ente nazionale della moda* ("National Fashion Authority") published the anthropometric studies by doctor Nicola Pende which subdivided Italian women into "Alpine," "Mediterranean" and "Adriatic" races.[40]

---

36 On May 22, 1941, Ascension Day, Pope Pius XI announced the "Crusade of purity" and spoke to four thousand girls of the Women's Youth groups of Catholic Action.
37 Gentile, E., *The Struggle for Modernity*, op. cit., p. 43.
38 Robiola, E., "Plasmare e proteggere la bellezza," *Bellezza*, n.1, January 1941, p. 100.
39 Calzini, R., (edited by), *La bella italiana: da Botticelli a Tiepolo*, supplement to *Domus*, n. 84, December 1934, p. 5.
40 Pende, N., "La tipologia normale della donna italiana feconda," in *Bollettino d'informazioni dell'Ente nazionale della moda*, III, n. 16, 1938, pp. 3-7.

Bellezza had nothing to do with rural housewives, aspiring to compete with Hollywood and Parisian styles. According to the ENM fashion system, as articulated by *Bellezza*, the fashion line (*"linea"*) – or *silhouette* – didn't flourish, each new season, from the free play of the couturier's mind, as was the case in Paris, but was something that the ENM, i.e. the state, established with its authority and "submitted" to a curated selection of dressmakers, those who had managed to obtain the *Marca d'oro* ("Gold Mark"). Fashion creators were therefore called upon to interpret, rather like journalists, the *linea* established by the bureaucratic elite of the ENM. It is no coincidence that in Gio Ponti's private correspondence regarding *Bellezza* one can witness the ongoing clash between the editorial staff's desire to publish the names of the dressmakers and regime's unwillingness to call into question both the non-commercial essence of *Bellezza* and the anonymous character of state fashion, whose ultimate creator was understood to be Mussolini, the only true *grand couturier* of the nation.

For its part, Gio Ponti thought the imitation *en mass* of the American lifestyle and the elite taste for French fashion were the outcomes of a provincial state of mind, a "disease" that infected both Italian elites and mass society. *Bellezza* was to offer them an alternative aesthetic and moral ideal of "sober elegance," where the neurosis of contemporary life was suffocated into a "truly modern" lifestyle. In this timeless *mirage*, which drew from fashion and from things themselves a notion of silent elegance, the excesses of French fashion, its frills and its Schiaparelli-esque clowneries became the political symbol of the moral degradation of defeated France, a threat for the creation of the "new Italian."

The desire for integrity in design "seems to have arisen in the second half of the eighteenth century, after the decline of the fashion for Rococo, in connection with the Enlightenment."[41] In that case, the reference to classical design evoked the strength and clarity of Greek democracy and Roman technology, which had become erotically and politically seductive; while for the regime

---

41 Hollander, A., *Sex and Suits. The Evolution of Modern Dress*, Knopf, New York 1994, pp. 5-6.

Introduction

the reference to classical aesthetics took on new connotations of discipline, health, obedience, timeless beauty and self-sacrifice. During the war, the values of "elegance" and "simplicity" were strongly promoted in women's magazines, from those dealing in high fashion to those targeting the middle and working classes. Commenting on an exhibition of colonial women's clothing in the pages of *Fibre tessili* ("Textile Fibers"), journalist P.H. Coronedi praised "the practicality and elegance of the clothing, distinguished by the Italian taste for harmony."[42]

In this regard, historian Emilio Gentile advocates caution with the use of the widespread concept of the "aestheticisation of politics" developed by Walter Benjamin in his studies of totalitarianism, since one of the most important aspects of fascism was in fact its "politicisation of aesthetics." Studies of fashion under fascism, in their treating fashion as detached from politics and fascist institutions end up aestheticizing fascism, "with the effect of relegating to the background, and therefore trivialising, its political nature,"[43] while exalting its modern appearance. Fashion, like Americanism, was significant for fascist culture in regard to its attitude towards modernity.[44] As an expression-metaphor of both modernity and the West, the positions around it can be interpreted as variations of the fascist controversy on modernity. Fashion is fundamental for interpreting fascism's attitudes towards the modern world and for understanding the history of Italian fashion and modernity in the immediate post-war period, when fashion was at least in part created by the same people. In September 1950, producers of woollen fabrics and clothing designers organized the fashion show *Sarti italiani e industrie della lana sfilano insieme* ("Italian Dressmakers and the Wool Industries Show Together"), where

---

42 Paulicelli, E., *op. cit.*, p. 116.
43 Tarquini, A., *op. cit.*, p. 45.
44 See Gentile, E., "Impending Modernity: Fascism and the Ambivalent Image of the United States," in Gentile, E., *The Struggle for Modernity, op. cit.*, pp. 161-180, originally in *Journal of Contemporary History*, 28, n. 1, January 1993, pp. 7-29; and Griffin, R., *Modernism and Fascism. The Sense of a Beginning under Mussolini and Hitler*, Palgrave, New York 2007.

the participants were the same fashion creators – Biki (Elvira Leonardi Bouyeure), Vita Noberasko, the Fontana Sisters and the Rivella company, with woollen fabrics by Marzotto, Rossi, Schio, Mabu, Zignone, Fila and other Biellese companies – that during the war had already appeared in the pages of *Bellezza*. Others – like Veneziani, Vanna and Marucelli – took part in the *First Italian High Fashion Show* of the 12th of February, 1951 – in the *alta moda* section – organized in Florence by Giovanni Battista Giorgini, that showcased Italian fashion to international audiences at the same time as the Paris collections.

From the second half of the 1930s, and with greater intensity during the war, the regime managed and indeed "occupied" the national fashion industry to an ever-increasing extent, developing its own myths of female appearance. During the war, the model of *militant female citizen* "with specific characteristics expressing the revolutionary and vital culture of fascism, [...] actively involved in the life of the regime" took shape.[45] For the *militant female citizen*, "being beautiful" in wartime became a duty and a form of militancy itself.

---

45 Tarquini, A., *op. cit.*, p. 159.

1
TOWARDS A TOTALITARIAN FASHION

Wartime fashion and, more generally, the fashion of the 1940s are periodically subject to processes of glamorisation and fetishization[1] by the media, but when studied in their original context they tell a more complex and less glamorous story. Unlike what we see in the fashion magazines of the time, the historical imagery of women under fascism is dominated by the figure of the "rural housewife," a perception that derives from the exclusion of fashion and the body[2] from studies of fascism and from the belief that fashion – this driving force of modernity[3] – was not part of the fascist culture:

> To be modern – Marshall Berman wrote – is to find ourselves in an environment that promises us adventure, power, joy, growth, transformation of ourselves and the world – and, at the same time, that threatens to destroy everything we have, everything we know, everything we are. Modern environments and experiences cut across all boundaries of geography and ethnicity, of class and nationality, of religion and ideology: in this sense, modernity can be said to unite all mankind. But it is a paradoxical unity, a unity of disunity: it pours us all into a maelstrom of perpetual disintegration and renewal, of struggle and contradiction, of ambiguity and anguish. To be modern is to be part of a universe in which, as Marx said, "all that is solid melts into air." [4]

---

1 A brief survey of online fashion magazines, social media and YouTube channels dedicated to vintage fashion will suffice to see this.
2 "Fashion is about bodies: it is produced, promoted and worn by bodies", cit. in Entwistle, J., *Fashioned Body. Fashion, Dress, and Modern Social Theory*, Polity Press, Cambridge 2015, p. XIX.
3 As in Marshall Berman's definition of it as a system of ideas and visions that aim to make human beings both subjects and objects of modernisation.
4 Berman, M., *All That is Solid Melts into Air. The Experience of Modernity*, London & New York, Verso 1983, p. 15.

As fashion historians Cristopher Breward and Caroline Evans argue, fashion is essential to the modern condition.[5] Fascism's interest in and progressive "occupation" of Italian fashion and its drive to modernise are crucial aspects of the "totalitarian modernity" of the fascist state, hostile to liberal and democratic modernity.[6] For this reason, I disagree with the following assertion, contained in *Fashion at the Time of Fascism*:

> The result is not a book on fascism, but on fashion in the Fascist period, from the march on Rome in 1922 to the fall of Benito Mussolini in 1943.[7]

A point of view shared by Eugenia Paulicelli's title, whose focus is "fashion under fascism."[8] But since Italian fashion had been increasingly shaped by totalitarianism, a book on fashion "*at the time*" or "*under*" fascism *is* a book on fascism. Furthermore, this forced separation of fashion and fascism lends itself to an aestheticization of politics.

Italian fashion during the fascist period – as culture, material identity, commodity and national myth – therefore presents an opportunity to explore the experience of fascist totalitarian modernity. Understood as an expression of the "will to power" of the new Italian "race," fashion clothed the emerging elites with prestige and power, mingling them with the old liberals, imposing aesthetic models on the population, peddling dreams and desires – especially to the young –, offering an identity through the production and consumption of "Italian" products and images, modernising Italians from a sartorial point of view, feeding the myth of victory and of the power of the Empire.

As costume historian Anne Hollander stated:

---

5   Breward, C., Evans, C., (edited by), *Fashion and Modernity*, Berg, Oxford 2005, p. 2.
6   Gentile, E., (edited by), *Modernità totalitaria. Il fascismo italiano*, Laterza, Bari 2008.
7   Lupano, M., Vaccari, A., *Una giornata moderna. Moda e stili nell'Italia fascista 1922-43*, Damiani, Bologna 2009.
8   Paulicelli, E., *Fashion Under Fascism, op. cit.*

The history of dress or the study of clothes has no real substance other than in *images* of clothes, in which their visual reality truly lives, naturalized, as it were, by the persuasive eye of art.[9]

During the fascist period, the photos and illustrations in women's magazines, books, films and the windows of department stores were the tool that allowed Italians, especially those of the younger generation, to consume the myths of appearance that fascism orchestrated for them and to see the "new Italian" as an ideal and yet physical thing.[10] Through their physical and visual existence, clothes exert pressure on the wearer's body and on the bodies of others, both literally and metaphorically, while their social aspect is influenced by the culture and involves expectations about clothing as it is commonly perceived. The two aspects are only separable in an abstract way:

> Fabric then, in its close proximity to the body, carries enormous social, cultural, political, and moral weight. It is closely bound up with individual anxieties and broader social and historical concerns about the regulation of bodies in social space.[11]

The choice of *orbace*, a sheep's wool fabric typical of Sardinia, for the making of fascist uniforms,[12] their butterfly-like silhouette, the obligation to use fabrics produced in Italy, the promotion of local craftsmanship, the design of the garments and the way they were worn were all ways in which fascism reified its fashion culture. Women's magazines, the mannequins in the windows and cinema established – not without contradictions – the body, character and sartorial tone of the "new Italian" with the aim of regulating the circulation of desire and bodies in social space.

---

9   Hollander, A., *Seeing through Clothes*, The Viking Press, New York 1978, p. 454.
10 See Muzzarelli, G., Riello, G., Tosi Brandi, E., (edited by), *Moda. Storia e storie, op. cit.*
11 Entwistle, J., "The Dressed Body," in Evans. M., Lee, E., (edited by), *Real Bodies. A Sociological Introduction*, Palgrave, Hampshire 2002, p. 144.
12 Pericoli, U., *Le divise del duce. Tutte le divise e i distintivi del fascismo dalle origini alla caduta*, Albertelli, Parma 2010.

1.1 Ente nazionale della moda

With Law n. 1618 of the 22nd of December, 1932 the fascist regime established the *Ente autonomo per la mostra permanente nazionale della moda* ("Autonomous Authority for the Permanent National Fashion Exhibition") in Turin. The decision was the result of a power struggle between the cities of Rome, Turin and Milan in which Milanese personalities like Vittorio Montano, director of the Ventura fashion house, figured prominently.[13] Mussolini's accompanying speech to the Parliament explained how, given the success of the *Mostra della moda e dell'ambiente* ("Fashion and Interiors Exhibition") held in June of the same year, the law was a response to the city of Turin's desire to make the exhibition permanent. The exhibition, he said, demonstrated "the good taste, refinement of concepts and technical ability and exemplary equipment of the national clothing industry."[14] The staging of the *Mostra della moda e dell'ambiente* exhibition had been entrusted to architect Levi-Montalcini – part of a group linked to architectural functionalism which at the time was busy giving Turin a new face, perhaps the least provincial of the period – with the help of the high-society gentlewomen charged with curating the sophisticated setting for these events, which aimed to attract the common people.

On June the 19th, 1932, *La Stampa* newspaper announced that on the 2nd of June, Mussolini had granted an audience to Umberto Ricci, prefect of Turin, the mayor and other representatives of the city, in which he accepted the proposal to create a permanent fashion salon.[15] Actor Mario Castellani communicated the news to a live audience from one of the stages of Turin's *Teatro della moda* ("Fashion Theatre") in the middle of a revue show entitled *La moda vuol così* ("Fashion Likes It That Way"):

---

[13] Vittorio Montano, head of the Ventura fashion house and the Italian High Fashion Union.

[14] «Il testo del disegno di legge con la relazione del Duce», *Stampa Sera*, 26-27 November 1932, p. 1.

[15] «Il Salone permanente della moda», *La Stampa*, 19 June 1932, p. 6.

The "mannequins" who brought to the lighted stage the freshness of the most exquisite summer fashions created by several highly respected houses in our city, did not appear alone, but were accompanied, as well as by "jazz," by a first-rate "presenter," Pia Spini, and the actor Castellani; Carletto Thieben performed some of his characteristic dances to much applause; and finally the whole company sang the glories of Zanzibar fashion and the "soubrette," Castellani exalted the graces of the Turin dressmaker in a much-applauded song and to conclude, maestro Frondel, the "jazzers," the artists and the "mannequins" left the stage to start the dance to the sound of Corvetto's latest modern song: *"Tripoli bel suol d'amore!"*[16]

On the 15th of October of the same year,[17] once again in *La Stampa* newspaper, further mention was made of relations with the Milan *Salone dell'abbigliamento* clothing fair, whose authorisation had been revoked, the Turin authority being obliged to reimburse the expenses incurred up to at that moment.

Yet Turin was a city of fashion and of fashionable ateliers such as Bellom, Sacerdote, De Rossi, Borgialli, Giobergia and De Gasperi, who had always enjoyed close – perhaps, for the regime's tastes, too close – contact with Paris. In 1911 it was a city of milliners and dressmakers, with 798 workshops and 4,925 workers, and the place where Camasio and Oxilia had set *Addio Giovinezza!*, a popular sentimental comedy centred around the unhappy love affair between a working class dressmaker and a bourgeois university student. Being a dressmaker was a popular job among girls from Turin's working class and artisan families, even socialist ones. Maria Bronzo recalled the experience as follows:

> I have worked in several high fashion ateliers, at Bellom and Rubioglio. I went to Rubioglio because it was the only large atelier that paid a little more than the minimum wage. There were almost a hundred of us girls there [...]. These seamstresses had their own way of thinking. They were practically all the daughters of workmen but, who knows why, perhaps because of the fact that they were always around beautiful clothes or wealthy people, they all wanted to marry a lawyer or a doctor, etc. Who were the students they hung around with and who then dumped them [...]. Despite these ideas, my workmates were quite sophisticated, for example almost

---

16 *Ibid.*
17 "L'organizzazione del Salone della moda", *La Stampa*, 15 October 1932, p. 7.

all of them loved the theatre very much and we went often, sometimes skipping dinner. As soon as the doors opened there was a great rush up the stairs to get to the gallery where there were very few seats and if you didn't get one you would be standing all evening. But we went all the same.[18]

But perhaps the things about Turin that irked Mussolini and made him prefer Milan, the cradle of fascism, played their part in the eventual decision to make Turin the capital of Italian fashion. In October 1930, in the report sent to the new National Secretary of the party Giovanni Giuriati, the Federal Secretary of Turin Ivan Bianchi-Mina specified how his office aimed to achieve the "minimum general dissent" rather than the "maximum unilateral consent" in a city

> (…) Where the old traditions and the old function as the nation's capital have not yet suppressed, in the local mindset, the ancient distinctions between the classes. It would be a mistake to entrust the party in Turin to an authentic representative of the warrior aristocracy that returned decorated from the victorious war. It would be a mistake to entrust the Party, in Turin, to an authentic representative of the Revolution, who comes from *squadrismo*, autodidacticism and work. A wealthy bourgeois of the commercial or industrial class would similarly be a mistake. In order for the Party to be credible in Turin, it must be personified by modesty, absolute

---

18   Tranfaglia, N., (edited by), *Storia di Torino VIII. Dalla Grande Guerra alla liberazione (1915-1945)*, Einaudi, Turin 1998, p. 34; Guidetti Serra, B., *Compagne*, I, Einaudi, Turin 1977, Maria Bronzo in Negarville, pp. 310-11. On fashion and workers in the sector in Turin, see Bondi, A., "La capitale della moda" and Gambarotta, B., "Modiste e sartine", in Castronovo, V., (edited by), *Storia illustrata di Torino XI. Società e costume*, Mondadori, Milan 1995, pp. 3201-20 and pp. 3221-40, for further bibliographical information. In the special issue of *La donna* dedicated to the Universal Exposition of 1911, where there were huge numbers of Turin dressmakers, we read: "From now on it will no longer be necessary to move from our usual place of work or business or undertake long boring correspondence with foreign houses to dress with solid elegance." For the hypothesis that the birth of an 'Italian fashion' as a mediation between haute couture and Italian taste should be traced back to the Turin tailors, see *L'alta moda capitale. Torino e le sartorie torinesi*, Fabbri, Milan 1991, pp. 17-39, 25, 30. One of the keys to the success of post-war Italian fashion is the concordance between the characteristics of Italian creations and the demands of the major Western market, the US, which was interested in "a revised and corrected Paris," see Morelli, O., "Il successo internazionale della moda italiana e l'esordio in patria del made in Italy post bellico", in Bianchino, G., Butazzi, G., Mottola Molfino, A., Carlo Quintavalle, A., *op. cit.*, pp. 58-71, 60.

integrity and authentic activity – the kind that produces results and which is beyond debate: none of which distant from a culture, an upbringing and a sense of Fascist fraternity that, in the difficult context of Turin, allow it to represent the Party as worthily in one of the five Courts of the Savoy as at a trade-union gathering or a meeting of representatives of the industrial technicism or intellectualism which continue to thrive in Turin.[19]

Despite the fact that the number of members of the National Fascist Party ("*Partito Nazionale Fascista*", or PNF) in January 1930 was double that of 1926, reaching 10,500 in the city, trade union membership exceeded one hundred thousand and the various municipal, neighbourhood and company *Dopolavoro* (afterwork clubs) had 75,333 members, the "vociferators" muttered against the regime, continuing to influence the public mood.

Bianchi-Mina was unequivocal in his report on fascism in Turin: "Hidden survival of the communist mentality in those living in the Barriera quarter," especially among metallurgical and textile workers, "a fairly positive mood among construction workers," largely of rural origin, "the survival, not always evident, of a social-reformist mentality in the petty-bourgeois classes," the survival of liberalism "with a democratic background seasoned with Giolittian nostalgia" in the middle and upper bourgeoisie, "whose interests were notably favoured at the time of Giolitti's parliamentary dictatorship and who today are out of necessity obedient to the discipline of the fascist regime."

Furthermore, the failures and restructuring of trade and industry together with an increasingly serious recession were resulting in high unemployment in the city, which had more than 30,000 unemployed in 1930, threatening Turin's newborn hopes of becoming a "fashion capital" and triggering a heated debate on the city's economic and cultural destiny. In the early months of 1932, Umberto Notari, writing in the *Gazzetta del Popolo*, identified "the foundations of the rebirth" of Turin in tourism, fashion and the establishment of a public credit institution along the lines of the banks of Naples or Sicily:

---

19 ACS, Pnf, b. 25.

> Turin – a true metropolis of the Alps, with its marvellous snowfields in winter and enchanting excursion destinations in summer, offers one of the most evocative attractions for skiers, mountaineers and tourists from all over Italy [...]. And after the mountains, fashion. Turin has a tradition of elegance with which no other city can compete. Only Turin can become a competitor to Paris in the creation and launch of an Italian fashion industry. Her ateliers, which are currently in serious trouble, can rise again and allow Turin's dressmaking industry to clothe all the elegant women in Italy.[20] [...] No antithesis, therefore, between the two Turins [...]. The Turin of today, builder of cars and machines of all kinds, can therefore look to the Turin of tomorrow, launcher of sports and fashions, with complete tranquility and sympathy.[21]

Thus, from 1933, the National Fashion Exhibition would be held in Turin – in two separate spring and autumn events – taking advantage of the customs and rail travel concessions provided by Royal Decree-Law (R.D.L.) n. 2740 of the 16th of December, 1923. Article 5 of the law was significant because it introduced a principle of temporary intellectual protection: "Industrial inventions, designs and factory patterns relating to objects that will appear in the exhibition will enjoy the temporary protection established by law no. 423."

The *Ente autonomo per la mostra permanente nazionale della moda* ("Autonomous Commission for the Permanent National Fashion Exhibition") was constituted with the participation of the Municipality of Turin, the Provincial Council of the Corporate Economy of Turin, the Provincial Federation of the PNF of Turin, the Fascist Industrial Union of the Province of Turin, the Provincial Fascist Commerce Federation of Turin, the Autonomous Federation of Artisan Communities of Turin and the Society for the Promotion of the National Industry of Turin. Its initial capital was 2,030,000 lire, of which 1,000,000 was provided by the city of Turin.

The commission was administered by a committee made up of delegates from the Ministries of Corporations and

---

20 Notari, U., "Nostra intervista", *Gazzetta del Popolo*, 9 March 1932, p. 6; "Della prosperità di Torino", *Gazzetta del popolo*, 26 March 1932, p. 7.
21 Notari, U., "La grande industria e la crisi", *Gazzetta del Popolo*, 13 March 1932, p. 7.

Communications and representatives of various fascist trade unions in the clothing sector.[22] The president – the Honourable Silvio Ferracini, president of the Fascist Industrial Union of Turin – was appointed by the head of the government and not by the committee members, and the body was under the supervision of the Ministry of Corporations. Mussolini watched the project with interest, as evidenced by a series of articles written for *Il Popolo d'Italia* by Lydia de Liguoro between the end of 1932 and the beginning of 1933, in all probability also to silence dissent, given their appeals to "fascist discipline" and references to tendencies opposed to the development of Italian fashion within the National Fascist Party itself.[23]

The fact was that Italy was the destination of a third of French fashion exports, to the tune of approximately a billion lire,[24] and the commission's ambitious goal was to turn this relationship on its head. In the meantime, Italian women were targeted by propaganda aiming to encourage patriotic consumerism, urging them to purchase Italian products and to be elegant and desirable "in an Italian way." As fashion historian Graziella Butazzi pointed out, this framing of the consumption of Italian fashion as a patriotic duty did not ease up even after Italy's entry into the war, and was directed at the entire nation, especially the aristocratic ladies of Turin and Italy, as elegant and sophisticated

---

22 The exhausting list includes: a delegate for each of the two ministries of corporations and communications, representatives of the municipality of Turin, of the provincial council of corporate economy of Turin, of the provincial federation of the Pnf of Turin, of the fascist general confederation of the Fascist General Confederation of Commerce, of the Autonomous National Fascist Federation of Italian Artisans, of the National Confederation of Fascist Industry Unions, of the National Confederation of Fascist Trade Unions, of the National Federation of Clothing, of the Fascist Industrial Union of Turin, of the Fascist Federation of Commerce of Turin, of the Autonomous Federation of Artisan Communities of Turin, of the Provincial Committee of Professionals and Artists of Turin, of the Provincial Delegation of Female Fascists of Turin, and of the Society for the Promotion of the National Industry of Turin.

23 De Liguoro, L., *Le battaglie della moda 1929-33*, Tip. Luzzatti, Rome 1934, p. 118.

24 De Liguoro, L., "Verso una moda italiana", *Il Popolo d'Italia*, 19 November 1932, p. 3.

as the models seen in *Vogue*, who represented the official face of the regime and the female archetype offered up by Italian high fashion.

The commission enjoyed powerful protectionism, as evidenced by RDL n. 2084 of the 31st of October, 1935,[25] which became law on the 11th of May 1936 and which modified the constitution of the Autonomous Commission, changing its name to *Ente nazionale della moda* (ENM, "National Fashion Authority") and tasking it with launching, coordinating and implementing initiatives aimed at favouring the progressive ascendency of Italian fashion, as well as consolidating and developing the industries and activities of fashion and clothing, both in Italy and abroad. To this end, the ENM was to collaborate with the textile and clothing sector, providing for the creation and launch of Italian manufactured products and models, promote measures to ensure the protection of new creations in the field of clothing (certification marks), organise and promote shows, exhibitions and conferences relating to fashion and regulate all similar initiatives undertaken by others, and function as a technical liaison body between the various bodies involved to facilitate and harmonise their trading relationships and help promote, also through the publications it would produce, Italian achievements. To this end, it facilitated and coordinated the action of these sectors in order to increase Italian fashion production destined to foreign markets, creating its own special information services. To finance its operation, the institution was given by the state an annual grant of two million lire, which was its main source of funding until its closure.

On the 18th of May, 1935, an article appeared in *La Stampa* newspaper[26] explaining to readers the functions of the new ENM[27] and the need to create a market in support of the annual

---

25 *Modificazione della costituzione dell'Ente autonomo per la Mostra permanente nazionale della moda*, R.D.L. 31 October 1935, n. 2084, G.U. n. 291, 14 December 1935.
26 "L'Ente della moda avrà più vasti compiti", *La Stampa*, 18 May 1935, p. 7.
27 Meanwhile, in 1935, the president of the ENM, Duke Thaon di Revel, former mayor of Turin, was transferred to the Ministry of Finance and replaced by Count Giriodi Panissera di Monastero, while Vladimiro Rossini became the the new general manager.

exhibition. The article clarified that the Clothing Corporation was scheduled to meet on the following 29th of May and that the occasion was a source of anxiety regarding the ENM's decisions on how to "regulate 180,000 companies for a total – including owners, managers, artisans and workers – of over 600, 000 workers." The first issue the Corporation would have to tackle was "establishing relations between the clothing industry and the textile industry for the purpose of increasing the use of Italian-produced fabrics. This is a complex problem that in turn affects many others, such as that of the relationship between the textile industry and high fashion, between the textile industry and mass-produced clothing, and between the textile industry and the ENM."[28]

The first part of the article looked at the relationship between dressmaking and industry. The challenges facing Italian fashion were clear and it was obvious that changes in this field could only be slow and gradual. One passage in particular underlined that fascism wished to export its own interpretation of international trends in taste rather than a national style:

> It is not a question of imposing Italian national fashion abroad, especially since fashion is broadly an international phenomenon; it is a question of gradually encouraging people to appreciate a specifically Italian interpretation of international fashion by drawing attention to the taste, the panache and the artistic talent of our fashion houses which, apart from anything else, once held undisputed primacy in the sector.[29]

The main problem was that of adapting the country's fabric production to the changing needs of fashion:

> For this reason, it is necessary to ensure that, alongside mass-produced fabrics, the textile industry produces new [state-approved] "types" which are constantly being updated so they can be offered, with privileged conditions, to fashion designers who in turn make use almost exclusively of these new Italian fabrics which, after the launch period, will become part of standard industrial production and will then be freely available for trade. In short, it is a matter of fostering an ongoing and dynamic connection – an intimate and continuous collaboration between fashion designers

---

28 Ibid.
29 Ibid.

and the textile industry. [...] Another field to leverage in order to gradually achieve the consolidation of a national fashion while achieving great sales of Italian fabrics is that of mass production. If it were possible to equip and strengthen the Italian mass-production industry and ensure its presence in foreign markets, it might constitute the vehicle for an initial affirmation of Italian taste and skill in clothing, preparing the way for the advent of an Italian fashion.[30]

Initially, the increase of the customs duty applied to "sewn items of clothing from abroad," which was considered too low, was seen as a way to promote the sale of mass-produced garments. In addition, it was clarified that it was the Clothing Corporation that managed and powered the ENM and that the intention was to entrust it with ever more extensive tasks and powers, making the ENM the technical, commercial, welfare and propaganda arm of the Corporation. It was also suggested that the fashion expo be accompanied by a clothing market – an actual fair that would bring manufacturers of mass-produced clothing and buyers together. The ENM would therefore have the task of regulating the activity of the clothing industry in both the domestic and foreign markets:

> It would be a question of selecting and grouping together if necessary the current fashion companies and subjecting them to special obligations which would be clearly linked to special benefits; to establish and award prizes for the best creations; to connect fabric producers and fashion designers so that industrial production follows the developments of national fashion with the necessary closeness; to target production at foreign markets.[31]

The article also covered the topics of working from home, apprenticeships and the export of gloves and hats. In 1930, the Italian clothing industry exported goods worth 900,000,000,000 lire, over half of which were leather gloves and hats, figures that shrank to 365,000,000,000 in 1933 and 315,000,000,000 in 1934. The ENM's goal was to stimulate the flow of exports via trade agreements and the establishment of quality guarantee marks.

---

30   *Ibid.*
31   *Ibid.*

The first article of Royal Decree Law n. 2084 of the 31st of October 1935 gave the measure of the ENM's power and the difficulties of implementing such a vast and ambitious programme, especially given fascism's tendency to bureaucracy. The new body was also placed under the supervision of the Ministry of Corporations and the text reiterated that positions in the ENM were unpaid; though, as can be seen from its financial statements, they were anything but – indeed, they were the singular voice that weighed heaviest on the institution's budget during the war years. And in fact, with Royal Decree Law n. 1559 of the 8th of July 1937,[32] which became law on the 13th of January, 1938-XVI n. 86, the funding went from 1,000,000,000 lire to 2,000,000,000 a year for four consecutive years.

In the statute of the ENM, approved by ministerial decree of the 13th of January 1936,[33] priority is given to the creation of a fashion documentation centre, both retrospective and contemporary, to guide industrial and artisanal activities, and the creation of a foreign information service in order to keep national industry informed about trends in international fashion and the situation of foreign clothing markets. It is clear that the regime had no intention of promoting the creation of a national fashion in a folkloric-regional sense, but rather of identifying international trends and "interpreting" or diverting them through the work of the ENM.

In a report from October 1944 on the ENM kept in the State Archives, it was noted that although ENM's practical utility and financial results were questionable, it should be kept in mind that it had been founded "at a moment of crisis in our economic history – that of the sanctions applied to Italy by most foreign states," and that it then continued to operate "in increasingly difficult times culminating in the declaration of war on the Allies in 1940."

---

32 *Finanziamento dell'Ente nazionale della moda*, R.D.L. 8 July 1937, n. 1559, G.U. n. 217, 17 September 1937.
33 *Approvazione dello statuto dell'Ente nazionale della moda*, D.M. 10 January 1936, G.U. n. 33, 10 February 1936.

In another report dated June 18th, 1945, the *Associazione nazionale produzione artistica abbigliamento* ("National Association of Artistic Clothing Production") wrote to the Ministry of Industry, Commerce and Labor, underlining the benefits of the institution:

> It has ended up carrying out functions likely to provide effective benefits to the sectors involved, namely its work protecting industrial intellectual property through authorising the use of the Hallmark for certain products, mediation between companies and the ministry for the purpose of registering designs, the protection of national products and of a category deserving assistance for its inventiveness and artistic genius, and also for the notable amount of exports which in certain European countries has, as is well known, overtaken the French competition.

1.2 *"Marca di garanzia"* and *"Marca d'oro"*

In order to achieve the goals of the ENM – though, given the difficulty of the procedure, in reality complicating things –, Royal Decree Law n. 13211 of the 26th of June, 1936-XIV, (*For the Regulation of the Production and Reproduction of Designs of Clothing and Clothing Accessories*), which became law on January the 18th, 1937-XV, established in its first article that "anyone who prepares or presents to their customers collections or samples of clothing designs, including clothing accessories, is obliged to report this to the ENM." The report was to be submitted through the respective trade union associations and the obligation extended to foreign companies present in Italy. This allowed the ENM to control the realities of the clothing and accessories sector in Italy, a task made difficult by its fragmented nature, which was made of up small, often artisanal realities scattered across the nation.

In addition, the ENM was authorised to establish a "Hallmark" for clothing and accessories that were recognised, both stylistically and materially, as Italian. The *Marca di garanzia* was in the shape of a red medal bearing the profile of Italy inside a rhombus delimited by two fasces and a label with the model number on it. It could be used by companies making regular reports and for designs of "Italian creation and production," without distinction between high and commercial, quality and mediocre, artisanal and industrial fashion.

The verification of these requirements was entrusted to judicial police officials, and the *Marca di garanzia* was to be applied not only on the original piece, but on all reproductions, and could only be removed when they were sold to clients. Collections and samples had to contain a minimum percentage of Italian designs bearing the *Marca di garanzia* – twenty-five percent or thirty according to some secondary sources – established by the Ministry of Corporations on the basis of a proposal from the ENM.

Those failing to report designs were punished with a fine of 500 lire, those using the *Marca di garanzia* without authorisation or applying it to non-Italian models with a fine of between 1,000 and 5,000 lire, and those including in a collection a lower than required percentage of designs with a fine ranging from 500 to 2,000 lire for each missing design, like those who presented to customers an insufficient number of designs. In addition, companies must keep a logbook of designs, provided by the ENM.

Upon the issuing of the certificate, the company must pay a fee of 10 lire for each certified piece of original Italian design and production and 2 lire for each reproduction, 20 lire for each fur design and 5 for each reproduction, 5 lire for each hat design and 1 lira for each reproduction. While establishing production of Italian origin was relatively simple, the concept of "Italian design" was somewhat more elusive and, unfortunately for the purposes of this book, it proved impossible to consult the ENM's reports, which might have helped shed light on the motivations behind the granting of the *Marca di garanzia*.

The meaning of "design" was specified in Law n. 17011 of 16 June 1939-XVII:[34] "Design means a garment or accessory existing in a single copy intended to be presented to commercial

---

34 *Norme integrative della legge 18 gennaio 1937, n. 666 sulla disciplina della produzione e riproduzione dei modelli di vestiario e di accessori per l'abbigliamento*, Law of the 16th of June 1939, n. 1701, G.U. n. 274, 25 November 1939.

or private customers for direct sales or for the taking of orders"; and collection: "By collection or sample collection we mean a set of designs of their own or others' creation that are presented by a company to private or commercial customers for the same purpose." It also specified that the *Marca di garanzia* was valid for nine months from the date of issue in the case of dresses or hats, and eighteen months in the case of furs, linens or accessories. Furthermore, when only the drawing was presented with the application because the design had not yet been made up, the company must send a photograph of the finished garment, the validity of the *Marca di garanzia* being annulled if they did not.

Concerns about the cumbersome nature of this procedure were voiced even among the ranks of those faithful to the regime, as can be seen from the case of champion of Italian fashion Roberto Farinacci and *Vita femminile* ("Feminine Life") magazine. *Vita femminile*'s editor Ester Lombardo was found guilty of having published eight photographs of French designs, and for this reason was punished with the impounding of the magazine's February 1938 issue. This was followed by an article in Farinacci's Cremonese daily, *Regime fascista* ("Fascist Regime"), which offered Lombardo the opportunity to highlight one of the problems of the ENM,[35] namely the supply of fashion photographs to the specialised press given the exclusion of foreign fashion and the ENM's monopoly of the fashion sector. Italian fashion houses being forbidden direct contact with the press for photo shoots of designs, the ENM was supposed to act as a link between the fashion houses and the press, but this could not happen because it was bound by professional secrecy.

The bureaucratic mechanism was further complicated by the corrective decrees that followed to define more precisely the functions of the ENM in controlling and protecting the originality of fashion designs, such as the institution of the *Marca d'oro* or "Gold Mark" (which lasted six months and was

---

35   Lombardo, E., *Vita femminile*, March 1938, pp. 9-10.

sanctioned by Law n. 1701 of June the 16th, 1939) to create a national register of high fashion houses. The aim of the *Marca d'oro* was to select a number of high fashion houses which created exclusively Italian-made designs, fabrics and materials and to distinguish between "high" and mass-produced fashion. According to the law, foreign companies doing business in Italy must present a visa from the Italian consulate at least ten days before beginning trading and the law specified that they could use the *Marca d'oro* for original Italian-designed garments produced using Italian fabric in order to stimulate exports of raw materials for clothing and the opening of branches of foreign fashion houses in Italy. Since 1937, Italian fabrics had also been branded as *Texorit*.

The Regolamento istituzione albo delle case di alta moda e della "Marca d'oro" ("Rules for Establishing the Register of Haute Couture Houses and the 'Marca d'oro'")[36] clarified that in order to be included in the register, fashion houses must have presented a minimum of twenty designs each season for two consecutive seasons at the special marking session, at least five of which must have obtained the *Marca d'oro* each season. Membership lasted for two seasons and the *Marca d'oro* applied to designs found – by a technical-artistic commission – to be deserving of distinction "for their originality and Italian style of creation, quality of execution and technical and artistic merits." For each design, the fashion house was required to send, seven days in advance, two copies of a photo of the piece, in at least two poses, which highlighted the characteristics of the design itself, a statement from the company's legal representative guaranteeing that the piece was original or not copied, and a sample of the fabrics used together with a declaration that the supplier was Italian.

The members of the commission remained in office for one year, with the option for their position to be renewed, and could not be owner or employee of a fashion company. Designs must

---

36 *Regolamento istituzione albo delle case di alta moda e della* "Marca d'oro", Accame, Turin, in ACS, ivi.

be presented at the ENM's headquarters in Turin and worn by models supplied by the company, with the costs borne by the companies. The commission's decision was "final and it (was) not required to communicate the reasons for its decisions to the interested parties." The approved designs were registered at the expense of the ENM for intellectual protection purposes.[37]

---

37 Italy had few provisions for the legal protection of fashion, and interest in the protection of industrial and artistic fashion products only emerged in the 1930s. See Bentivoglio, *La protezione legale delle creazioni di moda nell'abbigliamento*, Dir. Autore, 1937, p. 170; Caselli, P., *Codice del diritto d'autore*, Turin 1943, p. 14; Vercellone, *Arte figurativa e modello*, Rivista Dir. Comm., 1958, II, p. 172; Bonasi, Benucci, *Tutela della forma del diritto industriale*, Milan 1963, p. 284 etc. The legislative activity of the regime concerns the Law of the 22nd of April 1941, n. 633 (copyright law); the R.D. 25 August 1940, n. 1411 (law on industrial designs). In ACS I was able to see how there was a peak in the registration of fashion patents (hats and dresses) in 1941, most likely linked to the initiative of the legislator.

2
DRESSING ITALIAN

The idea of Italy being self-sufficient in the field of clothing which was summarised in the word "autarky" acquired relevance after 1935, on the occasion of the mild and distracted economic sanctions inflicted on Italy by the League of Nations for having attacked Ethiopia. The term, derived from the ancient Greek α□τάρκεια (*autarkeia*), meant "self-sufficiency" and was adopted to indicate the self-sufficiency of states after the severe economic depression of 1929:

> The decadent, international but individualistic capitalism in whose hands we found ourselves after the war has not been a success. It is not intelligent, it is not pleasant, it is not fair, it is not virtuous, and it does not keep its promises. In short, we don't like it, and we are in fact beginning to despise it. But when we ask ourselves what to put in its place, we are extremely perplexed.[1]

In a speech given at the end of the great manoeuvres for the invasion of Ethiopia on the 31st of August, 1935, Mussolini announced that Italy "will make it by itself," inaugurating the autarkic campaign. With the announcement of the sanctions, a period of intense mobilisation began for Italy in which consent for the regime reached its peak. In the speech of the 23rd of March, 1936 delivered at the Capitoline Hill, Mussolini proclaimed:

> The new phase of Italian history will be dominated by this hypothesis: to achieve the maximum possible autonomy in the economic life of the nation in the shortest possible time.[2]

---

1 Keynes, J.M., *La fine del lasciar fare: autarchia economica*, Utet, Turin 1936.
2 Mussolini, B., «Il discorso del Duce all'Assemblea delle corporazioni», *Assistenza fascista*, n. 1-2, 1934, pp. 137-142.

And from Berlin he specified:

> Without economic independence, the very political autonomy of a nation is compromised and a people with powerful military capabilities can be crushed by the economic bloc.³

Autarky acquired the characteristics of a religious crusade:

> The Italian people have sensed and understood not only the usefulness, but the, I would say, sacred necessity of the battle for autarky and, when I say the people, I include the inventors, producers, workers and consumers. All the divisions of this army have marched, some further, some less far, but today the speed of the march must be accelerated beyond the limits of what is possible. No energy must be wasted, all wills must be channeled, all sacrifices faced, all slow survivors or skeptics got rid of. The stakes of this game – which is anything but a game - are immense: it is a question of military power and therefore of the future of the homeland.⁴

and also involved the language of fashion:

> The inevitable function as propaganda that language assumes, even outside the field of commercial transactions, has caused the ENM, involved in work it is superfluous to illustrate here, to turn its attention to the discipline of the use of the word, considered a vehicle not only of spiritual influence but also, and especially in the delicate field of fashion, of materials imported from abroad. [...] The idea for this "Italian Dictionary and Analysis of Fashion" was born by spontaneous generation, and it is intended as an auxiliary means of propaganda and action in the struggle for the emancipation of Italian activities operating in the sector from influences and supplies from other countries.⁵

The *Commentario dizionario italiano della moda* ("Italian Fashion Dictionary and Commentary") was published in 1936 by journalist and writer Cesare Meano on behalf of the ENM, with the aim of purifying the Italian language and normalising approximately 1,600 fashion terms. The creation of the book was part of the linguistic policy of fascism, "focused on the

---

3 Speech given at the Berlin Olympic Stadium the 28th of September, 1937.
4 From the speech given to the Supreme Autarky Commission on the 18th of November, 1939, *Scritti e discorsi*, XII, pp. 244-45.
5 Meano, C., *Commentario dizionario italiano della moda*, Ente nazionale della moda, Turin 1936, p. IX.

preservation of the language from foreign influences, in parallel with the autarky and xenophobia implemented in the economic sector, and affecting both the lexical and the morphological sphere."[6]

In Italy, "autarkic politics could only be developed in the forms of a relaunch of the imperialist policy of preparation for war and an acceleration of the process of monopolistic concentration."[7] Furthermore, the war policy was necessary to strengthen the authority of fascism "against a capitalist bourgeoisie that is more willing to command than to obey and that only feels fascist to the extent that it has its hands free in the pursuit of maximum profit."[8] In the 1930s, the fascist regime broke away from the interests of the petty and medium bourgeoisie to try to identify itself, in the phase of its greatest political expansion and relative consolidation, with an industrialized and powerful Italy which was no longer prevalently agricultural and clerical.[9] Industrial manager Ettore Conti described fascist neo-capitalism as follows:

> In this period in which a desire to move towards the people is stated daily, a financial oligarchy has emerged in the industrial field that recalls ancient feudalism. Production is largely controlled by a few groups, each of which presided over by one man. Agnelli, Cini, Volpi, Pirelli, Donegani, Falck and very few others completely dominate the various branches of industry. In Italy we have more than 10,000 companies carrying out industrial activities which represent a nominal capital of 40 billion, 32 billion of which under the control of just 500 companies, that is, almost four-fifths of the capital is owned by 5% of the companies; and even in this modest fraction the same names often appear.[10]

The rural housewife could not serve the cause, and the aristocratic woman, who endured the Italian model "as if she

---

6   Bonadonna, M.F., "Il Fascismo contro i francesismi della moda. Il *Commentario dizionario* di Cesare Meano," *L'analisi linguistica e letteraria*, XXI, n. 2, 2013, pp. 191-206, p. 191.
7   Villari, L., *Capitalismo italiano del Novecento*, Laterza, Bari 1972, p. 376-377.
8   *Ibid.*
9   Ivi, p. 379. The regime's agricultural policy had failed and in 1937 Italy sent 30,000 agricultural workers to Germany.
10 Conti, E., *Dal taccuino di un borghese*, Il Mulino, Bologna 1986, p. 655.

were putting on a tunic, out of a pure spirit of discipline,"[11] was to fabricate and project fascism's image of power on the stage of the world.

2.1 Fashioning Fascism

It should be noted that Italy had a poor supply of raw materials and the Italian economy was, of necessity, open to other countries. In the 1930s, Germany returned to being Italy's main trading partner (29.4% of total imports in 1939), while the reduction in the importance of France and Great Britain continued and the importance of the United States decreased considerably.[12] Autarky in fashion had the ambitious goal of replacing Paris with Turin and of reversing the direction of flow of commercial relations in the field of fashion and luxury goods. In 1932, when the Chanel and Schiaparelli houses had opened their own offices in Turin, with the backing of Italian industry, a French source recognised the measures taken by the Italian government as "a real threat" to French dominance in fashion.[13] But the *haute couture* crisis was not just about Italy. After the stock market crash of 1929, the duties on imported goods prompted American buyers in Paris to buy "patterns and *patrons* protected by customs exception, obtaining the rights of reproduction."[14] The trade in patterns, in which a large part of the Italian dressmaking industry was involved, fed into an illegal system of copies which was added to the illegal copies of designs produced in real time. Throughout the decade, Italians were numbered among the most active copyists, even after the autarkic "new direction,"[15] and

---

11   Aspesi, N., *op. cit.*, p. 55.
12   Federico, G., Natoli, S., Tattara. G., Vasta, M., *Il commercio estero italiano (1862-1950)*, IV, Laterza, Rome-Bari 2011, pp. 34-50.
13   Garnier, G, *op. cit.*, p. 126.
14   Butazzi, G., "Gli anni Trenta. La moda italiana si mette a confronto, tra autarchia e nuove prospettive," in Chiarelli, C., *Moda femminile tra le due guerre*, Sillabe, Florence 2000, p. 12-19, p. 12.
15   Garnier, G., *op. cit.*, p. 81. Among these Ventura sent representatives including, apparently, Germana Marucelli.

Milanese seamstress Germana Marucelli, who had developed deep ties to French fashion, was among the most fervent. Her fanaticism after the sanctions acquired political overtones. When the fascist government obliged high fashion dressmakers to ensure ten percent of their production was Italian designs, her fashion shows were so often caught *in flagrante* – without the twelve mandatory designs – that "once they gave her a huge fine and she ended up in a trial that gave rise to even more copying of French designs.[16] In fact, Marucelli not only continued to copy French designs but actually began to sell them as fake originals to other Italian dressmakers, including the famous Ventura fashion house based in Corso Vittorio Emanuele in the premises of the Astra theatre and directed by the legendary Madame Anna. Despite the ban in force, in February 1940 Marucelli was still able to go to Paris – thanks to a permit obtained with the invented excuse of having to join an injured lover on the Maginot line – to buy for Ventura and other Italian dressmakers, taking advantage of Signora Fantechi's pass, one of her wealthy clients. After bombing damaged her shop during the war, Marucelli found refuge in an Hotel Regina's apartment in Stresa, where her most important clients, including the extremely elegant Flora d'Elys, stayed. With its beautiful, elegant young ladies who purchased her original designs, Marucelli had started experimenting and creating fashion for her increasingly demanding clients in the absence of Parisian ones, Stresa being a sanctuary in the chaos of war.

In the fashion sector, "the autarkic imperative"[17] assumed "a particular and significant character that was not restricted to the economic sector, but was coloured by interesting reflections of a higher order," because it was not a question "simply of producing a mass of products able to satisfy internal needs or to fuel exports, but of giving a specific and unmistakable character to the production so that it was in every respect, including aesthetically,

---

16   Pivano, F., *Le favole del ferro da stiro. Ricordi di Germana Marucelli scritti da Fernanda Pivano*, East 128, Milan 1964.
17   "Dalle manifestazioni del 'centro' di Torino si irradierà un'azione tesa al raggiungimento dell'autarchia," *La Stampa*, 27 November 1937, p. 4.

the direct expression of our world and of our sensibility." Fashion, which had "always been the fruit of these factors throughout history," must be even more so in an autarkic regime, since autarky did not mean "only independence of economies, but also autonomy of intellect, of taste and of aesthetic." But the industry was well aware of the international dimension of fashion; a study by the Fascist General Confederation of Italian Industry of 1929[18] highlighted how "the struggle between nations" that aspire to prevail in the fashion industry tended to "shift the field of creations and presentations; that is, to make it their own, rather than creating their own fashion to impose on other countries," because it was where these presentations took place that business was generated that involved all aspects of the fashion industry and determined profitable trade with foreign countries.[19]

At the centre of the battle for Italian fashion was the textile industry, with its autarkic fabrics. In the 1930s, wool production was traditionally one of the Italian economy's strengths, but the country relied heavily on imports for quality raw materials and Italian cotton production was also limited, expensive and largely dependent on imports from Turkey and Egypt. Italy therefore had to develop a strategy to overcome dependence. With the support of the fascist regime, the Italian textile producers led by the Snia-Viscosa company (the "National Industrial Company for Viscosa Applications") focused on the protection and expansion of the Italian domestic market while aggressively targeting export markets, mainly France. Efforts were concentrated on the development of synthetic fabrics, due to lower production costs and the lack of raw materials on national soil, the replacement of cotton fabrics with those made with locally sourced materials such as hemp and linen and local forestry programs to produce giant reeds that could provide Italy with a domestic source of cellulose, the raw material for the production of the rayon that Italy was forced to import. Regime propaganda boasted of the natural fibres obtained from local and colonial resources, fur

---

18   Confederazione Generale Fascista dell'Industria Italiana, *L'industria italiana a metà del XX secolo*, Castaldi, Rome 1929, pp. 563-564.
19   Ivi, p. 568.

(the regulations necessitated the use of native fox, dyed mole, sea otter and angora rabbit), rayon, China grass, Albene, Rhodia, Bemberg and Lanital. Some of these fabrics were given virile and evocative names such as Viritex and Raiontex by Zegna[20] and the posters advertising them used the colours of the Italian flag and imperial symbols. In addition, efforts were made to push forward the printing processes which, in the principal fashion-producing countries, had given good results with the production and adaptation to the new lines of soft and draped garments, where the effect of decorative motifs "in scattered harmony" was exploited as much as possible.[21]

The manufacture of autarkic textiles went hand in hand with the mass production of clothes[22] – as yet still underdeveloped in Italy –, the success of important creators and dressmakers, avant-garde experimentations and with the promotion of regional craftsmanship and handmade products linked to the rediscovery and protection of ethnographic traditions. Among the countless creations featured in fashion and architecture magazines,[23] the

---

[20] In a memo in the Zegna archive dated March 6, 1941 one can read that due to the war and the increasingly frequent sinking of steamboats, a long period of lack of wool was expected. For this reason it was considered appropriate, both for the future of the workers and of the company, to start the manufacture of rayon fabrics on a large scale, without expectations of large profits. As it would be detrimental to "the good introduction of our woolen fabrics," a company, Raiontex, was set up, which would buy the Rayon, have it processed by Zegna, and resell it abroad since "the Government most likely authorises the sale for the interior only of so-called State fabrics at controlled prices."

[21] Orsi Landini, R., in *La Galleria del costume*, V, Centro Di, Florence 1993, pp. 29-34; for Italian fabrics of the 1930s see Fanelli, G., Fanelli, R., *Il tessuto Art Deco e anni Trenta. Disegno, moda, architettura*, Cantini, Florence 1986, pp. 235-243.

[22] Lupano, M., Vaccari, A., *op. cit.*, 2009, p. 84-89; Paris, I., *Oggetti cuciti, op. cit.*, pp. 41-73; Tongiorigi, F., Torricelli, G., Principalli. M., (edited by), *Per una storia della moda pronta: problemi e ricerche*, Florence, Edifir 1991, pp. 167-168. Atti del V Convegno internazionale del CISST, Milano, 26 February - 28 February 1990.

[23] The principal magazines include: *Almanacco della donna italiana, Bellezza, Lidel, Fili Moda, Omnibus, Documento Moda, Modella, Raion, Rassegna dell'Ente nazionale e della moda*. Artificial yarns and some garments such as Pirelli mackintoshes are also advertised in *Domus and Lo Stile nella*

day dress in printed fabric, worn with a fur coat, was one of the most representative garments of the autarkic woman.[24] These simple and practical dresses in crepe, rayon, silk and hemp, and also designed for cycling, were worn across the social classes and represented a link between high-level dressmaking, the more modest dressmaking done at home or by the local seamstresses using paper patterns, and the dresses displayed in department stores.[25]

Among the fashion of the period, the unique creations of Anita Pittoni, Gegia and Marisa Bronzini and Fernanda Lamma from Bologna, whose creations were particularly significant with regard to principles of self-sufficiency and the use of natural and artificial fibres, stood out. At the end of the 1920s, Pittoni opened her decorative art studio in Trieste where, together with a select circle of artisans, she carried out structural and material research into rayon, hemp, jute and broom, and took new approaches to techniques such as knitting and crochet, with designs both for interior decoration and fashion.[26] Even the work of Gegia Bronzini, conducted with her daughter Marisa, fell somewhere between art, craftsmanship and avant-garde culture. Her artefacts – made with natural fibres grown in the Venetian countryside and spun and woven in the workshop – were sold in local shops and

---

casa e nell'arredamento; cfr. Dal Falco, F., *Prodotti autarchici 1930-1944: architettura, design, moda*, Designpress, Rome 2014, p. 159.

24 These are soft dresses, draped, cinched at the waist, with short sleeves and modest necklines, with light or dark backgrounds featuring coloured patterns (flowers, dots, palmettes, squares...) worn with a bandolier bag, wedge sandals, gloves, turban or hat. Other garments that define the feminine look of those years are the wool or Lanital dress worn with embroidered or masculine-cut shirts, the trouser skirt, the twin-set, the waxed canvas raincoat, the coat with accentuated lapels tightened by belts and autarkic rabbit, wolf, caracul, cat, leopard and silver fox furs; and for the evening the enveloping stage dresses of black or dark velvet, silk, satin and even wool, in ivi, pp. 177, 147.

25 Zingone, La Rinascente, Cim, Upim.

26 "Esempi di produzione italiana," *Domus*, n. 148, April 1940, p. 92; Cuffaro, R., Vasselli, L., Anita Pittoni, in Finessi, B., (edited by), *Autarchia, Austerità, Autoproduzione*, Corraini, Mantova 2015, pp. 82-85.

in Venice.[27] Also notable were the experiments of Lamma, who among her original wraparound dresses offered an evening dress in glass fibre cloth with sandals made of the same material.[28] The most interesting results with hemp were obtained by Anita Pittoni with the *Laboratorio artigiano triestino* ("Artisan Workshop of Trieste"), which presented creations for furniture and clothing at the Turin events. In the mid-thirties the regime undertook to launch hemp as a fashionable fabric at an international level, and it eventually appeared at the Paris fashion shows of spring 1935 as *Balilla*[29] hemp.

The regime created a mythology around national textiles. Autarky was not a definition but a "lifestyle," understood as a physical necessity and a form of spiritual obedience. In the creation of the autarkic style "the woman must become the guide and the initiator of everything. Action must start from the home, where the woman rules, and from there must extend everywhere."[30] On January the 31st, 1938 the important *Mostra del tessile nazionale* ("National Textile Exhibition") dedicated to autarkic fabrics, commissioned by Achille Starace and inaugurated by Mussolini on the 18th of November, 1937 – on the second anniversary of the sanctions – closed in Rome and for the occasion, the EIAR broadcast a commentary on the assembly of industrialists. As part of the exhibition, there were fashion shows from thirty Italian luxury fashion houses in the presence of a

---

27   Miglio, C., "Gegia e Marisa Bronzini," in Cuffaro, R., Vasselli, L., *op. cit.*, pp. 80-81.
28   "Abito da sera di vetro e sandali di vetro. Modello Fernanda Lamma," *Moda*, May 1935, p. 5.
29   *Balilla* was the nickname of Genoese youth who local legend held started the revolt against the Habsburg forces occupying the city during the War of the Austrian Succession and who gave his name to the *Opera Nazionale Balilla* Fascist youth organization.
30   *Cordelia*, November-December 1938, p. 442, cit. in Ruggiero, A., "L'immagine della donna italiana nelle riviste femminili durante gli anni del Fascismo", URL: http://www.officinadellastoria.info/magazine/index.php?option=com_content&view=article& id=350:limmagine-della-donna-italiana-nelle-riviste-femminili-durante-gli-anni-del- fascismo&catid=68:fotografia-e-storia.

delegation from the German fashion industry.[31] Edda Ciano, the international face of the regime, was there, as was Lucio Ridenti, who wrote for the occasion that "while making progress in terms of wealth and femininity, our fashion demands nothing more than dressing appropriately and making women look the way we wish them to: lively, nimble and proud of the health of their bodies – Italian, then, even on the outside."[32] The importance of Snia-Viscosa, leader in the production of viscose,[33] emerged at the exhibition, while rayon was defined as the "most Italian" and "most modern" fabric. The continuous references to the modernity of synthetic fibres, with modern techniques of processing hemp and broom, held real promise for the future, expressing above all the modernity of the regime and the myth of the power of the Empire risen again on the fated hills of Rome.

On the 11th of May, 1940 the gala evening organized by ENM for the *Mostra dell'abbigliamento autarchico* ("Exhibition of Autarkic Clothing") which would run from the 12th of May to the 9th of June, was held at *Teatro della moda* in Turin, inaugurating the venue. The inauguration included a presentation of collections by selected high fashion houses to an audience invited by ENM, with a certain number of paid seats. After the show, the programme included the ballet show *Sleeping Beauty* as adapted by Nives Poli with La Scala ballet company directed by maestro Norberto Mola. A few days later, again at *Teatro della moda*, the opera season was opened with Giacomo Puccini's *Turandot*, conducted by Maestro Tullio Serafin and directed by Mario Frigerio. Queen Irene of Savoy, Duchess of Spoleto, authorities, senators and national councillors and their spouses attended a parade of two hundred garments divided into morning-, afternoon- and evening-wear described as haute

---

31 On the German Fashion Agency, see chapter six of Guenther, I., *op. cit.*, pp. 167-202.
32 Aspesi, N., *op. cit.*, p. 81.
33 Balli, A., *La mostra del tessile nazionale*, Cesari, Ascoli Piceno 1937; Munoz, A., *Echi della mostra del tessile*, Palombi, Rome 1938; Doctor, M., «Le realizzazioni della SNIA-Viscosa e il miracolo di Torviscosa», *L'industria nazionale. Rivista mensile dell'autarchia*, n. 4, April 1941, pp. 19-21.

couture designs, the "motor of mass production." Participating fashion houses included Ajazzi and Fantechi, Biki, Buscaroli, De Gasperi-Zezza, Di Fenizio, Dragoni, Fercioni, Gabriellasport, Gori, Mattè, Trinelli, Ventura, Villa and Zecca.

For the occasion, the "logical" necessity of choosing Turin as the capital of fashion was reiterated on the basis of "the certainty of what tomorrow will be the changed political and economic conditions of Europe." The official aim of the exhibition was, in fact, to "reaffirm that tradition of elegance, refinement and good taste which is a universally recognised prerogative of the city of Turin,"[34] and for this purpose it was divided into eight sections: a fabrics hall, a hall of the Turin traders, a central hall, a hall of the Textile Agency, an automobile hall, a mass production hall, the Italviscosa hall and a floral exhibition. The clothes at *Teatro della moda* were not modelled in a parade as on a catwalk but moved freely on a raised theatrical stage. The first hall was undecorated, its white walls covered with Mussolini's pronouncements on the matter at hand, and its function was of introducing the exhibition and presenting the products of autarky, the fabrics on show being mixed-wool, silk and mixed-silk, hemp, linen and artificial. In front of the entrance there was an exact replica of the marble plaque commemorating "The enormous injustice of sanctions." Against the background of "a pale green that highlights the colours, soft, fluffy fabrics at the corners of the room give the space an elegant tone, in keeping with the exquisite and simple aesthetic of the event." The fabrics for men and women's clothes were "beautiful." Room number two showcased the production and launch at a fixed price of typical autarkic products selected by the Ministry of Corporations. In this room there were the special exhibitions of the Serta company for Atres fabrics, of Tulpizzo (Union of Tulle and Lace producers), of Cucirini Cantoni Coats and the installation of radio amplifiers for Radio Valenza in Turin. In the passage between rooms one and two there were the exhibitions of The Assembled Rubber Factories of Turin (FRIGT) and the detergents' demonstration section.

---

34 "Oggi si inaugura il Centro," *La Stampa*, 11 May 1940, p. 5.

In the third section, the central hall, linen for men and women, handbags, typical footwear, stockings, gloves, hats, jewellery and costume jewellery, filigree and coral, flowers and lace, feathers and ribbons were on show, in addition to the Carlo Pacchetti Institute of Rabbit Breeding of Alessandria and the Experimental Institute of Naples. The fourth room was occupied by the National Textile Body which, in addition to explaining to consumers the problems of autarkic materials, sought to educate them on the correct way to treat them: "Do not blame a fabric for the result it may have given you: rather make sure that the treatment used is the one best suited to it."[35] The fifth room was dedicated to Italian-produced automobiles, organized by RACI (the Royal Automobile Circle of Italy) and aimed to demonstrate the influence of custom bodywork on Italian fashion and elegance through the aerodynamics of both luxury and small cars, in which "the effort and tendency of our technicians towards a perfection which is not alien to reconciling the needs of the machine with aesthetics" was visible.[36] The sixth room was dedicated to mass-produced clothing, the first comprehensive review of the sector, in order to illustrate the future possibilities of "an orderly and artistic application of standardized production." In general, the exhibition was presented as a documentary review of technical importance in a sophisticated setting and exhibited a variety of products chosen from those considered most significant of Italy's progress in the application of autarkic plans. A peculiarity of the exhibition was the absence "of that static nature that usually makes those events which are destined to remain open for a certain period of time monotonous and rapidly lose the interest of the public,"[37] thanks to the rotation of the products on display every four days.

The open-air fashion theatre, which was opened on the 7th of July, 1938 hosted several thousand spectators. A singular construction, it implied a different vision of fashion from that

---

35 Puppo, G., "Mostra dell'abbigliamento autarchico al Palazzo della moda," *Turin. Rassegna mensile della città*, n. 5, May 1940, pp. 2-13.
36 Ivi, p. 11.
37 "Mirabile varietà di prodotti," *Stampa Sera*, 10 May 1940, p. 2.

of Paris, where a select few consumed fashion inside luxurious ateliers. The originality of the open-air theatre consisted of a dual stage, with two prosceniums facing one another, one of which opened onto the open-air theatre and the other onto the interior one. The creation of Ettore Sottsass, soon reduced to rubble when it was bombed on November the 8th, 1942 and July the 13th, 1943 it was part of fascism's attempt to create a mass liturgy in the fashion sector via rituals, events and exhibitions. Mussolini believed the fascist revolution must create new forms and festivals that would become traditions which would be considered essential for keeping the fire of the fascist faith burning.[38] The fashion exhibitions did not so much have the function of launching the designs of Italian high fashion as they did of rekindling the enthusiasm of the masses, in the knowledge that they were excited "more by a beautiful symbol than by a mediocre reality."[39]

In the fascist fashion system, every participant was an "artist in his or her field" and contributed to the overall harmony of the show, according to a totalitarian vision:

> It was necessary to create the chain, ring by ring: from the designer of fabrics to the person who weaves them, from the weaver of fabrics to the person who turns them into something capable of capturing the attention of women, from the fashion designer to the skilled seamstress who is able to see the design in a simple watercolour sketch and create it, just as the great actor creates his part, written in the script, and so on all the way up to the model, who is not an automated mannequin but an artist in her own right, who has to live that dress and bring it to life, and finally, to the photographer, to the fashion magazine, to the elegant lady who buys the model at a high price or to the mass produced product sold to the general public.[40]

In this regard, Giovanna Dompè,[41] author of the "fashion" entry in the 1934 Italian Encyclopaedia, clarified that it was the democratisation of fashion – which from aristocratic had grown bourgeois, and which suffered from "the lack of stylistic

---

38 Gentile, E., *The Struggle for Modernity, op. cit.*, p. 111.
39 Gentile, E., *op. cit.*, p. 112.
40 *Ibid.*
41 Author of *Storia della moda e del costume* in 1934.

guidelines" – which had "made it fall into a confusion worse than bad taste."

The regime's work to define a model of Italianness in fashion was extended to the showroom dummy, which must be in keeping "with the Italic race. Healthy firm women and well-proportioned men, not seductive and without flirtatious expressions:"

> A circular from the Ministry of Popular Culture sent to clothing retailers says that Italian women do not have slim hips or flat chests because motherhood is a coveted goal for them. And motherhood fills and firms up the gaps. The mannequins are inspired by the classic lines of Italian beauty that have the measurements of Apollo and Venus 1925 and 1940.[42]

The model of Italic beauty "has round breasts and hips, a graceful and regular face, not at all whimsical and haughty; a happy smile, joyful eyes." The autarkic mannequin was to be the image of health and life force. "The mannequin must be *simpatico*," an expression of good taste, of "real life," "of reality": "realistic humanity, lacking only the power of speech![43]:" "Grace," "joy" and "sympathy" were the words used in opposition to the *femme fatale* model that American cinema was promoting. This intrusion into the design even of mannequins exemplified the totalitarian politics of fascism "which regulated family life, clothing, greeting and speech, the very vocabulary of everyday language with intolerable license."[44]

Italy's first market conference for the millinery sector was held in Turin from the 23rd to the 28th of September, 1941. Turin newspapers rejoiced that the presentation was devoid of French influence and trumpeted the decline of the "humorous type" of hat and the affirmation of more highbrow artistic concepts. *La*

---

42 Below are the measurements, calculated in an unknown manner, of the Greek Venus and Venus 1925. Greek Venus (1940): height: 1.62 m., Weight: 61, 222 kg., Chest 0.86 m., Also: 0.90 m; Venus 1925 (peak of the crisis, era of "Sardine" women): 1,61 m.; 49,790 kg; 0.69 m.; 0,70 m. The Venus referred to is the Venus de Milo. Most likely the mannequin company was Rosa, Milano. "In a workshop of fake creatures ...», Stampa Sera, 28 May 1940, p. 4.
43 *Ibid.*
44 Monelli, P., *Roma 1943*, Einaudi, Turin 2012, p. 15.

Stampa railed against the "equestrian circus traditions dated 1937 in contrast with the present day which seeks ideas for original fashion statements in dignified aesthetic intentions, meaning no veils, flowers and fruits. Uncovered faces, covered napes,"[45] referring to the *Circus* collection of Italian Elsa Schiaparelli, whose surrealist eccentricities had sparked scandal even in Paris. Among the inspirations at the conference were "romantic motifs, apple trees, literary and historical allusions, nineteenth century opera; a widespread theatrical influence and the peasant styles of the Alpine valleys; halo shapes, medieval helmets with visible halos, the use of the central eighteenth-century diadems and Albanian costume: large, high turbans looming forward. The rhinestone is outdated, like the bags and huge hats from before the war."

The models and motifs of the millinery show abandoned "the tiny caps seeking an improbable equilibrium, the lampshade veils that obscured the faces of our ladies and the extravagant and sometimes buffoonish junk that has too often, and for too long, been the fashion," and welcomed privileged forms such as classical motifs taken from art and graceful and vaguely masculine sporty styles. The disappearance of decorations imitating jewels stimulated the use of tulle, which was not rationed, and traditional lace, "the pride and joy of the embroiderers." New raw materials made an imposing appearance at the exhibition: "an extremely telling index of the influence of new technical discoveries on our production."[46]

Later, at the same time as the high fashion events for foreigners, the ENM organized the second Millinery Market Show which was attended by eighty-five industrial and artisan companies:

> Artificial flowers were displayed alongside Barbisio's felts, the La Famigliare hat factory and SA Rossi Giuseppe [...] the artistic trimmings and beautiful ribbons of the *Nastrificio Italiano*, [...] the hides of the Furriers Tannery of Carignano, the fancy feathers, the special fabrics presented

---

45 "Anticipazioni sulle nuove fogge dei cappelli invernali delle signore," *La Stampa*, 9 September 1940, p. 2.
46 "Le modiste all'Ente della moda," *Torino. Rassegna mensile della città*, n. 10, October 1940, p. 61-62, p. 62.

by Calegari Cora and Vittorio and Della Serta, Tulpizzo's chenille, vaporous veils, lace and tulles; the precious velvets of the Cordani brothers and Gaspare Delleani. [...] Foreign influence is now nothing but a memory.[47]

On that occasion, the ENM recorded an increase in interest and the presence of "completely new" customers for Italy, in particular Swiss fashion houses and German buyers purchasing felt. There was also interest in a collective presentation of the straw industries of Florence and the lace industries of Orvieto and Rapallo, artistic trimmings in gilded metal and coloured stones, and the application of majolica for accessories, one of the exhibition's novelties.

In December 1940, the ENM published the colour charts for spring-summer 1941 which were to serve as the basis for the colour of clothing products. There were five charts in all: one for wool, one for silk, one for felt, one for rayon and one for straw. The wool chart featured twenty colours, including Tyrrhenian blue, Adriatic green, aquamarine green, mastic (somewhere between grey and beige), and silica grey. Among the most intense colours were rubber red, bark, grape must red, typhoon turquoise and "styx," an intense violet with hints of blue. The silk chart featured novelties such as Malacca red, Coconut (a refined shade of rosy hazelnut), and coppery Otter. The straw and rayon charts were identical, the only difference being that, while artificial straw's base color was white, natural straw possessed a compact sheen the artificial one did not. The names given to the colours evoked the myths of fascism, imperialism and the Mediterranean, from viticulture and the sea to Africa, and the press raved with its usual enthusiasm that the charts, especially the one for straw, had been the subject of numerous requests from foreign producers.[48]

The ENM's frenzy also extended to *manichine* ("mannequins"), as the regime called them, and in the same month in which the Millinery Conference was held,

---

47 Ivi, p. 50.
48 "Colori nuovi e sfumature inedite," *Stampa Sera*, 7 December 1940, p. 2.

the modelling course of the *Ente nazionale fascista di addestramento al lavoro commerciale* ("National Fascist Commercial Work Training Organization", or ENFALC) opened its doors, defining new professional criteria. At the same time, in January 1941, following the meeting of the Italo-Germanic High Fashion Committee which had the task of drawing up the directives for joint action of the two countries in the press, there was talk of an Axis fashion, which considered clothing proof of the level reached by "a form of life" and a demonstration of the superiority of the race. A national course for models, which attracted twenty-six participants, was established in the ENFALC school, as well as a course for fashion designers. The school was located on the four floors of a building in Via S. Francesco da Paola in Turin. The fashion designers were given a sample of fabric with which they had to develop a design such as an evening dress, while in the window dressing room they executed sketches on established themes before moving on to practical studies. The school was equipped with dress mannequins and cutting tables, while in the gym the models performed rhythmic exercises and were taught how to behave in society. There were fifty-six teachers and, as there were shifts of students in the day and in the evening, lessons never stopped, partly because many of the students worked during the day in businesses which were obliged to allow them to attend the lessons.

One of the most trumpeted autarkic achievements was in the field of furs. Autarkic fur had both economic and symbolic importance because even during the war it allowed a display of luxury without going against the tenets of the regime. New discoveries for the utilisation of Italian skins meant that the use of furs also spread to the lower social strata. The processing of skins with no particular qualities of beauty or colour allowed Italian industry to create cheap furs not devoid of aesthetic qualities alongside prohibitively priced natural furs, and was considered another demonstration of the fascist ability to get around Italy's lack of raw materials, highlighting the technical and artistic skills of the artisans capable of transforming low-quality leathers into objects of value. What counted was not the preciousness of the raw materials, but the ability of a nation to transform the little it had into beautiful objects with economic value.

2.2 There's a War Raging... But You Wouldn't Know It

From 1940 on, the regime banned fashion creators from traveling to Paris, because fashion should be aligned with the "discipline of war." This discipline provided for the adaptation of civilian customs to the "moral climate" of the war and a further squeeze on the fashion industry. French *haute couture* had received a huge blow with the occupation of Paris, although in part it would continue to work for the new collaborationist society of occupied France, and the ENM – as well as the New York Fashion Group – wanted to take advantage of this situation to replace Paris on the world fashion map of the future. To this end, the propaganda was intensified. Italian women must "dress Italian" at all costs, the war required it. Clad in embroidered dresses, straw hats, sequins and pearls, the most elegant women of the Axis gathered in Venice at the Summer 1941 *Rassegna del tessile e dell'abbigliamento autarchico* ("Autarkic Textile and Clothing Exhibition") – the word fashion having disappeared from the title – to present to the world a glamorous image.[49] Enthusiastic about the success of the exports of rayon to the markets of South America and South Africa, the periodical *La donna fascista* ("The Fascist Woman") wrote that the exhibition was a riot of bright colours, harmonious lines, kindness

---

49 At the beginning of the 19th century a radical change in the notion of luxury in Western Europe took place. In past centuries, excess had been one of the objectives of courtly fashion, before distinctive quality became refinement and style (without however abandoning cost). The waste of time and of goods connected with uselessness and costliness is a mechanism for gaining prestige among the upper classes, even primitive ones. See Veblen, T., *La teoria della classe agiata. Studio economico sulle istituzioni*, Einaudi, Turin 1949.

and grace; production was so abundant that it was exported abroad and, therefore, "there is no need to fear rationing,"[50] even though rationing would be announced a few days later. Despite the exhibitions and rhetoric about the *cittadine soldato* ("female citizen-soldiers") ready for the "carnage," the nation was unprepared to fight a war of this scale. *The New York Times* described Italy as the "land of fear," but the fashion and women's press never referred to fear or the tragic reality of war and its devastating effects on the population, instead insisting obsessively on women's duty to "be beautiful."

With Italy's entry into the war, anti-bourgeois propaganda intensified[51] as, consequently, did that against the culture, cinema, music, customs, fashions, oddities and immoral frivolities of France and the United States, even though Italian life seemed to continue as before in the summer of 1940, and on the Romagna Riviera and in Versilia they were dancing the fox-trot, which had replaced the fashion for the tango. "There's a War On...But You Wouldn't Know It," assured the caption of a July 1940 fashion report in *Dea* magazine. "Next to the sober evening wear of the two men, with black trousers and white jacket, the beautiful Rodia veil of the girl, fresh from a dance, envelops her like an airy cloud, making her even more seductive. A woman between two men: to whom the palm of victory?"[52]

In 1940 the number of Turin fashion awards multiplied, adding the ones for dressmakers and for the best dressed ladies at the journalists' ball, where artist Giulio Boetto had the task of portraying the woman wearing the most elegant Italian costume or dress, or the Elegance Award at a Nice-Morbelli show.[53] And already in February 1940 conferences were being held in

---

50 Gagliardini, G., "Autarchia dell'abbigliamento nella mostra del tessile a Venezia," *La donna fascista*, n. 44, 30 September 1941, p. 12.
51 An admonition in rhyme reads: "Weep, ye merrymakers, weep loudly for dancing is doomed to death."
52 *Dea*, n. 7-8, July-August 1940.
53 "Spettacoloso successo della festa mascherata al Teatro Carignano," *La Stampa*, 3 February 1940, p. 5.

preparation for total war at which autarky and its results were abstractly discussed.

Since 1940 there had been incessant propaganda regarding "discernment" and "good taste" in dress. Because of the war, beauty salons and hairdressers had "finally" stopped using foreign products and the good "Italian woman" took care of herself without falling into the excesses of the American, "because the Italian is more of an aesthete and a lover of beauty than other peoples and prefers a well-coiffed and well-dressed woman to manifestations of artificial simplicity that arrive even at nakedness. The secret is to avoid going overboard."[54] But there was no need to worry, because the Italian woman was "naturally" inclined to moderation and her preference was for Italian products that "make her an admired wife and mother, who, as Tasso sings, aims to increase her study and art – the natural beauty that shines in her."[55] On the other hand, it was recognized that fashion needed novelty, but this too was not a problem, because "novelties are our specialty."[56]

To celebrate Italy's entry into the war, a certain Mossotti had invented a special gas mask and a device that, Hollywood style, projected the *duce*'s face – framed by Italy's tricolour flag – into the fog. A distraught Paris was about to lose its dominance in many things, including fashion, and the thinking was that this was precisely the right time to bring out the famous fashion magazine:[57] "The city that until recent years exerted an unjustified fascination for ladies all over the world saw its chances diminished following the chaos caused by military turnarounds." As bizarre as it might seem, the declared goal of the ENM in the midst of war was, among other things, Italy's "primacy" in the field of fashion:

> We feel this not only through the communiqué but through clear signs. Positions must be maintained and they are not always maintained by re-

---

54 "Nel mondo degli incantesimi per la bellezza delle signore," *Stampa Sera*, 12 February 1940, p. 2.
55 *Ibid.*
56 *Ibid.*
57 Meaning *Bellezza*.

maining on the defensive. Having ensured customs borders are more watertight is a step in the right direction, but the goal goes beyond that, and autarky must become supremacy. There is the currency problem but above all a wager to be won, and that wager is the prestige of the nation, the profits of international trade and the strengthening of the various sectors. We must realise today that the wind is in our favour and make the task less difficult for the ENM.[58]

In an attempt to centralise control over fashion, the fascist government decided to create new local fashion committees through the *Federazione dei Fasci femminili* ("Federation of Female Fascists") with the task of developing initiatives for the promotion of high fashion and the totalitarian propaganda for national fabrics and mass-produced clothing, thus dismantling the committees of local patronesses. The task of cleaning up female mentality, of propaganda and implementation of the Agency's directives was given to the members of the Female Fasces.[59] Previous committees had in fact tended to escape central control and behave like miniature fashion agencies, not hesitating to take sides against the ENM and thus preventing the "birth of fashion," "a creature of the will to power."[60]

Since 1941, in conjunction with rationing, the *Corporazione dell'abbigliamento* ("Clothing Corporation") began to sell mass-produced popular fabrics and clothing of poor quality, with standard features and fixed prices, on the domestic market, to be distributed in certain selected stores. The standardised production was regulated by the ministerial decree of the 16th of March, 1941-XIX, supplemented by the decree of the 11th of August, 1941-XIX, which obliged companies to allocate 75% of the textiles at their disposal for internal civilian uses and to produce yarns which were "technically suitable for the manufacture of standard products." Textile type-products (*tessili tipo*) were divided into categories: A (109 types of various fabrics for suits,

---

58 "Si crea nella disciplina una nuova mentalità," *La Stampa*, 15 February 1940, p. 5.
59 The representative of the National Fascist Party in the organisation was Gina Federzoni, wife of Luigi Federzoni.
60 "Maria di Piemonte presidente onoraria dei comitati dell'Ente moda," *La Stampa*, 20 February 1940, p. 6.

linens, blankets, accessories), B (11 types of velvets), C (92 types of fabrics for men's and women's clothing), D (157 types), E (25 types of knitwear and panties), F (34 types of socks), G (47 types of luxury fabrics), H (36 types of bedspreads), I (32 types of patterned knitwear), L (17 types of gloves), M (14 types of canvas), N (48 types of canvas), O (four types of carpet). Men's hats and caps were also categorised. The war was touted as the event that would reveal an Italian "line," because "minds and hearts are tempered in deprivation, discipline and sacrifice," and it legitimised the policing of female appearances.

As part of the war discipline, the *Corporazione dell'abbigliamento* ("Clothing Corporation") issued a ban on women wearing long or short trousers except for reasons of sport or work, as well as banning dresses with trains, double-breasted jackets, men's waistcoats and long trousers or knickerbockers for boys. Furthermore, the directives of the Ministry of the Interior absolutely forbade female office staff to wear skimpy clothes, make-up or nail polish.[61] For the winter of 1941, the fashion houses "got in line" by presenting a type of flared skirt with raised ribs over shorts that went down to the knee, covering the leg, and a very flared skirt over a knitwear garment functioning as stockings and trousers that reached from the foot to the waist and was reminiscent of medieval chainmail – which, according to one journalist, could only be flattering. The trousers (though the ENM preferred the more autarkic word "*calzoni*" to "*pantaloni*") had what was called the "jump" style: straight

---

61 *La moda maschile*, June 1941, p. 1. The *Corriere della Sera* of November 1941 gives notice of two interventions by the magistrate of Novi. A girl was surprised in the sports field wearing men's shorts and sentenced to a fine of 250 lire, the same magistrate sentenced fifty-year-old Maria de Rossi, defined as a "mature young lady," to a 200 lire fine because in the courtyard of her house she wore a pair of men's long trousers. In 1942 the prohibitions became more severe. In Marina di Massa, the carabinieri referred to judicial authorities women and girls who circulated, on foot or by bike, wearing short beach shorts, which were seized from them. Cit. in Quercia, A., (edited by), *Donne d'Europa. Quali prospettive*, Luigi Pellegrini Editore, Rome 1999, p. 104.

legs that fastened under the shoes. The preferred fabrics were waterproofed gabardine and waterproofed corduroy.

On the 28th of June, 1941 the Prefect of the Province of Trento issued an order forbidding women to "show themselves in public or circulate wearing long or short men's trousers, though the use of pant-skirts for cycling and overalls for proven work needs is permitted," under penalty of being "stopped" for reasons of public safety and morality and having one's bicycle seized. A report to the judicial authorities pursuant to Article 17 of the Public Security law provided for imprisonment of up to three months or a fine of two thousand lire:

> As for the clothes, try to make them as large and as long as necessary or, better still, use the comfortable pant-skirts that are one of fashion's more useful inventions and facilitate the movements and efforts of those who travel by bicycle without harming... that which must remain intact: a correct appearance. In short, our girls should not force us to affirm together with Alfredo Panzini that "the modesty of women was invented by men," but should rather try to affirm in this area too, and especially at this moment, those qualities that are traditional of our girls and constitute one of the main prerogatives of our race.[62]

At the women's *Littoriali* games of May 1940, the emphasis was placed upon the elegance of the participants – "an elegance made up of those details that the fascist uniform grants to uniformity" – and upon the absence of trousers. The participants' clothes showed a trend against the masculinisation of fashion – which included the use of trousers, jackets and English fabrics – except for one Neapolitan woman, who was reported and singled out for public mockery. The fascist euphoria for autarkic fashion and mass sports performances was echoed by pope Pius XII[63] who at the end of May 1941 received four thousand girls from Roman Catholic lay association *Azione Cattolica*, inviting them to hold a "Crusade of purity:"

---

62 *La provincia di Bolzano*, 25 July 1941, *Bolzano scomparsa* online archive.
63 22 May 1941, in Cava, A., *Ineluttabile. Moda e mode*, Vita e Pensiero, Milan 1943, p. 7, 41.

A daring, indecorous fashion for a young woman brought up as a Christian; garments so skimpy or that seem rather made to emphasise what they should cover; sport, dances, shows, auditions where the desire for fun and pleasure increases the most serious risks. As long as certain brazen attires remain the sad privilege of women of dubious reputation and almost a sign by which they can be recognized, none will not dare adopt them, but the day they are worn by people above all suspicion, there will no longer be any obstacle to following the trend – a trend that will perhaps lead to the worst possible fall from grace.[64]

Despite having its hands fairly full, in the winter of 1941 the ENM found a way to deal with the winter ski season which, despite the war, continued with the Olympics in Cortina: for the 1941 ski season "the undisputed domination of trousers suffered a powerful shock."[65] The aesthetic dilemma that the sportswomen found themselves facing was the choice between skirts and "breeches." The ENM preferred skirts, a solution that followed the "logic of tradition," and indicated certain types that denoted "the advent of an intelligent combination of skirt and trouser, combining feminine elegance with practicality." The trouser-skirt adhered to a modern aesthetic where the movement of the skirt highlighted the body of the skier. The institution also noted that as well as having enthusiastic female fans, the trouser-skirt also had enthusiastic male supporters. As for other garments, the institution proposed two "well received" trends which served as a basis for the creation of long jackets, tight and coming down over the hips, or short, bulging and tight at the waist. These short jackets were made with shiny waterproof fabric and lined with brightly coloured woollen knit or in leopard skin and taupe, which was "not only very elegant but also very practical as it can be turned inside-out and worn both ways,"[66] while there were long gabardine or corduroy jackets in colours either matching or

---

64 Speech by Pius XII to the young women of Azione Cattolica, in Pio XII, *Discorsi e radiomessaggi di sua santità Pio XII*, III, Tip. Poliglotta Vaticana, Vatican City 1960, pp. 86 and sgg.
65 "Orientamenti della moda," *Torino. Rassegna mensile della città*, n. 12, December 1940, pp. 46-48, p. 48.
66 The anonymous descriptions are taken from the monthly municipal magazine of Turin.

sharply contrasting with the trousers. Another "very successful" model of anorak was made with waterproofed heavy pure silk in bright, lively colours such as lacquer red, purplish-blue, egg-yellow and jade-green, and was completed by a hood. Finally, the ENM reported a "brand new" jacket made with specially treated Tuscan lambswool. The double-faced jacket, dyed in the customer's favourite colours, was soft suede on the outside with a waterproofed lambswool lining.

Other novelties included doublets in hand-knitted wool lined with natural-coloured calfskin fur to match the bright colours of the outside, while others were in angora wool, another self-produced material, in pastel or intense colours, which "bring a necessary note of colour to the ski suits, brightening them up and bestowing a particular elegance upon the whole." Cloaks were an essential part of a lady's mountain wardrobe and the directions, again, were clear: they could be made of waterproof gabardine lined with Tuscan lambswool and play with colour combinations – "Blue and gray, brown and hazelnut, plum and gray, green and brown" – or lined with very thick selected fabrics in classic white. In the field of headgear, the ENM proposed a velvet cap inspired by the shape of jockeys' caps, a velvet hood completed by two joined scarves which, when wrapped around the hood, formed a turban, and a Russian *ushanka* model edged with fur. The newest models included one in angora wool reproducing the classic bonnet knotted under the chin. The caps and doublet must match the gloves and socks. Finally, it was specified that other new colours and combinations based on personal taste could certainly be used, but that they must be based on those indicated by the ENM.

"(Imagination), harnessed by the practical needs of sport, was liberated in costumes and hotel suits," full of "original creations." A model of wide flannel trouser in intense colours – red-plum, green-cypress, blue-violet and black – with a very flared leg worn with a three-coloured velvet scarf worn at the waist, a blouse and matching velvet shoes that tied at the ankle with ribbons in the same colours as the scarf, for example. Another "sure-fire hit" costume was the jumpsuit, made of corduroy or flannel, coloured or black. This winter review of sports fashion, which was given a tone of elegant formality, aimed to distinguish itself from the traditional "skirt-suit" by the use of several distinctive elements: the relationship of the dressed body with the environment, the preservation of elegance and grace in practicality, the attention to detail, the perfection of the cut, the preference for intense but harmonious colour, the adoption of experiments and the transposition of a "sporty mood" into formal fashion.

In 1941, for the first time, the ENM presented a number of high fashion models to two hundred representatives of foreign fashion houses from Germany, Yugoslavia, Switzerland and other unnamed countries.[67] The press spoke of the event as a milestone in the regime's progress in promoting Italian fashion internationally. After having seen the collections of the Turin fashion houses in their respective ateliers and the Roman and Bolognese collections in Turin hotels, the delegations, who arrived in Turin on the 3rd of February, went to visit the textile factory of the Piacenza Brothers in Pollone and the city's fashion houses: "Through fashion, Paris once influenced the spirit and mood, and imposed French taste. [...] That is now all over. The collective presentations of garment designs for international customers marked the beginning of a new direction[68]." The German delegation was led by the representative of Minister Ley, Dr. Manthey, the president of the Clothing Industry Federation Dr. Tenyelmann and the director of the Fashion Institute Dr. Keller. After visiting the collections in the Turin salons, the delegation was a guest of the ENFALC school, where twenty modelling students gave a practical demonstration: "In elegant blue costumes expressly created for them and lined up on the stage, they performed for that exceptional audience one of their lessons. That of rhythmic group movements and of individual walks that revealed the instinctive ease of these

---

67 "Convegni d'eccezione al Palazzo della moda," *Torino. Rassegna della città*, n. 2, February 1941, pp. 45-50.
68 Ivi, p. 46.

future promoters of the women's garments made by our great dressmakers."[69]

For the fashions of spring 1941, the ENM tried to impose a new line in which the waist was shifted slightly towards the hips,[70] the skirt lengthened and the shoulders rounded. Suits, cloaks and jacket costumes were to have drooping rounded shoulders, supported by padding only towards the arm, which "may seem an unsightly innovation but in reality gives the design a graceful nineteenth-century flavour which is very refined and elegant."[71] The afternoon and dinner dresses' sleeves should be elaborate, decorated with ruffles, appliqués or very loose and tight at the wrists. For skirts, the most common formula was that of pleats and the model of the half or full circle skirt. Featured fabrics included natural silks and printed rayons with original motifs like tropical flowers, horses and starfish, as well as classic polka dots. Among those in plain colours, mixed wools or lanital or rabbit fur, natural silk, rayon, linen, canvas, hemp, muslin and taffeta prevailed. In addition to the classic white, black and blue, the colours were shades of pastels, except for a hint of red. Among the most frequent combinations of colours were white and blue and white and red. One of the main features of the afternoon dresses were jackets, often decorated with embroidery, applications, trimmings, sequins, cut-outs and taffeta ribbons. Among the evening dresses, the ENM reported a gown with mid-evening skirt-suit completely covered in aubergine-coloured sequins and a white silk crepe dinner dress with a short-pleated skirt and bust embroidered in rhinestones, sequins and silver tubes depicting signs of the zodiac. For the evening, a very tight dress in black crepe draped on the front and adorned with a large central pocket embroidered in coloured beads reproducing an Asian ornamental motif and a "very tight" dress

---

69 "La delegazione germanica alle nostre case di moda," *La Stampa*, 5 February 1941, p. 5.
70 This aroused discontent at *Bellezza* and they were forced to adopt new solutions to comply with the imposition.
71 Ivi, p. 47.

in white mesh made of different-sized meshes all covered with applications of silver beads. Inspiration came from historical motifs: bulky shoulders, discreet necklines, wide and billowing skirts. The general tone was one of simplicity, with a "ban on the tacky complications" typical of xenophiles. Here too, the eccentricities of French and Hollywood fashion were viewed as negative and in opposition to traditional Italian good taste, the Italian summer fashions of 1941 being described as possessing "vaporous simplicity" and "enchanting lines." The fashion houses' presentations to national customers, both private and commercial, followed by international presentations at *Teatro della moda*, were considered significant due to the impossibility of buyers travelling to Paris: "For the first time, Italian clothing merchants were able to avoid trips abroad for the purchasing of designs with the advantage of obtaining supplies about a month in advance of the date of previous years."[72]

The ENM's initiatives, including the highly refined bi-annual publication *Documento Moda*[73], struggled with an apparent contradiction: on the one hand, the ENM had to reassure the industry and the ladies of high society that it did not intend to force women to wear a uniform, while on the other hand it needed to regulate the sector:

> *Documento* is literally what its title describes, a documentation of the current or future possibilities of Italian work and production in the field of fashion. Directing the creators, clarifying the "spirituality" of the new line and encouraging industrialists, artisans, traders and designers with the

---

72   "Nuove linee della moda estiva," *Torino. Rassegna mensile della città*, n. 8, March 1941, p. 60.
73   Vitrotto, G., (edited by), *Documento Moda,* year II, Grafitalia, Milan 1942. From the summary: Italy in arms: modern painting and printed fabric, with 12 colour plates by Carena, Carrà, Casorati, De Pisis, Ferrazzi, Ropes, Palazzi, Sironi, Vellani - Brands; Fabrics, with mm. pp. colours and applied fabric samples from Snia Viscosa, Salterio, Dafni De Angelis - Frua, Ente Nazionale del Tessile, ISA, Polo Visca, Piacenza & C., Tessital, Puricelli, Piantanida, Anita Pittoni, Stamperia di Camnago, G. Lucchini, A. Gatta, Seterie di Cugnasca, Nene Buratti, Serta, E.N.M., F.lli Cardani; Lace, millinery, accessories, hairstyles with 25 illustrations in colour and b/w from various companies; Footwear, with 15 illustrations in colour, almost all applied; Jewellery, with 5 illustrations in colour and 1 in b/w.

publication's specific character. It is, in short, a clear, concrete and persuasive word that admits no doubt or diversity of interpretation while at the same time admonishing those who look backward, deceiving themselves in their support of now-outdated positions. The aim is not to subjugate the freedom of fashion by creating a kind of uniform; [...] it does, however, aim to set appropriate limitations for the extemporaneous subjective vision of fashion which determines a kind of artifice that replaces the natural style of a people. An imposition, perhaps, but a necessary one for creating an unmistakable aesthetic.[74]

Documento Moda was a "code of elegance" which, in an unadorned and elegant typography that "goes beyond a mannered aestheticism,"[75] embodied the new aesthetics of fascist fashion. Aimed at Italian and foreign representatives of the sectors concerned, it was published until 1943 and the first issue, dedicated to spring-summer 1941 fashion, contained nine sections: colours, line, fabrics, millinery, linen, lace, jewellery, shoe-making and accessories. Inspired by principles of practicality and elegance, it was aimed at and subject to an idea of "style,"[76] a highly evocative word in fascist culture. The colours for spring-summer oriented the production towards harmonious combinations in order to eliminate violent contrasts such as "tomato red-billiard table green," which were considered vulgar and were replaced by delicate shades of pastel tones or by other more intense but never violent tones.

In the pages dedicated to the *Linea*, defined as the "leitmotif" of fashion, the directives were categorical. To signal the distance of the Italian woman from that of Hollywood and Paris, the institution used a photograph of the Venus of Cyrene. *Plastes*, an invention of Luigi Branchini, was a tool of sartorial measurement and discipline which aimed to eliminate error and save fabric by making female garments adhere to a body that reflected the

---

74 Lazzarini, L., "Documento-Moda dell'E.N.M.," *Torino. Rivista mensile municipale*, 1941, p. 23.
75 Ivi.
76 *Documento-Moda*, I, *op. cit.*; Lazzarini, L., "Documento-Moda dell'E.N.M.," *Torino. Rassegna mensile della città*, n. 7, July 1941, p. 33-38.

proportions laid down by the institution.[77] Despite the attempted progressive imposition of a state-approved *linea* (silhouette), the ENM stated that it did not want to "create a single standard way of dressing for all Italians," as infinite "interpretations" of the silhouette were in fact possible. In practice, the institution decided to move the waistline down towards the hips out of a hatred of the wasp waist that Mussolini had condemned in 1939 for being "anti-demographic": "Do not publish photographs and drawings of women with a so-called 'wasp waist'. Drawings and photographs must show voluptuous and healthy women."[78] The skirts of dresses with jackets had to be straight, longer and in some cases draped, with rounded and slightly drooping nineteenth-century style shoulders, and the jackets, cloaks and capes were to have straight lines.

Documento Moda invented and named colours for Italian fashion[79] which formed "a very varied and wisely chosen range [evoking] the brightness of our sun, the clearness of our sky and that haze of colours that seem to change with every hour, veiling

---

77 Vanessa, "Un'invenzione per eliminare l'errore e risparmiare stoffa," *Rassegna dell'Ente nazionale della moda*, VI, n. 5-11 (June).
78 Order sheet dated July 17, 1939. Other order sheets can be found in Matteini, C., *Ordini alla stampa*, Rome, Editrice Polilibraria Italiana, 1945; Flora, F., *Ritratto di un ventennio. La stampa dell'era fascista*, Bologna, Edizioni Alfa, 1965; Cesari, M., *La censura nel periodo fascista*, Naples, Liguori Editore, 1978.
79 By establishing an indissoluble link between the fascist imperial mission which had its roots in ancient Rome and the "Mediterranean destiny" of the House of Savoy, the myth of the Mediterranean Risorgimento gradually became a dominant motif in fascist publications and in the writings of distinguished personalities of the Italian intelligentsia. With increasing intensity, from the second half of the thirties, in conjunction with the Ethiopian enterprise, fascist culture was engaged in a cultural operation aimed at reinterpreting and re-reading national history in order to respond to the needs posed by the present. The futurists ventured into southern Italy with the intention of reshaping the ancient Mediterranean landscape in accordance with their modernist vision. Modern European architects, in particular Le Corbusier, Josef Hoffmann and Bernard Rudofsky, traveled the Mare Nostrum, in their writings and sketches. The modern landscape became a commodity to be consumed, as evidenced by the diffusion of landscape architectures by Bernard Rudofsky, Le Corbusier, Gio Ponti, Maria Teresa Parpagliolo, Lina Bo Bardi (architect and illustrator of *Bellezza*).

our landscape with an impalpable tenuity. This is how the colours of fashion were created." Light airy shades such as pink and pastel green, pink and grey and white and grey were preferred, along with "dark, vague, nebulous backgrounds upon which the artist will position touches of rare, precious colour with a certain sense of the dramatic."[80] To guide fashion designers, a coloured star indicated the contrasting hue and a coloured circle the hue that was matching. The *Linea e Colori* ("Line" and "Colour") booklets set "the tone of Italian fashion" for 1941 and, together with that of the *Tessuti* ("Fabrics"), were considered the most important.

The section dedicated to fabrics featured various state-approved fabrics in natural and artificial fibre, while in the *Modisteria* ("Millinery") section, "clownish" excesses were replaced by pictorial inspiration that framed the female face. Among the novelties of the *Biancheria* ("Underwear") section were sober short nightgowns and pyjamas with short pants designed to highlight "the harmonious agility of the female body." The articles featured in the pages of *Gioielleria* ("Jewellery") were considered "worthy of the masters of the Renaissance" and the *Calzolerie* ("Shoes") booklet, which took into account the limitations of the use of leather, illustrated the various applications of "our" fabrics – not "substitutes" – such as wood, cork and domestic raw materials.

In addition to its documentary function, *Documento Moda* had the purpose of stimulating a spirit of competition on the part of fashion houses or textile companies by providing them with a "code of elegance" aimed at defining an Italian style that represented fashion in a "sincere expression of art." The ENM brought in the best painters and designers for the creation of *Documento Moda* because "their creations offer and practically impose on industrial manufacturing the imponderable but indispensable element of 'style'."

---

[80] In order not to overload the text with notes, when a long quotation is broken up in the text, the reference in the footnote is repeated only once.

In June 1941 the organization published the new colour charts for wool, silk and felt for autumn-winter 1941-42 with the aim of obtaining "a harmonious whole, skilfully matched and therefore essentially elegant and at the same time designed according to a single, integrative criterion capable of eliminating any unnecessary waste." Bright colours were added to the duller ones as a decorative accent. Among the new colours proposed to Italian industry were "abyss grey," "olive grey" and "stagnant green."

In August 1941, Italian designs were once again presented to foreign buyers – according to official sources, two hundred exponents of the fashion houses of Germany and Switzerland arrived in Turin.[81] Upon arrival they were received at the Principi di Piemonte hotel, where they were welcomed by national councillor Gabriele Parolari, vice president of the Clothing Corporation, the managers of the Clothing Industry Federation, managers of the fashion houses of Turin, Rome and Bologna and the president of the ENM, Count Giriodi Panissera. The patriotic black cherry and various shades of green stood out in descriptions of the presentations, along with black with decorative elements of gold and silver. Printed and textured velvets were preeminent among the fabrics, with nineteenth-century trimmings, beaded embroidery, straws, lace, fringes, tulle and shaved furs, and novelties included a muff hung around the neck with a velvet ribbon to leave the hands free.

2.3 The Clothing Card

So little study has been devoted to the rationing of clothing in Italy during the Second World War[82] that, in his book on 1940s

---

81 G. P., "L'industria dell'abbigliamento e la moda. Presentazione dei modelli alla clientela straniera," *Torino. Rassegna mensile della città*, n. 8, August 1941, p. 43.
82 In international books or essays concerning the relationship between fashion and the Second World War, the rationing of Italian fabrics and clothing is rarely mentioned. Rationing is mentioned in Gnoli, S., *op. cit.*, p. 163-168. But its concrete effects and functioning, in conjunction with the introduction of the new state-approved textiles and the price freeze, remains to be explored.

fashion, historian Colin McDowell states there was no rationing of clothing in Italy.[83] Although it failed to meet the needs of the population, rationing did however take place in Italy from the end of September 1941, the regime's autarkic policy identifying in a strategy of controlled prices, grouping of clothing types and individual rationing its main tool for disciplining the textiles and clothing sector[84] to cope with galloping wartime inflation.

In 1941 a decree established the characteristics of the fabrics for the domestic market. Wool was destined for soldiers and for export and the use of leather and hides was strictly prohibited. In addition, the Clothing Corporation issued a series of regulations that attempted to limit waste, framing itself as part of the anti-bourgeois campaign and prohibiting the use of woollen fabrics for summer dresses, long evening dresses, trains for wedding dresses, double-breasted jackets and waistcoats.[85]

Rationing of textile and sewn products arrived with the ministerial decree of the 29th of September, 1941 *Discipline of the Distribution of Textile Products and Manufactured Articles, Footwear and Other Articles of Clothing*. Article one decreed the suspension of any sale or transfer to the public "of textile products, articles made of textile materials, other articles of clothing and footwear of all kinds." The companies in the sector were required to take inventory of the goods present in their shops or warehouses and note the quantities in a special register provided by the trade union associations, which were to constitute each company's initial stock. The trade union associations were in turn to communicate this information to the provincial council of the relevant corporations. Even industrialists, artisans and wholesale traders were obliged to suspend the sale of products and take inventory of the goods in stock.

The reason lies in the autarkic perspective of fashion studies during fascism, see Merlo, *op. cit.*, p. 65.

83 McDowell, C., *op. cit.*, p. 81: "In Italy, for example, there was no rationing during the war."
84 «Si estende la tipizzazione tessile», *Tinctoria*, XII, December 1942; for the rationing, "Il tesseramento tessile e del vestiario," *Quaderni della rivista Maglieria*, II, 1943.
85 Mafai, M., *op. cit.*, p. 118.

A ministerial decree of the 23rd of October, 1941-XIX established a corporative committee for the distribution of textile products and clothing[86] – headed by national councillor Achille Castelli – with the task of "regulating the production, distribution and consumption of textile products in general, articles of clothing and footwear of all kinds," and on October the 30th, 1941 the Ministry of Corporations issued the *Rules for the Rationed Distribution of Textiles, Clothing and Footwear*. Distribution to the consumer would take place through an "individual clothing card," which came into effect on November the 1st, 1941 after sales had been blocked for a month for inventory, and which was part of the general war economy framework to minimise civilian consumption of textiles in the light of the growing needs of the armed forces. From that date, the sale of textile products, other articles of clothing and footwear of all kinds indicated in a table denominated 'A' could not take place except through the "individual card" or special "purchase coupons". The products listed in table B were not rationed and could therefore be freely sold or purchased. The individual cards were of five types: a "diamina butterfly brown" 'A' card for men (over 15 years); A purple 'A' card for women (over 15 years); a "diamina butterfly green" 'B' card for children (5 to 14 years), a "Victory blue" 'B' card for children (1 to 4 years). The type A cards contained 120 coupons, the type B cards contained ninety-six and the type C card eighty-two. Inspired by the British rationing system, it was a cumbersome approach. Each card had coupons of three types: coupons with *Arabic numerals* for shop yarns (for knitting and crochet), fabrics of all kinds, packaging and personal linen, clothing items made of textile material and footwear, coupons

---

86 This was composed of a representative of the Ministry of Corporations, a representative of the Garment Corporation, a representative of the Textile Products Corporation and a representative for each of the following organizations: Fascist Confederation of Industrialists, Fascist Confederation of Traders, Fascist Confederation of Industrial workers, the fascist confederation of trade workers, the fascist confederation of credit and insurance companies, the fascist national cooperation body, the national textile body, the national fashion body, the national silk body, the Italian cotton institute.

with *Roman numerals* for household linens, furnishing fabrics, carpets and tapestries, suitcases, bags and handbags, in leather or leather, and coupons with *letters of the alphabet* from A to F, valid for sewing, embroidery and darning threads. The cards were issued by the municipalities in accordance with the same rules governing ration cards, the difference being that they were not issued to children under one year and were nominative even for those in "stable cohabitation," "meaning, those who cohabitate on an ongoing basis where they do not have their own clothing items for individual use during the period of time in which they are hosted or hospitalised." Upon presentation of the card, the vendor removed as many coupons as there were points assigned to the item. Since household linen "is part of the family trousseau, some items of this category, larger in size or with a longer duration, cannot be claimed with a single card, as the number of coupons corresponding to them exceeds that (30) attributed to an individual card. The purchase of these items therefore requires coupons from two or more cards belonging to members of the same family." The card was valid for one year – from the 1st of November, 1941 to the 31st of October, 1942 – whatever the date of issue and the year was divided into three four-monthly periods, in each of which the consumer could use a maximum of one third of the coupons with Arabic and Roman numerals. For blankets, the purchase of which involved spending more than ten coupons, the use of a higher number of coupons was allowed from the first four months.

Goods which could still be freely traded included footwear for children up to 12 months, furs for children up to 5 years, fox skins made to be worn around the neck and embroidered fabrics "with absolute prevalence of embroidery on the fabrics."[87] One of the system's strangest rules was the exclusion from rationing of newlyweds, who were granted extra coupons for clothes and linen for the home as well as for sheets, but only if double. According to a bizarre and discriminatory logic, consistent with

---

[87] "Precisazioni per la vendita dei prodotti di abbigliamento," *La Stampa*, 10 November 1941, p. 5.

the ideology of the regime, newlyweds could also be issued coupons for the purchase of a coat, a skirt-suit, a skirt, two shirts, two pairs of underwear, six pairs of socks, six handkerchiefs and a pair of shoes for both men and women. In addition, the bride and groom could obtain coupons for certain items of household linen: two pairs of double sheets, four shams and four pillow-case, a double bedspread, a double blanket, a double padded, two tablecloths for six, six napkins, six towels, six kitchen towels. Obviously, exceptions were foreseen in the case of advanced pregnancy to provide for the needs of the new-borns.

There were those who could circumvent the rules by purchasing poor people's cards, though women of wealth could always modify their husband's suits for themselves, and the rationing system had a number of flaws which women were adept at discovering. For example, cork shoes with fabric uppers, the only ones on the market, cost from forty to sixty coupons while leather bags, from which the uppers could be made, cost only two and cork soles, if bought separately, were not rationed.

As well as cases of hoarding (like three Roman tailors who were sentenced to three years' imprisonment for hiding cuts of fabric to be resold at higher prices), there was also the purchase and sale of rationing cards, with which one shopkeeper in Turin "taking advantage of the fact that the less well-off barely use their clothing cards" was planning to organize a trade of cards by asking an accomplice in Naples to buy thousands of them up for forty lire each.[88] On March the 23rd, 1942 *La Stampa* newspaper[89] reported a very long list of traders, arrested and fined for not respecting the rules while the situation of retail prices was illustrated in a comic strip by Guareschi – the creator of Don Camillo – showing a gentleman in a coat and hat walking into a haberdashery and coming out half naked, captioned: "With prices shooting up, the gentleman goes to buy a wool sweater."

After war had been declared, a 1942 decree from Mussolini prevented women from wearing mourning to avert the Italian

---

88 "Illecito traffico di un negoziante," *La Stampa*, 14 March 1942, p. 2.
89 "Ultime notizie," *La Stampa*, 23 March 1942, p. 4.

people from realising the actual number of deaths. In the summer of 1942, a *New York Times* journalist reported from Italy that skirts were shorter and skimpier and hats smaller and more bizarre than ever. According to the journalist, Italian women were wearing increasingly extreme fashions – though not trousers, which in fascist Italy were the exclusive prerogative of men –, lipsticks of dubious quality and imitations of woollen stockings turned out "by the millions."[90] Municipalities could issue coupons for fascist uniforms at the request of the interested parties and with the approval of the federal secretary, while the provincial councils of corporations could issue employers coupons for clothes, overalls, aprons and work shoes for their workforce and articles of sportswear upon request approved by CONI, the Italian National Olympic Committee.

The tables of the ministerial circular distinguished between packaged ready-to-wear items and tailored fabrics. The articles made for women and girls were wool or wool-like skirt-suits (60 coupons), one-piece wool or wool-like dresses (40 coupons), wool or wool-like jackets (36 coupons), blouses (6 coupons), wool skirts (18 coupons), coats, cloaks and overcoats of wool or wool-like fabrics, excluding gabardine overcoats (65 coupons), raincoats and overcoats of gabardine (35 coupons), cellophane or synthetics (20 coupons), bathrobes (50 coupons), pyjamas (15 coupons), wool robes (40 coupons), Italian-produced consumer goods furs, lamb, rabbit, cat, mole (25 or 40 coupons depending on the model, jacket or cloak). Non-Italian-produced furs cost 60 coupons for a jacket and 90 coupons for a cloak.

As far as fabrics and yarns were concerned, woollen fabrics involved greater expenditure of coupons – 24 per linear meter over 600 grams – while muslin and organza were worth 2 coupons per linear meter, and fabrics for raincoats and gabardine 12 coupons per linear meter. Non-standard footwear with a leather upper and leather sole for women cost 80 coupons, almost an individual's entire card, standard footwear a little less at 65, while those with

---

90 "Italy aids women to keep looks while Nazis impose dowdiness," *The New York Times*, 3 June 1942, p. 19.

textile uppers and rubber soles cost 20 coupons and those clogs excluded from free sale 10 coupons. Bags and handbags for ladies in leather or hide cost only 2 coupons.

Linen and vestments for the exercise of worship, bracelets and mourning ribbons, lace, tulle and embroidery, except embroidered fabrics, busts and sheaths, "bras and girdles of any kind," trimmings, gloves, hats for men and women, berets, felts for hats, umbrellas, all small haberdashery items – woven, braided or twisted – used to decorate garments, buttons, zippers, buckles, fabrics and articles of straw, paper, cellophane and wood shavings, completely wooden clogs with at most a small median strip to secure them to the foot, footwear without leather or rubber, used clothing items provided they are sold by firms authorized by the public safety authority were all exempt from rationing and therefore could be sold freely.

The list of rules, rationing and prohibitions favoured the spread of a popular aesthetic and influenced fashion design. Wool, destined for military use or for export, ended up disappearing from public use in favour of wool-like fabric and autarkic furs, which cost 20 coupons. Synthetic fabrics such as rayon were also favoured, while accessories such as hats, gloves and belts and decorative elements such as buttons, trimmings and small haberdashery, feathers and felts, lace, tulle and embroidery, being exempt from rationing, were available as "details" and for the embroidery and "freshening up" that was encouraged by the fashion female press.

As the war progressed and the situation worsened, a circular dated March the 27[th,] 1942 from the Ministry of Corporations introduced the rationing of hats, gloves and ties: felt hats were worth 4 coupons, leather gloves 2 coupons, those of other material 4 coupons, ties 1 coupon. In July 1942 the clothing rationing cards were reduced to two types and the number of coupons subject to revision. One type was valid for men, women and children aged 5 and over (120 coupons with Arabic numerals for yarns and packages, 30 coupons with Roman numerals for linen, 24 coupons with letters of the alphabet), the second for children from 1 to 4 years (72 coupons with Arabic numerals, 30 coupons with Roman numerals and 24 coupons with letters).

In 1942 the conditions of the Italian population as regarded clothing were dramatic. The press spoke of war fashion in soaring rhetoric, their words magically multiplying one garment into a thousand and a thousand into one of infinite durability and resistance, the watchwords being mending, repair, conservation and reuse. The regime urged Italian women to be chic at all costs, the repair of a worn or worn-out garment being an indication of wise domestic management and not of poverty, and meaning being able to transform old things into novelty ones: "No pining for English fabric or Parisian patterns, and no complaints that the Italian press offers nothing beautiful." The style of the Italian woman must eliminate all forms of exhibitionism, dissipation and ostentation.[91]

The aim of this invitation to creative reuse was to suggest how to maintain a smart, fashionable look so as not to depress morale in the family and in public. For example, in the case of a light wool sweater with the elbows worn through, the suggestion was to unpick the sleeves up to above the elbow and finish the work with two straight and two reverse sides to make the sleeve puffy. Instead of buttons, one could use a zipper and a hem in a contrasting colour that ended in a bow around the neck. If a heavy wool sweater was moth-eaten, it should be unpicked and the best parts saved to remake the sleeves, yoke and waistline. For a bodice, for which there would not be enough wool, one could buy seventy centimetres of heavy fabric – the so-called *pelle di diavolo* or "devil's hide" – in different colours to be cut into strips six centimetres wide and attached to the knitted pieces. If a knitted dress were worn out, it could be taken to the seamstress to be made into a skirt with four flared panels, tight at the hips and belt and the jacket will have an elastic yoke, patch pockets and smooth masculine sleeves. Finally, one could embroider very delicate lines in grass stitch in wool on the jacket that looked woven, thus providing a touch of elegance. The

---

91   *La donna fascista*, 15 October 1941.

motif could then be repeated on the hem to simulate the addition of fabric.[92]

According to the fashion press, the Italian woman[93] demanded sobriety – "the sign of distinction in every age" – and discipline without skimping on femininity and elegance. The situation called for "flair but not whimsy, no buttons, bows, lace, trim, pleats or fluttering frills. This way women will know how to do it themselves or will take advice from a seamstress. It is necessary to create our own fashion that is moderate, national and personal within limits. The dress must adhere to the body as style adheres to the mind," and the line must not be overly angular "like some twentieth century furniture."

Elegance and simplicity in dressing were at the heart of what was on offer at department stores *La Rinascente* and *Upim*.[94] Bringing fashion to life in wartime was no easy thing but, as *La Rinascente* assured, fashion – "the powerful creative engine of the nation"[95] – had not stopped. The most important role now was played by fabrics, as the new materials required less coupons. "We middle-class female workers don't need sumptuous things to be well dressed!" proclaimed *La Rinascente* house organ, certain that those who spent large amounts of money were envious of the young saleswoman with her innate elegance that could not be bought. What really mattered was the elegance of one's demeanour in one's modest overcoat made of state-approved fabrics and one's state-approved shoes.

For the department stores, which spoke in paternalistic tones to the urban and provincial public, the real elegant women of Italy were the working women: the office workers, the typists, the saleswomen. Women, who had the right and duty to be elegant, must adopt a simple style, because showy garments

---

92 Silvia, "Rimettiamo a nuovo i vestiti a maglia," *La donna fascista*, 30 October 1941, p. 15.
93 Gaudenzi, V., "La moda femminile in tempo di guerra," *La donna fascista*, 15 July 1942, p. 9.
94 Simonetta, R., "Eleganza e semplicità nel vestire," *La Famiglia Rinascente-Upim*, February 1941, n. 1, pp. 25-27.
95 Simonetta, R., "La moda e i prodotti tipo," *La Famiglia Rinascente-Upim*, January-March 1942, n. 1, pp. 21-22.

were for those who had many. All you needed was a single dark dress, which could be freshened up with accessories that could be bought in department stores. Those who worked in an office must have a very simple wardrobe: a skirt-suit with jacket and a skirt in *"principessa di lana"* wool to alternate with the dress, another dress for holidays and a cheap Italian-produced coat or fur. Any accessories must be modern but simple in order not to attract attention and to be worn for months, always giving the impression of elegance and never of seediness. True elegance lay in "rightness" and "simplicity."

La Rinascente organized numerous practical demonstrations for the "fight against waste." At the *Upim* in Palermo, a certain "Dr. Tocco" gave a lecture on the tasks of women in war organized as part of a series of War Propaganda Courses to explain to clients the tasks of fascist women. It was necessary to consume, but buying a lot was only permissible when the general conditions allowed it. Waste, on the other hand, was always condemned – even in times of abundance – in the name of social equity and out of respect for the less fortunate. There was no lack of good intentions, but what was missing was experience in the techniques of home economics and for this reason, from the 8th to the 21st of March, *La Rinascente* in Milan organised an initiative for a propaganda campaign that had as its centrepiece an exhibition on the second floor where ladies were taught how to make a pair of autarkic shoes.

La Rinascente's home economics conferences[96] played a role of no small importance in a situation in which traditional knowledge was not enough: "To understand their importance, we must understand the situation housewives found themselves in as a result of rationing." Many had in fact taken advantage of the confused situation, and while the 1941 campaign against waste had the commercial purpose of clearing out the goods in stock, a year later advertising seemed inappropriate; *La Rinascente* therefore became an adviser on rationing economies, secrets and tricks.

---

96 Ivi, p. 18-19.

In the meantime, the department store's ready-to-wear shows did not stop,[97] with one hundred and forty designs featuring "notes of lively elegance within the framework of stately simplicity and evening gowns that were smooth and simple but with exquisite lines." Peacetime clothes were replaced by the "brilliant idea of a house dress and comfortable housecoats." The designs were characterised by sportiness, practicality and elegance. There were afternoon cloaks with fur trimming and the inevitable furs, jacket and princess dresses, shorter skirts, stiffer jackets, elongated princess waists, a round-shoulder coat clinched at the waist by a belt and with very high padded shoulders. There was an attempt to return to late nineteenth-century fashion, both in shape and colour, with wide necklines in the garments, sequinned trimmings, embroidery, golden studs, draperies; eccentric pockets positioned on the back where the buttoning is also placed, hyper-decorated afternoon dresses with fur appliqués, velvets on woollen and fur buckles.

The description of *La Rinascente*'s second home economics exhibition[98] is heart-rending, the house magazine offering advice to readers on how not to die of cold: wooden-soled slippers made with scraps of old clothes and yellow piping taken from military trousers, half-wool and half-fabric dresses, gaiters, baby clothes "using daddy's shirts," a winder to spin the wool of domestic waste, a dozen newspapers sewn in layers and wrapped in cloth as a waistcoat. In order to make some money, in 1944 *La Rinascente* founded APEM (Artisan Export Production Milan) to promote exports of ceramics, wood, metals, lace and straw. *La donna fascista*, the magazine of Fasci femminili ("Female Fasces"), railed against the ostentation of luxury, in particular against flashy jewellery, and tried to make it clear to women that one could be elegant without going overboard with accessories: "A ban on vain luxuries, but only during wartime. Get in line." *Fili*

---

97 Simonetta, R., "Presentazione dei modelli primavera-estate," La Famiglia Rinascente-Upim, April 1941, n. 2, pp. 40-42.
98 "Prepariamoci ad affrontare l'inverno," *La Famiglia Rinascente-Upim*, July-September 1942, n. 3, pp. 17-20.

moda[99] also invited Italian women to base their lives around the seriousness of the current moment, but specified that austerity did not mean sloppiness. Women must take care of their appearance in order to make the home more serene, without pointless and harmful frivolities. They must avoid lavish, original designs, which were unsuitable at the present time, and woe betide anyone purchasing raw materials intended for military uses.

There were many pages dedicated to illustrating the useful work to protect the soldiers from the cold on the Russian front, emphasising that women should dress themselves as well as the soldiers. In a building scheduled to be demolished at the Roman Forum, several hundred workers toiled, both in person and from home, in the laboratory of the Rome Federation of Female Fascists, an organisation which produced packs of clothing for soldiers, grey-green and black uniforms for fascist women and garments for the needy. Through the intervention of the governorate, the factory was later moved to a huge room at the permanent exhibition site in via Nazionale equipped with Necchi sewing machines and a refectory with a radio. Inside they sewed camisoles for children and rural housewives, hundreds of uniforms for fascist women and garments for the military produced for the use of the armed forces.[100]

---

99 *Fili-Moda*, n. 2, 1941. In 1941, tastes were oriented around autarkic inspirations and fashion journalist Maria Pezzi had the task of creating a series of colour double-page spreads dedicated to the traditional costumes of the Italian regions. Two years later the bombing of Milan began and the offices were moved so Maria was forced to go by bicycle every week to deliver her sketches to Domus which, displaced to Bergamo, published the magazines *Fili Moda* and *Fili Ricamo*. It was her first important job and not only consisted in illustrating the latest fashion news, but also in contributing with original ideas and advice on how to adapt the clothes hanging in wardrobes. Added to this was her work with Rizzoli's *La Donna* magazine and the creation of advertising designs for various companies. These were hard times, shared with friends like Camilla Cederna, Emilio Radius, Crespi, who came together to listen to Radio London. Cit. in Morini, E., *Maria Pezzi, giornalista di moda. L'Europeo 1947-58*, Società per l'Enciclopedia delle donne, Milan 2017.

100 Argnani, L. M., "Il laboratorio 9 Maggio (Federazione dei Fasci Femminili dell'Urbe)," *La donna fascista*, n. 3, 30 November 1941, p. 5.

Even those who had nothing must contribute. *Per voi signora* ("For You Madame") magazine, which was closely aligned with the regime, pointed out that the enemy was unfamiliar with the Italian woman, "otherwise he would not threaten her that she would soon have nothing to wear. Italian women know that production is constantly on the increase and distribution more equitable. Saying that Italian women want peace is a trick! Poverty and hunger, another bogeyman of English propaganda." Thus, in *La donna, la casa, il bambino* ("Woman, House, Child"), Narciso Quintavalle urged the eradication of disobedience and obstinacy. And it didn't matter if the wool didn't reach the soldiers, because "they will be warmed by the fervent unity of a people fighting for their destiny."[101]

Numerous letters addressed to the *duce* testify to the seriousness of the situation as regarded clothing:

> Excellency,
> I the undersigned, P Dina. Farmwoman Podere Valona, did not want to disturb you in this moment of war and pain: but desperation obliges me, forgive me: I find myself with six children all small under 13 years old And for Christmas I will give birth to the seventh child. I have 4 who go to school and without clothes: and many times I cannot send them because I don't have anything for them to wear without shoes, without proper clothes and with no money, have pity. I know that your heart is always ready to help the poor, I sincerely thank your beloved wife Donna Rachele who will help me to dress my children a little. I sincerely thank you, wishing you with a mother's sincerity an iron health to you and to all your very distinguished family. Thanking you a second time.
> Your Dina P. Farmwoman Valona. daughter of M Giovanna[102]

Right until the end of the war, women's and fashion magazines, whether aimed at the wealthy or the working classes, published editorials, articles, illustrations and photographs of morning and afternoon dresses, for lunch, theatre, dance parties, of hats and furs. Ironically, clothes were everywhere – newspapers, magazines, movies – except on the streets.

---

101 Cit. in "Rassegna della stampa riguardante la vita femminile," *La donna fascista*, n. 1, 30 November 1941, p. 12.
102 28 November 1941, URL: http://secolodelledonne.altervista.org/le-donne-e-il-duce.html

Fig. 1, 2, 3 Dress Tizzoni, hat Zanollo *Marca d'oro* (*Bellezza* n. 2, 1941) Courtesy of Library Fiamma Lanzara of the Accademia di Costume e Moda in Rome

Fig. 4 Trinelli (*Bellezza* n. 3, 1941) Courtesy of Library Fiamma Lanzara of the Accademia di Costume e Moda in Rome

Fig. 5 Hat Zanollo (*Bellezza* n. 24, 1942) Courtesy of Library Fiamma Lanzara of the Accademia di Costume e Moda in Rome

Fig. 6 Dress Radice "Apparently simple but studied in the cut" (*Bellezza* n. 15, 1942) Courtesy of Library Fiamma Lanzara of the Accademia di Costume e Moda in Rome

Fig. 7 *Linea 1941* (*Bellezza* n. 2, 1941) Courtesy of Library Fiamma Lanzara of the Accademia di Costume e Moda in Rome

Fig. 8 Example of *Linea 41*, ensemble by Moro.
The skirt is made with recycled men's ties silk (*Bellezza* n. 5, 1941) Courtesy of Library Fiamma Lanzara of the Accademia di Costume e Moda in Rome

Fig. 9 Gambino *Marca d'oro* (*Bellezza* n. 9, 1941) Courtesy of Library Fiamma Lanzara of the Accademia di Costume e Moda in Rome

Fig. 10 Vanna *Marca d'oro* (*Bellezza* n. 9, 1941) Courtesy of Library Fiamma Lanzara of the Accademia di Costume e Moda in Rome

Fig. 11 Tizzoni *Marca d'oro* (*Bellezza* n. 9, 1941) Courtesy of Library Fiamma Lanzara of the Accademia di Costume e Moda in Rome

Fig. 12 Noberasko (*Bellezza* n. 5, 1941) Courtesy of Library Fiamma Lanzara of the Accademia di Costume e Moda in Rome

Fig. 13 Gegia Bronzini (*Bellezza* n. 19, 1942) Courtesy of Library Fiamma Lanzara of the Accademia di Costume e Moda in Rome

Fig. 14 Trinelli (*Bellezza* n. 5, 1941) Courtesy of Library Fiamma Lanzara of the Accademia di Costume e Moda in Rome

Fig. 15 Royal School of Lace, Burano (*Bellezza* n. 29, 1943) Courtesy of Library Fiamma Lanzara of the Accademia di Costume e Moda in Rome

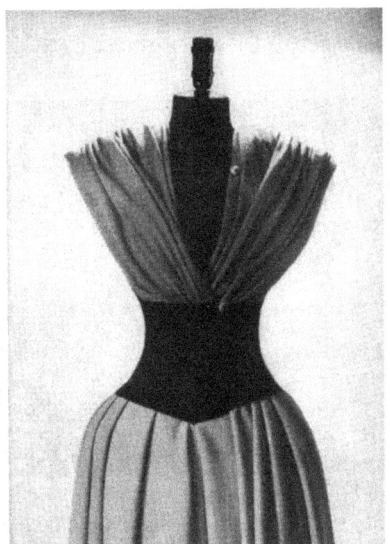

Fig. 16 New 1943 line (*Bellezza* n. 32, 1943) Courtesy of Library Fiamma Lanzara of the Accademia di Costume e Moda in Rome

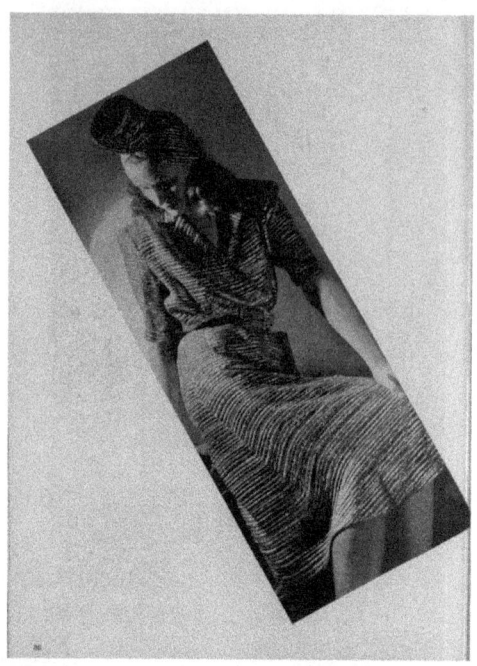

Fig. 17 Biki, evening gown (*Bellezza* n. 1, 1941) Courtesy of Library Fiamma Lanzara of the Accademia di Costume e Moda in Rome

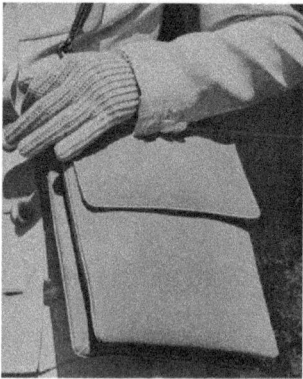 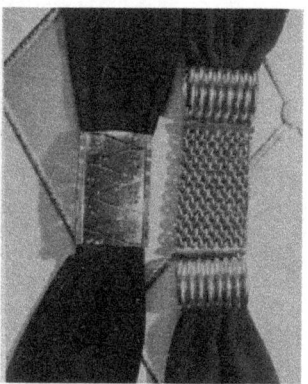

Fig. 18 Gucci, white leather bag (*Bellezza* n. 5, 1941) Courtesy of Library Fiamma Lanzara of the Accademia di Costume e Moda in Rome

Fig. 19 Ceriano (*Bellezza* n. 10, 1941) Courtesy of Library Fiamma Lanzara of the Accademia di Costume e Moda in Rome

Fig. 20 Hat Gauturon (*Bellezza* n. 3, 1941) Courtesy of Library Fiamma Lanzara of the Accademia di Costume e Moda in Rome

Fig. 21 Melozzo da Forlì, detail

Fig. 22 Favro (*Bellezza* n. 49, 1945) Courtesy of Library Fiamma Lanzara of the Accademia di Costume e Moda in Rome

Fig. 23 Franco Bertoli (*Bellezza* n. 29, 1943) Courtesy of Library Fiamma Lanzara of the Accademia di Costume e Moda in Rome

Fig. 24 Cavestri (*Bellezza* n. 37, 1944) Courtesy of Library Fiamma Lanzara of the Accademia di Costume e Moda in Rome

Fig. 25 Vanna illustrated by Brunetta (*Bellezza* n. 3, 1941) Courtesy of Library Fiamma Lanzara of the Accademia di Costume e Moda in Rome

Fig. 26 Fercioni illustrated by Gian Giacomo Dal Forno (*Bellezza* n. 3, 1941) Courtesy of Library Fiamma Lanzara of the Accademia di Costume e Moda in Rome

Fig. 27 Jacket Vanna, hat Guerci, jewellery Fratti illustrated by Federico Pallavicini (*Bellezza* n. 37, 1943) Courtesy of Library Fiamma Lanzara of the Accademia di Costume e Moda in Rome

Fig. 28 Stage fashion: gown Ventura, photo Emmer (*Bellezza* n. 1, 1941) Courtesy of Library Fiamma Lanzara of the Accademia di Costume e Moda in Rome

Fig. 29 Assia Noris. Publicity still of *Un colpo di pistola* (R. Castellani, 1942) by Vaselli. Costume design by Maria De Matteis (*Bellezza* n. 13, 1942) Courtesy of Library Fiamma Lanzara of the Accademia di Costume e Moda in Rome

Fig. 30 Costume design fantasy illustrated by Federico Pallavicini (*Bellezza* n. 27, 1943) Courtesy of Library Fiamma Lanzara of the Accademia di Costume e Moda in Rome

3
ALL THAT IS AIRY TURNS INTO STONE
Bellezza's Code of Elegance

3.1 *The Birth of* Bellezza Mensile dell'alta moda e della vita italiana

Women's lives in Germany and Italy were extremely difficult during the war, with one odd difference: "German women have resigned themselves to Nazi-imposed dowdiness for the duration of the war, women in Italy are encouraged to keep themselves attractive to the menfolk – though the means at their disposal are extremely limited." While the *New York Times* article grasped fashion's active role under fascist rule, much of the discussion around fashion centres on its *reflective* properties and many historians seems to agree that fashion simply reflects broader cultural changes. I would argue instead that fashion plays an active role in bringing about cultural change. Through the aesthetic world of fashion, the modern system of cultural dissemination of fashion and the concept of "taste" and its relationship to modern identity, fashion was a genuine force of fascist culture in that it created a verbal, visual and material world through which what was airy became solid.

During the war, Italian women who flaunted fashionable looks were accused of "servility," "self-interest" and of attacking the "conscious body of the nation."[1] Female devotion to the currents of international fashion was one of the ways in which the fidelity of women to the regime was measured and, in the misery of war and "with a revolutionary spirit – that is, with sacrifice and dedication,"[2] they were called to beauty. The viciousness

---

1   Gentile, E., *Il culto del littorio, op. cit.*, p. 279.
2   *Ibid.*

of the fascist press towards women guilty of following fashion is explained by the fascist state's ideal of the "good citizen" as a "social individual" who is willing to sacrifice his or her "*particulare*" for the common good, unlike "therefore not only the anti-fascist but the bourgeois of individualistic, skeptical, materialistic morality"[3] whose behaviour fed "a seething black market where anything can be sold for ten times its value, with petticoats, handmade pure silk shirts and nightgowns going for $35, $50 and $75."[4]

After the 1936 reshuffle of the ENM and its being assigned new responsibilities – which made it the backbone of the regime in the fashion sector – publishing activities increased, reaching their peak during the war years. Among the most prestigious publications were Cesare Meano's *Commentario dizionario della moda* ("Fashion Dictionary and Commentary"), the monographic issues of *Gazzetta del Popolo* edited by Lucio Ridenti and the prestigious *Documento Moda*. *Bellezza* was added to these publications in 1941 as the official organ of the ENM.[5] For their part, the Clothing Corporation asked for support for high fashion and its promotion in order to encourage exports and the Ministry of the Interior lifted the blockade of passports for industrialists who could prove that they were going abroad to sell Italian fashion.

In the first year of the war, the most prestigious fashion event was the Venice *Rassegna del tessile e dell'abbigliamento autarchico* ("Review of Autarkic Textiles and Clothing") organized for high-ranking Axis officials and staged by Erberto Carboni, one of the most popular architects of the time. The organization of exhibitions, architecture and urban planning, was "a genuine *arte fascista*, where fascism most effectively realised its totalitarian and monumental conception of the political

---

3   Ivi, p. 173.
4   Packard, E., Fleischer, J., "Italy Aids Women to Keep Looks," *op. cit.*, p. 19.
5   The first issue, published by EMSA (Edizioni moda società anonima) in Turin, came out in January 1941 under the title *Bellezza. Linea*, which turned into *Bellezza* from its second issue, was subtitled *Monthly of High Fashion and Italian Life*. It was published until September 1970.

integration of the arts through an eclectic syncretism of styles"[6] and which responded to a unitary principle: that of reifying the myths of fascism in "contingent monuments." *Bellezza*, whose editor was – unsurprisingly – an architect, had the advantage of being small and light, a souvenir rather than a monument, and enjoyed a small international circulation in Germany (where the press had already talked about the "Italian line"[7]), Switzerland and Spain.

Bellezza's fashion photography was designed to create a mood for the clothes, and was framed and shot in such a way as to increase the prestige of Italian creations. The main editors were Elsa Robiola, Federico Pallavicini and Lucio Ridenti and the magazine's contributors included journalists Irene Brin, countess Elena Celani and Luigi Barzini, writers Emilio Cecchi and Maria Pezzi, illustrators Brunetta Mateldi, Federico Pallavicini and artist Edina Altara. With its simple layout, *Bellezza* presented a vision of fashion inspired by the present and shot through with echoes of the historical-artistic past and a keen interest in fashion details, Italian printed fabrics, the harmonious use of colour and accessories, the classicism of the line, embroidery, lace, local craft traditions and art, music, theatre and cinema understood as showcases for fashion.

Bellezza was born from the fusion of two magazine projects: Gio Ponti's *Linea* and the ENM's *Bellezza*, which would eventually merge into *Bellezza*, the official magazine of the ENM from January 1941 to February 1945. The ENM had been planning a luxury magazine for some time. In December 1939 the *duce* had received

---

6   Gentile, E., *op. cit.*, p. 164. On the exhibitions see Russo, A., *Il fascismo in mostra*, Editori Riuniti, Rome 1999.
7   Issue n. 1 of January 1938 of *die neue linie*, dedicated to Italian fashion. The first German lifestyle magazine which appeared in 1929 and whose design and typography were the work of Herbert Bayer and László Moholy-Nagy, two important Bauhaus artists. Bayer designed a total of 26 bags.

the fascists Count Giriodi-Panissera, national councillor Ezio Maria Gray[8] with the lawyer Pacces, respectively president and managing director of the Turin publishing company,[9] who submitted to him the plan for the establishment of the limited company *Edizioni Italiane Moda*, which will soon launch a grand Italian fashion magazine whose editorial and organizational capabilities will be fully capable of delivering what the Corporation voted for and promoting the artistic production of the nation in the clothing sector.[10]

Meanwhile, in a letter addressed to film director Enrico Fulchignoni, Gio Ponti had clarified *Linea*'s mission: "To represent a top-tier documentation of Italian taste in order to validate Italian styles and import them into the New Europe. We must have prevalence in the fields in which France once operated. This is the demonstrative battle that *Linea* and *Stile* will undertake." Ponti considered the wartime isolation of Paris as a unique opportunity to launch Italian fashion in Europe and around the world through a monthly that competed with the American *Vogue* and *Harper's Bazaar*. But the ENM promptly intervened to block the launch of *Linea* and merge the two magazines *Bellezza*

---

8   Leading figure of fascism (deputy, member of the Grand Council in 1925 and 1926, vice president of the Chamber of Fascists and Corporations, director, in the RSI, of the *Gazzetta del Popolo* of Turin), for which after the Liberation he was tried and sentenced to death. Granted amnesty, he resumed political activity within neo-fascist political party MSI, for which he was an MP (1953-58) and senator (1963-68).
9   Alberto Beneduce called in Eng. Cenzato, exponent of the Southern Group and president of the Union of Industrialists, to restore the SIP. It was on this occasion that he gave two of his best staff members to SIP: Eng. Selmo and the lawyer Pacces, see Russo, G., (edited by), *L'avvenire industriale di Napoli negli scritti del primo '900*, Guide, Naples 2004.
10 "Importante iniziativa per l'autarchia," *Il Messaggero*, 24 December 1939, in ACS, Secretariat of the Duce, 3669, b. 380, f. 137888. The magazine was to be published in the first half of the fascist year XVIII and Ugo Ojetti was appointed as president. A comment on the article reads: "It is not enough to recommend autarky in the clothing sector; but it is also necessary to direct the public towards the national product by educating its taste and regulating its preferences. At the same time, it is necessary to offer the clothing industry, our highly skilled craftsmanship, a publication that will enable it to find the necessary information for an activity that must be able to hold its head up with the best foreign production. [...] Hence [...] the need for today's programme [...] which will finally be able to implement a longstanding aspiration of the country."

and *Linea* into a single monthly periodical entitled *Bellezza*,[11] appointing national councillor Gomez,[12] a journalist and brilliant man of culture, to make "extensive contacts with the national directorate in Rome and textile manufacturers in Lombardy, with the aim of consolidating Turin as the capital of fashion." The chairman of the management committee was painter Cipriano Efisio Oppo, while Ponti held the unofficial role of creative director, with a monthly salary of five thousand lire. It was established that the first issue of *Bellezza* would be released in January 1941 and the first two issues would be printed at Alfieri & Lacroix in Milan. Contributors included artist and jewellery designer Luciana De Reutern as Rome correspondent, Vittorina Bianchi from Florence, photographer Lina Haake, "fashion expert" Beatrice Celani, "pattern designer" Eva Carocci, "painter" professor Ciuti, "director of a large model agency" Carla Guido, "painter" Michaelles Ernesto, Tancredo Tancredi for men's fashion, Rome correspondent Stefanella della Sciarra, "worldly advice and contacts with patronesses" by Gabriella Bosdari di Robilant and "fashion reportage expert" Elsa Robiola. The photographers were Bricarelli for Turin and Pavanello and Rodolfo Alvino for Florence. The steering committee included the painter Cipriano Efisio Oppo as president, Alberto Francini, critical editor of newspaper *Il Messaggero* and Lucio Ridenti. The head of the editorial staff was Elsa Robiola, with regular

---

11 Renata Paganelli of the CEIM submitted to Ponti a compromise scheme relating to the merger of the two magazines *Bellezza* and *Linea*, letter of the 23 December 1940, ivi.
12 A journalist and brilliant man of culture, fluent in French, English and German, he was among the protagonists of Florentine social life. He immediately and enthusiastically joined the fascist movement, for which he also carried out important diplomatic missions abroad. In June 1935 he went on an official mission to England where he met Mosley (British Union of Fascists) and invited the English Fascists to join the Universal Fascism Movement. In 1932 he was the head of Florentine craftsmanship. After being elected president of the "Istituto Pio X Artigianelli" in Florence, he established a school for professional training for young people and founded the handicraft exhibition. An official of Confindustria and then of the Fascist National Federation of Artisans, in the second half of the 1930s he was elected to parliament and collaborated with Giuseppe Volpi, becoming president of his film company.

collaborations from Irene Brin, Vera Rossi Lodomez and Elena Celani, illustrators Brunetta Mateldi, Maria Pezzi, Federico Pallavicini, Edina Altara, Paolo Garretto, Lina Bo and Anna Evangelisti and writers Anna Banti, Luigi Barzini, Alberto Savinio, Emilio Cecchi and Massimo Bontempelli. The editorial office was in Via Spiga 25 in Milan, and the management in Via Roma 24, Turin.

The publicity campaign for the launch was formidable and showed how important the ENM considered *Bellezza*: circulars, letters to booksellers, posters, railway billboards, letters to major dressmakers, circulars to minor dressmakers and shops, letters to the most important textile industrialists and hat makers, minor industrialists, ladies' hairdressers, radio announcements – at 15:30 and 19:30 from the 10th to the 30th of January 1941 – "a grand letter to the princesses," to women's boarding schools, advertisements in national newspapers like the *Gazzetta, Stampa, Corriere, Popolo d'Italia* and *Giornale d'Italia* and in provincial and regional dailies like the *Gazzettino, Piccolo, Nazione, Tevere,* and *Regime Fascista* and telegrams and letters to artists and art producers. In addition to sending the magazine to all newspapers and ambassadors, the "centralised action" included a press release from the Stefani Agency and the Ministry of Popular Culture announcing the launch and agreements with Lati, E42, FFSS, Ala Littoria and INA. There was even the creation of "beautiful headed notepaper with the title *Bellezza* in red Bodoni capitals."[13]

According to Ponti, Germany would dominate the fields of heavy industry in the Europe that would arise in the aftermath of the war, while Italy should "affirm and conquer primacy in the spiritual and artistic fields. Without this we will be – to put it bluntly – the land of sunshine, Chianti, oranges and citrus fruits." To achieve this goal, Italian society must be mobilised:

> The other classes must aim for the sole purpose of enhancing the arts, artists, work, crafts, art productions, textile and construction industries. If we are not able to claim for ourselves this primacy in the Axis and are

---

13   Filippo Gomez to Gio Ponti, *Ibid.*

unable to snatch it from France, which sees it as the source of its recovery, we will have won the war but lost the victory. This is our moment. France prostrate, no art of creative value in England either or America, nor in Sweden or Spain: but the pre-eminence of our values over Germany in terms of painting, etc. the precious presence in Italy of international masters (De Chirico, Campigli, Severini, De Pisis), a vibrant artistic climate, etc., are things we must promote as much as possible around the world, arousing in Italy an awareness of the values that determine it and that without which it is no longer Italy.[14]

But Italy, Ponti complained, looked abroad and lacked awareness of its own artistic resources:

This is the aim of the other magazine I have started, *Linea*, dedicated to fashion and which must counter the penetration of *Harper's Bazaar* and *Vogue* both in Italy and in Spain, Germany, Hungary, Romania and Yugoslavia (*Linea* is also translated into other languages). Scope. Fashion is not presented there as a mere series of photographs and fashion sketches but as a function of Italy's extremely refined artistic, social and civil climate. This is the only thing that confers prestige upon fashion! Fashion has no nationality, it is neither Italian, nor German, nor French, nor American: but it becomes the force (and what a force!) of a nation if its spiritual prestige is superior. *Linea* will therefore assert the values of art that must determine the prestige of Italy.[15]

But the differences of opinion within the magazine did not take long to surface. First, there was the issue regarding the publication of magazine's members names and the colophon. Gomez would have preferred that the name of the editor-in-chief not be published, given that the magazine was the result of collective work. Oppo strongly opposed the idea but proposed printing at least the names of the president and co-director because "given the precedent of *Linea,* which Ponti ran by himself, and since I suppose Ponti is the editor, people would think that the magazine has changed only its name. It cannot go out blank."[16] Oppo's vision for the magazine also differed from that of Ponti,[17] who thought "*Bellezza* must be a vehicle for creative work, and

---

14   *Ibid.*
15   *Ibid.*
16   Cipriano E. Oppo to Filippo Gomez, letter of the 26 January 1941, ivi.
17   Cirpiano E. Oppo to Gio Ponti, letter of the 27 January 1941, ivi.

not for the ambitions of a class of rich Italians in the fashion sector." Gomez was also careful to set some coordinates for the future in a political-economic memo whose first point concerned wartime discipline:

> We need to acknowledge that ever wider classes of the Italian public consider it their duty to reduce their standard of living so as not to offend the sensibilities of the less fortunate who lead a life that borders on discomfort, and for this purpose it is fascist and corporate, and in accordance with the present moment to insist on formula "The luxury, clothing and fashion industries provide employment for thousands of workers and artisans, selectors and qualifiers of labour and exalt all classes without humiliating anyone."[18]

It was necessary to adopt a "policy of using substitutes and of supporting the official corporate approach in the matter of products made with raw materials which are not widely available," even though prohibited fabrics such as wool, leather and hide would continue to appear in *Bellezza*. Furthermore, "to keep high fashion linked to the coefficients of European collective life, we should launch a series of articles on women's uniforms, as they were created for the civil services and Axis parties."[19] Ponti, who had "many enemies," sought assistance, writing in a memo addressed to Mussolini:

> of our allies who give us such an example as to incite us to a chivalrous but spirited emulation if you want my opinion. [...] As in the attachment to this letter, they take a position in the sector of fashion (fabrics) and of taste (crafts, art, furniture, glass, ceramics, art editions) but this is a sector in which we can fight to win Italian primacy. Committed Italians always win when they want to succeed.[20]

Ponti's statement was forwarded to the Ministry of Corporations, which did not hesitate to reply:

> This office was sent a copy of your report, dated March 3 and addressed to the Duce, in which you signal the position taken by Germany in the fashion sector and urge action aimed at forming a national awareness of

---

18 *Ibid.*
19 *Ibid.*
20 Gio Ponti to Osvaldo Sebastiani, letter of the 27 January 1941, ivi.

the importance of the problem. In this regard, the ministry would like to remind you that the ENM has been in operation since 1935.[21]

Ponti and Elsa Robiola would be forced to "fight hard"[22] and with the passing of time, enthusiasm gave way to disillusionment:

> You know that in *Bellezza* I saw not a job but a mission to beat the foreigners and to make Italy triumph. It is very disheartening to see a car with an engine that could make it go at 200 per hour running instead at 20: and all this when you have far more than enough means at your disposal.[23]

Oppo did not understand Ponti's concerns about running *Bellezza* according to methods of economic efficiency because penny pinching would mean "gradually killing the magazine, and in any case it is not our problem."[24] Furthermore, he was annoyed by the constant references to *Vogue* and *Harper's Bazaar*:

> We have to make an Italian magazine and not take these UNATTRACTIVE foreign publications as inspiration. You and all the Italian ladies can think what you want but I find those magazines unattractive. And if we have (not overly) imitated them so far, it was only so as to not point out to them the deficiencies of their foreign magazines. But it will be increasingly necessary to be Italian: from the typefaces of the printing and publishing, to the drawings to the paintings to the designs (the main and real goal).[25]

Oppo was convinced it was a mistake to advertise individual dressmakers in the magazine: "For us, fashion follows the directives of the ENM and not of private individuals." Referring to a drawing of a beach scene by Brunetta he wrote: "It is not what we had seen and will certainly cause scuffles with the race office. They are black, not tanned. The rule must be that we see a finished draft of everything. Much nonsense would be avoided even in the copy."[26] To the ENM, which considered

---

21 Renato Ricci to Gio Ponti, letter of the 24 March 1941, ivi.
22 Gio Ponti to Elsa Robiola, letter of the 31 January 1941, ivi.
23 Gio Ponti to Avv. Pacces, letter of the 30 December 1941, ivi.
24 Cipriano E. Oppo to Gio Ponti, letter of the 13 June 1941, ivi.
25 *Ibid.*
26 *Ibid.*

some of the companies mentioned undeserving due to their lack of compliance with ENM edicts, Ponti replied:

> The criticisms of *Bellezza* are refuted by its decisive success, which surpasses and eliminates that of any previous publication and therefore also fashion. The choice of and comment on the designs were carried out by the most competent people in Italy, namely by Countess Celani: a member of the *Marca di garanzia* commission, who dealt with and wrote about fashion in Paris for the most popular French magazines; Pallavicini: designer, painter and model maker who has always been involved in fashion in Vienna, Berlin and Paris. He has designed clothes for Vanna, Villa and Ventura and creates fabric designs made by Gandini Satam. He collaborates with the finest German magazines; Emilia Kuster Rosselli: fashion editor for three years at *Corriere della Sera* and then founder and director of *Fili* for eight years; Elsa Robiola, head of the fashion column at *Secolo Sera* for eight years and knows perfectly the directives of the institution, good and bad. Photos as beautiful as those in *Bellezza* have never before appeared in Italian magazines. The comprehensibility of the designs has not been accentuated because high-class dressmakers do not provide designs to copy but want beautiful photos that increase their prestige. The function of *Bellezza* is not to provide patterns to make clothes at home but to exhibit high-class Italian creations with the utmost prestige. The first issue was delayed due to the ENM's negotiations. *Bellezza* has every novelty coming out of the dressmakers. To say that the material is from undeserving companies is in contradiction with the competence of the editorial staff and absurd when the companies presented, from Ventura to Ferragamo, are NOTORIOUSLY the best in Italy. The ENM complains that much coverage has been given to companies that contravene its guidelines, but the ENM has never bothered to communicate them, and in any case, why are Ventura and Biki not eligible? It is incorrect to say that unknown companies have been favoured repeatedly because they correspond to a list given to us after two issues by the ENM on which only two of them were not included, and they are anything but unknown. In the first editions, the *Marca d'oro* had not yet been allocated.[27]

A year after the publication of the first issue of the magazine, Ponti was embittered and disappointed:

> Today we limit ourselves to taking pictures with little conviction because we do not know which will be accepted and how they will be laid out. Things will be very different when we are making those decisions! The current layouts now do not correspond to our needs or those of Oppo. Ridenti will not be given photos to be completed with captions and sketch-

---

27 Gio Ponti to Cipriano E. Oppo, letter s.d., ivi.

es to be laid out. The meetings are too short for the results to not contradict the taste and directives of Oppo, which we have obeyed to the point of humiliation. You know that I saw in *Bellezza* not a job but a mission to beat the foreigners and make Italy triumph.[28]

And he defended the work of Elsa Robiola and her team because it was they who, despite the countless difficulties of the war, made the magazine function.[29] The only editorial office of *Bellezza* worked thanks to the assiduous presence of Robiola and Pallavicini, and this alone allowed the freedom and advice of Countess Celani and permitted the management to lay out in a few hours a magazine containing between sixty and eighty photos and the technical writings that made up "seventy-five percent" of Italian fashion activities:

> It is absurd that Robiola, who has lost her father, and who supports her family, whose property is in danger of being destroyed, who has already suffered the expense and painful disturbance of being evacuated to relatives, in order to come in Milan for us has to pay for a train pass from Vercelli to Milan and endure three hours of uncomfortable daily travel in the cold (it has to be experienced to be believed!), lives like all of us practically without real heating, has to pay for her breakfast outside her home and has to live and work with what she earns each month. The same goes for Pallavicini. To him we owe all the photographs and a constant interest in *Bellezza* in the field of ideas and tailoring. He has no heating and like everyone else has to go down to the shelter at night, being able to count on only 1,300 lire per month plus 250 lire for each picture drawn, and he cannot do more than 3 or 4 (in certain editions there is only one or none at all). Now is the time to act! It is time, out of human and national solidarity, for the management to intervene in person (in relation to a national institution).[30]

From the summer of 1943, Milan underwent severe bombing and the fashion houses were forced to evacuate. Ponti sent out a circular to all the companies – more than fifty in total – to find out where they would be and would present their collections, to ensure that their efforts would be matched by those of *Bellezza*. The new political situation and the progressive disintegration of

---

28 Gio Ponti to Avv. Pacces, letter of the 30 December 1941, ivi.
29 Gio Ponti to Cipriano E. Oppo, letter of the 3rd of December 1942, ivi.
30 *Ibid.*

the fashion world would influence the writing of *Bellezza*, which hosted new names and new styles. There was still the desire to bring the magazine to life and get past the crisis, but things were getting worse. The most serious issue concerned paper: "The (paper) we had got burned and I am desperately trying to find more for the next issues."[31] At a certain point, in February 1943, Ponti evacuated the entire staff of *Bellezza* in order to allow it to function better than it would if staff were evacuated individually. Finally, in May, he announced his resignation, since his work no longer seemed necessary. Oppo appeared surprised and saddened: "It is true that I have been troubled by your dissenting stubbornness and apostolomaniac graphomania. It is true that I have railed against your tendency to send cautionary and professorial circulars to colleagues. Other times I have told you that it is not on the ephemeral fashion ground that we can debate art and thought."

From issue 36 of 1944, the names of the management committee disappeared completely and for all intents and purposes the magazine was in the hands of Elsa Robiola and Lucio Ridenti, who were "clinging to the machines, and I think we are managing to do something, by which I mean, being useful,"[32] and perplexed about the future of the magazine. "I am handling the whole thing. The printing works moved to Cossato (SET factory, Volpe Cossato district, Biella)."[33] At the beginning of 1944, continuing to publish *Bellezza* seemed a desperate anachronism, but "the initiative has established itself, employs many people, and I think offers possibilities of work not only in the typographical field but for the evident uses of propaganda in a sector in which we had reached a high level of production."[34] Despite his resignation, Ponti was more active than ever, as can be seen from his detailed analysis of the March issue, page by

---

31 Avv. Pacces to Gio Ponti, letter of the 29th of December 1942, ivi.
32 Lucio Ridenti to Gio Ponti, letter of the 28th of May 1943, ivi.
33 Lucio Ridenti to Gio Ponti, letter of the 4th of August 1943, ivi.
34 Avv. Pacces to Gio Ponti, letter of the 15th of January 1944, ivi.

page,[35] where he declared that the new direction *Bellezza* had taken as a "dream for displaced people" was unacceptable:

> March's poor results derive from the vain persistence of the old directives. *Bellezza* should not engage with certain topics, it must be a fashion and culture magazine – the way to do patriotism is by producing splendid issues, not by printing patriotic articles. Too much imagination and too little taste in the titles of the articles. Banish frivolity, which risks inelegance. A fashion magazine doesn't need that kind of thing. The opposite is necessary. Being alive with the life of today. And the echoes of yesterday (and a very questionable yesterday). Sometimes I think of Gomez's words; Italian life is not a dream for displaced people, it is in the resources of those who work, why don't you take pictures of some redone shops and many other things? Life! Life![36]

But his ideas were also in contrast with those of Lucio Ridenti, who accused Ponti of not understanding *Bellezza*'s audience, of not knowing how to distinguish between a forty-cent readership (*Illustrazione del popolo*), a two lire readership (*Dramma*) and a forty lire readership (*Bellezza*).[37] For this reason "the article *Disappearance of the Lady* should not be illustrated with modern sculptures by today's artists," as Ponti had wanted, "but in order that it not offend our ladies or those who believe themselves to be such and pay 40 lire, can only be illustrated with reproductions of those women that our ladies still admire nostalgically because they regret no longer being like them."

In the meantime, *Bellezza* was in disastrous financial conditions, with debts of two million lire and 70,000 lire worth of dubious credit abroad ("Germany, Romania, Greece, Bulgaria, etc."), confirming that Italy had exported its fashion to Europe. In this situation, "given that *Bellezza* was chosen by the Ministry of Popular Culture to continue its publishing in the fashion sector,"[38] two solutions were envisaged: continue to publish *Bellezza* and face further losses, or liquidate the company and give the magazine to third parties. On the 5th of March, 1945

---

35 Ponti's notes in the "Friends of *Bellezza*" column of the March issue, letter of the 13th of April 1944, ivi.
36 *Ibidem.*
37 Lucio Ridenti to Gio Ponti, letter of the 5th of May 1944, ivi.
38 *Ibid.*

the ENM, in the person of commissioner Roberto Leumann, renounced its right of option, noting that since *Bellezza* had been created as the official magazine of the ENM, given the current conditions it should suspend publication.³⁹ *Bellezza* would return to newsstands from November 1945 under the direction of Michelangelo Testa, with a renewed graphic design, the subheading *International Magazine of High Fashion* and with its publishing offices in Milan. After the war it would establish itself as one of the most important Italian *haute couture* magazines and would continue to be published until 1970. The first issue of the new launch was inaugurated with an editorial by Gio Ponti entitled *Is the Superfluous Superfluous?*⁴⁰

Bellezza's readership was made up of professionals and the wealthy women who turned to them to forge their own daily appearance. Among them were those of the varied elites of the new fascist society: lesser and greater stars of the regime's film industry, billionaires and the wives and lovers of high-ranking functionaries and rich industrialists:

> Those who at the time spoke, with passion or skepticism, of Italian fashion certainly did not have in mind as the target of this nascent fascist propaganda either the rural housewife, who was asked only to work harder, nor the war widow or mother of a fallen soldier, who continued to be the most exalted female figures in street speeches and schoolbooks. Nor was it the young and carefree female workers that the National After-Work Club was pushing strongly towards low-priced consumerism. [...] And certainly even the salaried woman was not the target of the nascent national fashion: in recent years she had seen her pay check dwindle. [...] In that textile industry which must free itself from shameful French taste, the weaver who in 1926 earned 20 lire a day, in 1929 earned 12. A tailored dress cost from 1,000 lire upwards: the distance was thus unbridgeable. Italian fashion would therefore be for the ladies the regime had always favoured, and which the propaganda always showed absorbed in good works: the aristocrats, the haute bourgeoisie, the nouveau riche, those who, not very patriotically, seemed determined to dress only in the French way.⁴¹

---

39   Leumann to EMSA, registered letter of the 5 March 1945, ACS, *Ibid.*
40   Ponti, G., "È superfluo il superfluo?," *Bellezza*, n. 1 (new series), November 1945, p. 45-46, p. 45.
41   Aspesi, N., *op. cit.*, pp. 26-27.

A magazine modelled on *Vogue* conferring prestige on Italian clothing and acting as a mirror and a form of cultural legitimation for the regime's aristocracy should come as no surprise. According to historian Lynn Hunt,[42] clothing is one of the most contested arenas of revolutionary cultural politics because it is the most visible sign of adherence and resistance to new political and social concepts. Among other things, fascism revalued the aristocracy, like any other hierarchy, with the entry of many members of the regime's armed forces and industrialists into the ranks of the nobility.[43]

Bellezza's readership was the epitome of that worldly and cosmopolitan life which, despite Italy being at war, showed no signs of slowing down. The reluctance of these women to give up the conspicuous signs of that luxury condemned by the fascist press was made acute by the war and by the emphasis given by the regime to social hierarchy and clothing as a sign of national distinction. The party officials exhorted the popular classes to low-cost, autarkic consumerism while the elite indulged in a luxurious and decadent lifestyle, of which Mussolini's mistress

---

[42] "Freedom of dress" is not usually counted as one of the inalienable human rights central to modern democratic politics. It might be related to Jefferson's "pursuit of happiness" in the Declaration of Independence, but freedom of dress hardly seems central to life, liberty, or the protection of property. Even so, dress, with both its freedoms and constraints, turned out to be one of the most hotly contested arenas of revolutionary cultural politics. It provided the most visible marker of both adherence and resistance to new social and political conceptions, including notions of gender definition. See Hunt, Lynn, "Freedom of Dress in Revolutionary France," in Melzer, S. E., Norberg, K., *From the Royal to the Republican Body Incorporating the Political in Seventeenth and Eighteenth-Century France*, University of California Press, Berkeley 1998.

[43] On the increase of the aristocracy in institutional positions during fascism see Passamonti, L.S., "La nobiltà della stirpe: il sogno di un'Italia aristocratica e fascista", *Diacronie*, 27, n. 3, 2016 URL: http://journals.openedition.org/diacronie/4235; Jocteau, G.C., «I nobili del Fascismo», *Studi Storici*, n. 3, 2004, pp. 677-726; Rumi, G., "La politica nobiliare del Regno d'Italia 1861-1946", in *Les noblesses européennes au XIXe siècle*, Actes du colloque de Rome, 21-23 November 1985, École Française de Rome, Rome 1988, pp. 577-593.

Claretta Petacci was the personification.[44] General Giacomo Carboni, of the Office of Strategic Services (OSS), remembered her wearing an eccentric white hat which her sister[45] had tried to launch as a fashion in her first film and two showy silver fox stoles:

> ...Petacci seemed to me an insignificant creature, with an upturned nose, two small lively black eyes, a pale face without make-up, and thin lips. She wore an eccentric white hat that her sister, actress Miriam di S. Servolo, had tried to launch in her first film; on her shoulders were two showy magnificent silver fox stoles... When on the 14th of July I learned from Donadio himself that Petacci had been - for the third time - expelled from Palazzo Venezia[46], I insisted that he accompany me to her, as he had promised me. After calling by telephone, I obtained an appointment with her at Via della Camilluccia for the next day at noon... At 12 noon on the 15th of July I went to the Camilluccia. The maid, Ersilia, was barely able to open one of the grandiose sliding windows which, covering the entire facade of the villa, made the property look like a large box sitting on a block of ice. I was ushered into a huge hall with glass doors, as large as the walls and with windows that, as with the entrance, formed a single wall of glass from one corner to the other. There were about twenty soft armchairs. In one corner was a grand piano and a harp. Against the wall was a very ugly picture of an ugly little girl. A frescoed wall divided the living room from a sitting room with a fireplace and a very long sofa with feather cushions. On the right was large wooden door. The floors were all marble. The wait was long - so long that, finding myself alone, I ventured into the right side of the house. I found myself in a princely bedroom. Each wall was covered with mirrors and there must also have been a mirror on the ceiling which had then been detached, probably at the wish of the exceptional lover! Pink furniture; the low bed on a dark wooden base covered with pink veils and very fine feather-filled blankets. The kind of thing you see in American films, but obviously in bad taste. I realized I was in the alcove. Pushing open a mirrored door, I found myself in a bathroom all in black marble. In the centre was a level swimming pool decorated with mosaics. A separating wall concealed the toilet, also in black marble. Lights in all corners. In a corner of the swimming pool there was a telephone socket. The glitz of the nouveau riche! At about 1 pm the maid came to call me and took me along a carpeted ramp (there were no stairs in that house, but only very long ramps to avoid the effort of climbing steps) up to the upper

---

44   De Felice, R., *Mussolini l'alleato, I, vol. 2: L'Italia in guerra (1940-43). Crisi e agonia del regime*, Einaudi, Turin 2008, appendix, pp.1536-37.
45   The actress Miria di San Servolo.
46   During the fascist period Mussolini used the palace as his seat of government and private residence.

floor in a dining room where there was another antechamber. Here, too, I spent my time observing the luxurious furniture and went as far as the terrace that overlooked the large outdoor swimming pool; on the terrace was gymnastic equipment. At 1.15 pm I was finally received by Petacci in her private bedroom. A large bed with silk blankets and the finest linen; a bedside table upon which there was a large colour photograph of Mussolini; a cabinet with a large quantity of medicines (Petacci later confided to me that she was afflicted by many imaginary illnesses); a bookcase; a dressing table. Clad in a very low-necked dressing gown which revealed part of her bosom, Petacci invited me to sit on the bed with her. Her mother, a big woman, stood in a corner, leafing through correspondence that she piled up in [a] drawer. These were petitions, some of which addressed to Her Excellency Clara Petacci. Petacci then forwarded on the petitions to Buffarini and De Cesari to get rid of them...[47]

It is a sarcastic and merciless portrait of the lack of good taste of Claretta Petacci who, however, had her dedicated fans. In *Io son te*, Luigi De Vincentis, a friend of the powerful Petacci family, remembers how his wife was dazzled by the sight of Claretta's wardrobe:

Clara's clothes hung behind immense sliding doors in the huge walk-in wardrobe. My wife was literally dazzled: before her eyes, hundreds of dresses appeared in iridescent shades, dark tones and delicate and lively colours. A vision which, especially for a woman, was truly captivating. The elegance and good taste of those dresses was beyond question and it was undoubtedly the wardrobe of one of the most elegant women in Italy. She could wear a black tulle dress, three-quarter jacket with delicate white embroidery on the pockets and on the bodice. Her black dresses were enlivened by trimmings of shiny sequins, her suits were rich in furs, her summer dresses decorated with embroidery and lace. Her showiness in her dress was however always tempered by very fine good taste.[48]

---

47 *Ibid.*
48 De Vincentis, L., *Io son te*, UTAC, Milano 1947, cit. in Aspesi, N., *op. cit.*, p. 159-160. About Claretta Petacci see Serri, M., *Claretta l'hitleriana. Storia della donna che non morì per amore di Mussolini*, Longanesi, Milan 2021; and also Sarfatti, M., *My Fault. Mussolini as I Knew Him*, Enigma Books, New York 2014, p. 129. The finding of ladies of the regime with jewels, exquisitely cut dresses and furs is a recurring motif. After the war, British soldiers found Frau Höss, wife of Rudolf Höss, commander of the Auschwitz concentration camp, hiding in an abandoned sugar factory amidst a huge amount of high fashion clothing and furs owned by the victims of the camp.

But the glamorous face of international fascism was Edda Ciano, nicknamed "the lady of the Axis," who on the 24th of July, 1939 appeared – gaunt, pale and dressed in black – on the cover of *Time*, which spoke of her as the brain behind the regime's foreign policy:

> Although Signor Mussolini's favourite and eldest child, Edda, has done her duty to the State by giving birth to two future soldiers and one future housewife, she has not toiled unduly in the kitchen and has not hesitated to enter the male province of international politics. [...] the role that Edda Ciano, née Mussolini, has played in the momentous recent realignments of European nations, has been half concealed by a regime which refuses to admit women in politics.[49]

Described as "high-spirited, witty, gay," Edda Ciano had little respect for convention. She is said to have caused an "uproar at a full-dress diplomatic dinner in Peking by showing up in a tailored skirt-suit while her husband wore a dinner coat". She was fond of dancing and going to nightclubs and, as the Foreign Minister's wife

> became dashing, chic, smart. At times she was a brunette, at other times as is fashionable in Rome, a blonde. She wore heavy, fashionable make up — except when she went to see her father. The circular rolled hairdo she adopted means a daily visit to famed Hairdresser Attilio on the Piazza di Spagna. All one winter she wore a sable coat everywhere. During her junket to Vienna and Budapest in 1936 she was seen in ermine, morning, noon and night. In Poland last winter she wore mink. While she patriotically orders Roman, rather than Parisian, clothes, she prefers French perfumes and creams but was only slightly disturbed when Italy stopped importing these items. Her comment: "The Ala Littoria (Italian civil air service) boys will bring them to me.[50]

After her marriage to Count Galeazzo Ciano, she had entrusted her image to a woman of great talent known in the world of Italian fashion as Madame Anna, who was considered the finest seamstress in Rome, where she worked as a première

---

49   "Foreign News: Lady of the Axis," *Time*, 24 July 1939, https://content.time.com/time/subscriber/article/0,33009,771660-1,00.html. Accessed 17 august 2022.
50   Ivi.

for the Ventura fashion house. Of Franco-Dutch origin, Madame Anna wanted to launch herself as a creator of fashions and, for this purpose collaborated with Edda. In reality, notwithstanding autarky, Edda's model was the diva of American cinema Greta Garbo. She studied Garbo's clothes and poses and, somewhat unpatriotically, hired Ventura to create her a wardrobe like that Garbo wore in her films and in the photographs of her in fashion magazines.[51] In 1938, the Italian ambassador to Brazil Lojacono was forced to prevent the publication of photos of Edda that showed her dancing enthusiastically, drunk and flirty, while the Nazis in Berlin organised scientifically calibrated schedules to prevent her from getting bored. Between 1944 and 1945 Edda found refuge in Switzerland, where the *Basler Nachrichten* newspaper published reports of the parties and receptions in which she took part and where she is said to have married her fashion designer friend Emilio Pucci, one of her Florentine admirers who she met in Capri in the summer of 1941.[52]

Galeazzo Ciano's parents, Donna Carolina and Costanzo Ciano, were known in Livorno for their presumptuous ignorance and vanity, considered typical of the *nouveau riche*, and Maria – Galeazzo's sister who had married the young diplomat Massimo Magistrati – was nicknamed "the scarecrow" by Mussolini. He used to speak of her thinness as a warning: "A woman without wide hips is like a bed without pillows — very uncomfortable. Look at that poor Ciano. She was so full and pretty at sixteen. She then went on a diet, despite the efforts of her family. She lived on half an artichoke a day to keep herself lean. Then she got sick and became a living skeleton. She has lost her health, beauty and joy. So sad!"[53]

The aristocratic ladies – who often featured in the press in the guise of benefactors and inspectors of women's fascist groups and at sumptuous receptions and premieres – were the official image of Italian elegance and their wardrobes were exemplary –

---

51 Sarfatti, M., *op. cit.*, p. 140.
52 "Edda Ciano Remarried to Wealthy Florentine," *New York Times*, 4 December 1944, p. 8.
53 Sarfatti, M., *op. cit.*, p. 151.

like that of the Marquise Barbara dal Pozzo of the Orsi Mangelli family, which, among other things, included:

> A long, low-cut black silk knit dress; a loose dress in black tulle with black organza roses; a black otter cape; a beaver fur cape; a skirt-suit with a mink collar; a purple satin house dress with a fuchsia belt; a silver laminate evening dress with a silver fox jacket; a cloak of black cloth with a black woollen gown; a suede-coloured wool cloak with matching skirt and blouse; a tartan morning dress; a black draped afternoon dress.[54]

In her memoirs, Margherita Sarfatti recalls that shortly after seizing power, Mussolini had sworn to her there were two things he would never ever get involved in: religion and fashion. "If women decided they were going to wear petticoats that only went down to their hips you could even kill them but you would never make the petticoats go an inch lower." However, even the freedom to choose what to wear would disappear in the ensuing years, with the help of the young Galeazzo Ciano who had brought a breath of energy and novelty first to the press office and then to the Undersecretariat for Press and Propaganda, introducing an approach that followed the organization of the German Propaganda Ministry.[55] Upon his death on the 11th of January 11, 1944[56] Galeazzo Ciano was one of the richest men in

---

54   Aspesi, N., *op. cit.*, p. 164.
55   Propaganda was the tool for the exercise of propaganda in the fashion press. In 1939 (July 17, 1939) a statement read: "Do not publish photographs and drawings of women depicted with the so-called "wasp waist." Drawings and photographs must represent prosperous and healthy women," in *Le veline di Mussolini*. In July 1941 (18/7/1941) it was forbidden to publish articles and campaign against women without stockings, also in the same year it was forbidden to publish photos of regime hierarchs in civilian dress, photographs, articles and news about Bette Davis, Mirna Loy and the MGM film house. The ban on showing queues dates back to November 1941 (12/11/1941). On May 4, 1943, the Ministry asked to lengthen the skirts of the drawings slightly below the knee. The sketches and photos of fashion and women's magazines, such as *Grazia* e *Bellezza*, were left a margin of freedom in the design of the sketches, often with a slim, wasp-like waist, and the choice of models, even if, in this case, the physical shape was less slender and the hourglass shape was never accentuated.
56   Galezzo Ciano was shot in Verona after having voted against Mussolini in the sitting of the Great Council between the 24th and 25th of July 1943.

Italy. Andrew Noble, secretary of the British embassy in Rome from 1933 to 1938, commented on his death:

> Costanzo Ciano was notoriously corrupt and greedy. And so was his son, Galeazzo. His father ran what was known as the Ciano Group. This coterie was nothing more than a gang of thieves who took advantage of Costanzo's inside information.[57]

The social life of the Italian elites revolved around the Ciano Group in several select places on the peninsula, including Capri. Two months after the German-Italian attack on the Soviet Union, the bathing season was at its peak in Capri. *La Voce di Napoli* newspaper of the 4th of August, 1941 recorded the visitors to the island enjoying "the restorative bathing and heliotherapy treatments... despite the contingencies of the war, in this corner of paradise in the middle of the ocean you can enjoy the most perfect tranquility."[58] Edda adored Capri and the secret reports sent to her father spoke of a dissolute life: "People are surprised that the Countess circulates the island, carefree and in skimpy attire, wearing bright colours, as if her brother Bruno were not so prematurely and tragically dead. She does not respect his mourning. The countess has not even given up dancing, as if her homeland were not at war."[59] In short, despite the

---

57 NAUK, FO 371 Italy 1939, 23826 R5522, note by Noble of the 7th of July, 1939.
58 *Voce di Napoli*, 4 August 1941, cit. in Mannucci, E., *Il marchese rampante*, Baldini&Castoldi, Florence 1998, p. 192-193.
59 *Ibid*. A few weeks after the death of his son Bruno, in a tragic accident the 7th of August 1941 during a test flight, Mussolini wrote the book *Parlo con Bruno* (I Speak with Bruno). Guests at the *Quisisana* included: "Baron and Baroness Karl von Klemm, Countess Lydia Cini and family, Baron and Baroness von Chamler-Glisczinski, Prince G.B. Caracciolo-Carafa, countess M. Campello, marchesa G. Granafei, lady gen. E. von Rintelen, comm. Alberto d'Agostino and family, prince and princess del drago, Donna Lucienne De Cardenas, comm. C. Pignatti and Signora, comm. L. Malabarba and family, count G. Airoldi, marquis V. Cattaneo Della Volta, prince and princess Carlo Filomarino di Bitetto, count and countess G. Bosdari, s.e. Guglielmo Rulli, comm. lawyer M. Gazzoni, count and countess B. Blanci di Roascio, count and countess L. Lucchesi Palli, count Cesare Celani, duke Luca Caracciolo d'Acquara, etc. Roberto Farinacci, cons. nat. Mario Varenna, with. nat. Luigi Candiano, cons. nat. Alberto Calza Bini, count

"contingencies," what with the luxury hotels and private villas, life in Capri at the time was good: "It was awakened from [...] sleep by the noise of the second, great world war; but since this too was the bearer of infinite suffering, the island, a land immune to pain, remained more than ever 'abroad' – its neutrality, now, hermetic, and definitive."[60]

But the war eventually changed everything, even in Capri, and by 1944 the "nights at Forte dei Marmi and in Turin and recently at the Bosco in Rome"[61] were a distant memory. The stars of the island had already fled a few days after the start of the war. Barbara Hutton, a friend of Edda, was luckier than Mona Williams and Gracie Fields, and found a place on a ship bound for America thanks to the intercession of Galeazzo Ciano, who obtained for her eight first-class cabins on the transatlantic Conte di Savoia, departing from Genoa to New York.[62] On October the 16th, 1939 the New York Times announced the return, aboard the Rex, of Mona Williams who, in 1941, was denounced as part of

---

Ugo Pellegrini, prince Carlo Maurizio Ruspoli, count Casimiro Kulczicki, countess Marina Rossi-Martini, count and countess L. Treccani, marquis M.C. Dal Pozzo, baron Diego Calcagno Féraud, duke R. Caracciolo of San Vito, count T. Fani, marquis sen. Rome Delle Torrazze, comm. A. Rosset Desandré, Marquise Capece Minutolo di Bugnano, general Leo von Bayer and Madame, cons. nat. Cornelio di Marzio, comm. Arturo Guttinger and Lady, Baroness M.L. Boris, Mrs. M. Toeplitz de Gran Ry, Alice Ravà and Marino Turchi." The *Splendido* was empty in comparison: "Viscount di Modrone Galeazzo, Rossetti family, sig. Roberto Squatriti, Mr. Mario De Crescenzo"; like the *Vittoria Pagano*. Prof. Enrico Prampolini was staying in *La Palma*. The most elegant seems to have been *Villa Le Terrazze*, judging by the guests: "Prince and Princess Ubaldo Barberini di Sciarra, Princess Lola Giovannelli, Prince Ranieri Bourbon Del Monte, Princess Marinetta Ruffo, Bettina Varè and daughter, Countess Sita di Sambuy, Marchesa Delia Di Bath and family, Maritaine Marita Guglielmi, Miss Gioia Marconi, frigate captain Manlio Lazzeri, Freiher von Sirschberg director Dekafilm of Berlin, baroness von Hirschberg, first att. Joannes Riemann and Madam, first att. Hermann Pfeifer, Herr Karl Doese and Mrs. Laura Solari, Marquis Lt. Emilio Pucci, Com. Alessandro Aristeo, Dr. Cav. Tito Lebreton, Dr. Cav. Annibale Scicluna, Mrs. Diana Torrieri."

60 Cerio, E., *Guida inutile di Capri*, La Conchiglia, Capri 1946, in Mannucci, E., *op. cit.*, p. 194.
61 Ivi, p. 176.
62 Heymann, D., *Poor Little Rich Girl*, Lyle Stuart, New York 1984, p. 143, 164.

an elite group that welcomed wealthy pro-Nazis to Palm Beach. In the spring of 1942 "all tourism in Capri ceased, revenues fell enormously due to the lower water consumption of the hotels, the lack of travellers, as the bulk of the traffic was due to hotel guests, and the lower consumption of energy in hotels, private villas, the funicular railway and the aqueduct."[63] From 1943, Villa Palazzo a Mare was occupied by American troops, the British and then the Americans arrived at Castiglione – the Ciano family's villa – and the island became a rest camp for General Clark's troops. Soldiers and nurses walked through the rooms of the Ciano family and the caretaker was scandalized by the soldiers of the Women's Army Corps (WAC) who wandered naked through the luxurious salons. Since 1943 and the German occupation, clothing had become a matter of life and death:

> When the first light of dawn begins to lighten the sky - writes Franco Levi - here is the border network: one stretch is knocked down and there is a heap of earth that favours the passage between the trampled bushes. Once we are a few metres past it, with a great sense of relief and a sudden drop in psychological tension, we stop. The smugglers are in a hurry, and with good reason. We are in the land of the free; here we will deliver ourselves as prisoners but, god willing, to human creatures! I began to walk feeling like someone who emerges into the open air for the first time after a long illness and with the strange impression of being watched, even though the place seemed deserted. I had not traveled a kilometre and was starting to enter the wooded area when I saw two soldiers with rifles in hand, running down with great strides from the steep wood to the left, and who seemed to be Germans, partly because they were shouting "Halt! Halt! Halt!" It wasn't until I saw the Swiss cross on the buttons of their jackets that I could breathe a great sigh of relief.[64]

The writer Paola Masino remembers how during the German occupation of Rome, a colour or a particular cut, however dull or modest, could acquire a character of danger and threat, perhaps simply from its ubiquitousness, "the way a sound, however low, does if it is prolonged to excess":

---

63 Leone De Andreis, M., *Capri 1939*, Unpublished, Rome 2002, p. 401.
64 Broggini, R., *Terra d'asilo. I rifugiati italiani in Svizzera 1943-45*, Il Mulino, Bologna 1993, p.93

> We tried to change our clothes the way we changed lodgings. With discretion and apparent ease we went from a hotel to a hovel, from a grey skirt to a brown blouse, from a dubious apartment to a convent, from a blue coat to a tartan skirt-suit.[65]

The colours in the streets of Rome were muted and the only bright things, "like an empty eye socket, were the flat napes of the necks of the German patrols." In order not to be noticed, Masino had some "little dresses" made of rayon dyed. One of these was:

> A two-piece dress in heavy dark blue crepe consisting of a collarless bolero with short sleeves and a skirt straight on the back and with a wide godet on the front, tied at the waist by a wide band that twisted at the hips and finished in a bow under the chest. Underneath I wore a black chiffon blouse with a scarf collar adorned with small ruffled leaflets, very eighteenth-century and not at all austere.[66]

At the end of the war, fashion was nothing more than a memory: "It is very difficult to keep your hair combed when you live in constant terror of being caught, tortured and killed. [...] At night you sleep badly, half-dressed so as to always be ready to escape, your skin and clothing crease on you and take on indelible folds."[67] For the writer, pre-war clothes were relics of a bygone world and bygone feelings: "Fashion had not yet had time to come back to life and impose its diktats, but who was thinking of fashion?"[68]

3.2 *Costuming Fashion*

To understand the way in which *Bellezza* perceived its role in the Italian fashion system, it is useful to start with the celebratory issue of 1960 dedicated to the magazine's twentieth

---

65 Masino, P., *Album di vestiti*, Lit Edizioni, Rome 2015, p. 203.
66 Ivi, p. 204.
67 *Ibid.*
68 *Ibid.*

anniversary.[69] In it, a series of testimonies from those involved and other observers told the story of *Bellezza*'s origins. Elsa Robiola described the time she spent there as "dizzying but exciting like little else." The war years, although "cruel and frightening," had not been enough to turn "everything dark" and the memories glowed with enthusiasm "for the impetuous will of Ponti to finally create in Italy a fashion and lifestyle magazine that could hold its head up with the foreign ones [...] which in that moment were unable to publish in Italy."[70] The war was spoken of as a period of "coming together" in which "every initiative was given the attention it deserved" and ideas and products bloomed, so much so that never before had fashion been close to "intelligence and culture, technique and artisan traditions, ingenuity and inventiveness," and if Italian fashion after the war had international success, it owed it to the "ferment of those years caused by the problems of Italian fashion."[71]

For Arturo Tofanelli, who in 1960 was co-director of *Bellezza* with Elsa Robiola, *Bellezza*'s task was to "invent an Italian approach, and smuggle its ideas across the border."[72] Giovanni Battista Giorgini confessed that he used the photos in his conferences to prove that Italy was already at the forefront of the creation of fashion in the early 1940s. Alfieri & Lacroix, who had printed the first two issues of *Bellezza*, remembered the "cold January morning of 1941" when Ponti, Lucio Ridenti, architects Bo and Pagani, Elsa Robiola and others had started *Bellezza* in its offices. Among the testimonies there was also that of Francesco Ilorini Mo who thanked *Bellezza* for helping launch the Agnona company. For Irene Brin "Italian fashion was born poor," midwifed by a group of women who worked to "bring Italian elegance out of the ruins of Italy."[73] After the war, the only one with adequate equipment was Gabriella di Robilant who, like Gabriellasport, had for some time installed herself in the

---

69   *Bellezza*, n. 4, 1960.
70   Robiola, E., "Dopo vent'anni," ivi, pp. 26-27.
71   *Ibid.*
72   Tofanelli, A., "Storia di venti anni fortunati," ivi, p. 25.
73   Brin, I., "Come nasce l'alta moda," ivi, p. 31.

Ventura premises in Piazza di Spagna, but "the others began with two sublet rooms in via Veneto, a mezzanine in via Sistina, or a warehouse in via Gregoriana." They were readers of *Bellezza*, experts on their own wardrobes, trying their hand at fashion production: "We must immediately mention Donna Aurora of the Giovannelli noble family and Donna Stefanella of the Colonna di Sciarra noble family; donna Simonetta Colonna of the dukes of Cesarò; Giovanna of the Caracciolo-Ginetti noble family; Countess Dessalles and Baroness de Reutern."[74] During the war, *Myricae* of Rome had dressed her clients with handcrafted sheets dyed using Indonesian batik technique and thus, according to the marchioness Teresa Massel of Caresana, two trades – crafts and fashion – became one.[75] During the war, out of necessity or out of a need for distraction, *Bellezza*'s readers and testimonials became fashion creators.

The magazine had already celebrated its pioneering role as a courageous architect of Italian fashion in 1949 in an evocative drawing by Brunetta. In the drawing, *Bellezza* is represented as a multi-storey building inside which the staff carries on the work of the magazine as if in some busy desert oasis while outside the bombs fall.[76] The drawing celebrates the heroic role of *Bellezza* in the creation of Italian fashion. In fact, for the protagonists of the war years, Italian fashion was born before 1951. Tizzoni recalls that "*Bellezza* was close to us during the war, in every sense of the word: we bravely endured bombings and evacuations together under the same roof [...],"[77] and Carosa adds: "When I became part of [the world of fashion] *Bellezza* already existed and I knew its character and style [...] I know that, despite the enormous difficulties of those grim times, *Bellezza* managed to live and survive thanks to a few of its staff who worked miracles."[78] Despite the difficulties of the war, *Bellezza* enjoyed lavish funding and had an original formula, with continuous

---

74 *Ibid.*
75 Myricae, ivi, p. 30.
76 *Bellezza*, 1949.
77 Tizzoni, G., *Bellezza*, n. 4, 1960, p. 59.
78 Carosa, ivi, p. 31.

leaps between languages and materials, and the various parts of the magazine used different colours, textures and weights of paper for translations into Spanish and German, the concluding sections of articles, the pages by Lucio Ridenti and the internal fold-out which reported the most important events of the Italian social calendar. The typefaces changed frequently, as did the magazine's logo and the cover style. The layout continually offered new approaches, such as the ingenious idea of presenting seventeen high-fashion designs in an envelope with a wax seal containing photos of the garments. Over time, the progress of the war and the loss of Ponti's artistic direction, the flexible layout and the stylistic variety veered towards messiness and inconsistency, a context in which artwork was prioritised over photography. The prevalence of artwork was probably linked to its greater adaptability to editorial needs, the scarce availability of fashion photography and its power of artistic and narrative synthesis.

In the field of photography, *Bellezza* produced the most cutting-edge photographs of its day, promoting a modern idea of the fashion monthly as a creative agency at the service of dressmakers and brands. In fact, in the first issue, between advertisements for Coty and Elizabeth Arden, there was a double page spread illustrated by Pallavicini showing two designs by Ventura and Gori with the caption "*Bellezza*'s art office creates artwork for your advertising." In general, *Bellezza*'s photography has a theatrical flair, with art direction like that inside a studio even when the photos are shot outdoors. The war and the teeming life of the world do not appear. Photography is used not in its documentary and scientific function, but as a way of mythologising the garment as much as possible. The constant presence of columns, mirrors, masks, shadows and baroque furnishings has an evocative function and connotes the setting as an almost magical place of artifice, dramatizing the presence of the garment-actor, enhancing it as an object of art. The photographs depict a life in costume, the assiduous presence of mirrors placing fashion in a mythopoetic dimension. Here the mirror does not have the function of showing the workings of the garment, as it would for *Grazia* and *Novità* after the war, but of multiplying reality and immersing the onlooker in a ritualistic atmosphere which fashion designs seemed to be lacking. The covers featured the work of famous artists such as De Pisis, author of a treatise on elegance[79], or Enrico Prampolini,[80] with mixed results. Inside, there were Lina Bo's doodles, the archaism of Dal Forno,[81] whose approach echoed the work of Campigli,[82] and the stylized solutions of Prof. Ciuti, which accentuated and flattened the colours in a context of refined references. Brunetta's

---

79   De Pisis, F., *Adamo o dell'eleganza. Per una estetica del vestire*, Abscondita, Milan 2019. In it, De Pisis affirms that "the intimate essence of elegance is something *eternal* and unfathomable," p. 13.

80   One of the best known exponents of Futurism, to which he subscribed from 1912, contributing 'manifestos' and polemical writings.

81   Gian Giacomo Dal Forno was born in Catania on the 21st of December 1909 to a Veronese family. The following year he moved to Milan where he completed his classical studies, graduating from the Brera Academy of Fine Arts. As early as 1930, he began showing in group exhibitions; in the decade from 1930 to 1940 he was present at the Milanese trade union exhibitions, the Lombard interregional exhibitions and the four-yearly Roman exhibitions; in this period he obtained his first recognition: the 1933 L'ambrosiano Prize for "Drawing," the 1934 Gold Medal at the Triennale di Milano; the1938 Medardo Rosso Award and Fumagalli Award from the Brera Academy. Dal Forno achieved his first important official statement on a national level with the task of frescoing a wall of 100 square meters. at the VII Triennale di Milano in 1940. The artist, then thirty years old, painted a choral theme: *Women's work,* a composition of about three hundred life-size figures painted with his colleagues Sironi and Carrà. The execution of the fresco earned him a gold medal at the Triennale. Referring to this episode Franco Passoni writes: "With this piece the young painter had brought to completion his personal style, that style characteristic of him, which became a constant in his plastic and figurative process." In 1940 he also began his career as a teacher: at the del Castello Higher School of Art, and a few decades later, in 1968, he taught figure paining at the Brera Liceo Artistico and later at the Academy. Among the prestigious achievements of his youth, two First Prizes should be mentioned: the 1941 Cremona Prize and the 1942 City of Verona Award. In 1942 he was invited to the XXIII Venice Biennale. In that period (1937) he was a founding member of the 'Milanese Group of the Ten' and in subsequent years he participated in the *Movimento della Rotonda* and the *Gruppo del Gatto Nero* groups. The first individual show we know of was held in 1944 at the Galleria Borromini in Como, followed by another in Milan in 1945.

82   Cfr. Wolbert, K., *Massimo Campigli. Mediterraneità e modernità*, Mazzotta, 2003. The catalogue was published for the exhibition that was held in Darmstadt at the Institut Mathildenhöhe, 12 October 2003 - 18 January 2004.

art had the advantage of not simply capturing a garment on paper in the same way as a fashion sketch, but of using the models as a way of looking at changing habits.[83] Brunetta was able to adapt her design and adopt different styles to suit the title of the article and the needs of the text. Her women were not mannequins and presupposed a body in motion, a lifestyle and a way of relating to the world around them.[84] Federico Pallavicini,[85] on the other hand, conceived of the illustration as tapestry or interior design, flattening everything into the two-dimensionality of the page, with background and dress literally on the same plane forming a single arabesque. Given the excellent work of the illustrators, according to Ponti:

> We can be profoundly Italian in our work by and still be international, it is vain naivete to believe that it is necessary to imitate Hollywood or Paris to be understood by the Americans or the French: both will distinguish us better and appreciate us more easily if we present ourselves as ourselves,

---

83   Impressionismo, École de Paris, Eric e Bouché; see Blackman, K., *100 Years of Fashion Illustration*, Laurence King, London 2007.
84   *Grazia*, n. 3, 1949, pp. 34-37.
85   Federico von Berzeviczy-Pallavicini, decorative artist, set designer and artistic director, died in Manhattan on November 13, 1989 at the age of 80. Pallavicini's sophisticated, delicate and imaginative designs appeared on wrapping paper, porcelain and textiles. They have also been translated into elegant costumes and theatrical sets. In 1950 he created *Flair* magazine for Fleur Cowles. The short-lived magazine's design was unusual, using techniques such as opening pages to reveal images and a foldout sheet that revealed a cross section of an apartment building. He was also a stylist for *Look* magazine, exhibited paintings in galleries in New York and Chicago and, in 1955, became the artistic director of Elizabeth Arden, the cosmetics company. From 1956 to 1965 he was an art consultant and interior designer for Helena Rubinstein and decorated the rooms of her apartment on Park Avenue. In 1978, Pallavicini created the sets and costumes for the Vienna State Opera's production of The Young Lord. Born Friedrich Ludwig von Berzeviczy on April 12, 1909 in Lausanne, Switzerland, Pallavicini studied fine arts in Vienna. At the end of the 1920s, architect Josef Hoffmann introduced him to Demel, the famous pastry shop, for which Pallavicini created imaginative display cases, gift wrapping paper and packaging. In 1936 he married Klara, a niece of Anna Demel. After moving to Italy in the late 1930s, Pallavicini adopted his mother's name and embarked on a career as a magazine illustrator and artistic director, working for publications such as *Bellezza*, *Domus*, *Fili* and *Scena Illustrata*. He moved to America in the 1940s.

without resorting to disguises that might end up being grotesque. Who would have the courage to replace St. Mark's Basilica with an American-style skyscraper? It may be that some of us think that Florence, Assisi, Perugia are only provinces; but they will never understand that Giotto's bell tower is much more international than a swing song that sounds almost American. For *Bellezza*, fashion is never just the invention of a style, but the material and evocative whole that includes the accessory, the jewellery and the fabric, all taken to the highest quality level.[86]

From at the latest 1936 on, the ENM, at the behest of Mussolini and in compliance with the Clothing Corporation, strove to create a totalitarian fashion, as stated in the second edition of Cesare Meano's *Commentario*. Under the "fashion" entry in the *Commentario* it can be read that fashion consists of "minimal" and "lazy" variations of the costume that do not change its fundamental characteristics. Costume history

> is explained by political history: the basic shapes fit into the framework of their day with perfect harmony. Hence the peplums and chlamydias of Hellas, as well as the togas and tunics of imperial Rome... There was one great time for fashion: the Renaissance. Universalism existed also in fashion, it was nothing more than the mirror of the various original civilizations. This is Europe.[87]

Meano compared the era of fascism to those that preceded it, implying that fascism would eventually produce its own "costume" that would not be the result of couturiers' freedom of creation, because no tailor "has ever invented a fashion but rather has interpreted it, [...] with the designs or patterns that bear his signature. Fashion is created by forces far greater than those of a man's talent or a woman's whim. [...] In our days, fashion is generated by current events."[88] In Italy, fashion was under the control of the ENM which did not exclude, and in fact "considers probable [...] in the not too distant future the achievement of a totalitarian national production, that is the extension of the *Marca di garanzia* to all the collections created by our producers."[89]

---

86   Moravia, A., "Via Condotti," *Bellezza*, 1949.
87   *Commentario Dizionario italiano della moda*, op. cit., p. 142.
88   *Commentario, op. cit.*, 1938, p. 147.
89   Ivi, p. 292.

Immediately after the war, Robiola looked regretfully at the "period when, isolated by the fiery circle of war, every piece in Italian collections was unique and the dressmakers, intoxicated by our wonderful fabrics, cut and attached buttons and pockets, each admirably in their own way,"[90] condemning the "collective conditioning" that had infected the Italian tailors and dressmakers who had returned from the pilgrimage to Paris.

Gio Ponti's vision of fashion was consistent with that of the *Commentario*. In 1928, in one of *Domus*'s first editorials, he stressed that the modern home should not simply be a matter of *fashion*, understood as the expression of the whims of a designer, but of adherence to the life and culture of one's time.[91] A few years later, on the occasion of the second *National Fashion Show* in Turin in 1933, Ponti stated that the point where architecture and fashion meet is in their both being an expression of the style of an era and of its customs, with the difference that architecture "surpasses the expressions of art and customs that have over time created it," making "these transitory human phenomena an expression which is alive only insofar as it is eternal" – "a perennial monument" – while fashion "predeceases the general and human phenomenon that generates it," making "an eternal phenomenon a living expression only insofar as it is transitory"[92] – "a contingent monument." According to Ponti, a modern way of life should correspond to a modern way of living and dressing, a modern "costume," even if "as a dress, though fashionable, can be made – alas – by a bad tailor and be ugly, so modern architecture can also be beautiful or ugly depending on the talents of the architect" – but here, he adds, "we pass from style to art."[93]

Ponti's position was echoed by that of architect Bernard Rudofsky who considered fashion an inhuman inclination, referring to the difficulty of it becoming an expression of

---

90   Robiola, E., *Bellezza*, n. 16, 1947, p. 15.
91   G. Ponti, "La casa di moda," *Domus*, n. 8, August 1928, p. 11.
92   G. Ponti, "*L'architettura e la moda*," in Autonomous Agency for the Permanent Fashion Exhibition, *II Mostra nazionale della moda*, October, Roggero and Tortia, Turin 1933, pp. 35-36.
93   *Ibid.*

contemporary civilization.[94] In the summer of 1940, someone – perhaps Ponti – hiding behind the pseudonym Arital had announced in Daria Guarnati's magazine *Aria d'Italia* that the moment of the "Italian style" had come: not "a futile and capricious fashion," but a style that "represents absolutely an Italian creation, reaffirming those great rights to prestige and primacy in all the vigorous expressions of art that have been fully recognized in Italy in the past."[95] The Italians, "with the wonderful fabrics of Ferrari and Lisio, with its magnificent silk weavers and silk printers (Frua is the best in the world), with its great rayon and hemp industries, with its exceptional footwear (as Ferragamo shows)" were born "for this sector, which is imagination, art, creation, invention and brilliant execution."[96] The first issue of *Bellezza* opened with an editorial by him entitled *Costume and Civilisation*:

> Costume is the living mirror of civilization. Civilisation is above all an interior, human order of the spirit and of the heart; it must however express itself and express itself with three things: elegance, grace, beauty.[97]

Elegance is education, grace is art, "the sublime expression of civilization," and beauty is "a mirror of education and art, and a mirror of the intimate sense of physical and spiritual dignity;" "A great civilised people must be a beautiful people." According to Ponti, the mission of civilisation was the achievement of beauty for all through the physical and spiritual culture of the person, education and the elevation of taste. There should thus not be a succession of fashions but a taste that "accompanies the changing

---

94   Rudofsky, B., "La moda: abito disumano, *Domus*, April 1938, n. 124. Rudofsky, in 1944, curated an important fashion exhibition at the Moma from the 28th of November 1944 to the 4th of March 1945, *Are Clothes Modern?* The exhibition's press release stated that this was not a fashion show nor an exhibition of costumes. The aim was to provide a fresh approach to the question of clothing, as if it were a new phenomenon, removing the blinkers of tradition to see that certain conventions are completely irrational and uncomfortable.
95   Arital (G. Ponti), "La foggia italiana," *Aria d'Italia*, n. 3, summer 1940, pp. 59-60.
96   Arital (G. Ponti), "Moda," *Aria d'Italia*, n. 4, autumn 1940, p. 74.
97   Ponti, G., "Costume e civiltà," *Bellezza*, n.1, January 1941, p. 1.

shapes of a nation and an era." *Bellezza* would have the task of showing this taste "in the Italy of Fascism" because "the reason for the rise of *Bellezza*" lay "in the timely and indispensable preparation for the fortunes – even beyond our borders – of the future expansion of our activities." Consistent with this approach, the payoff of an advertisement for Lineoleum floors read: "To each age its costume, its floor, its decoration," and an image, showed, as in Ponti's designs, a woman of composed and modest elegance standing in a statuesque pose on the threshold of a door in a black lace house dress accessorized with a showy artistic necklace, while the Barbara Gould brand of Casalecchio di Reno and Elizabeth Arden promised fast and modern beauty routines.

For Ponti, then, the goal of *Bellezza* was not so much to document the varying whims of fashion as to testify and help create an Italian style, understood as an expression – one which was universal – of the Italian civilisation:

> A fashion cannot triumph if it is not the mirror of an elevated, cultured, spiritual 'lifestyle', whose elegance derives from a choice exercised by people of taste, who represent a culture expressed not only by their garments, but by their background and culture.[98] Fashion as the expression of an aristocracy less of class and more spiritual, of culture and taste.

All the more reason then that with the shrinking of the fashion market due to war, Ponti thought the mission of the magazine should be based on culture, morality, costume, home and art, without sacrificing the number of garments presented.[99] In fact, he conceded that the creations of the main Italian fashion houses were increasingly oriented towards "a line, a style of simplicity, of true taste, of interpretation of today's life that is a prelude to a real Italian fashion" based on the formula: "Excellent style in a costume suited to modern social life."[100] The garments featured in *Bellezza* were a small sample – what today one might

---

98   Ponti, G., "La moda nella nuova Europa," *Stile*, n. 3, March 1941, p. 99.
99   Gio Ponti to Cipriano E. Oppo, letter of the 6th of April 1942, Gio Ponti Archives, APM, D5cp.
100 Ponti, G., "Scelta di bellezza," *Bellezza*, n. 16, April 1942, p. 3.

call a capsule collection – whose composition was informed by aesthetic and moral principles. And so, partly in response to complaints from some of the most intransigent parts of the regime, Ponti reiterated that the choice to publish strange hats and imaginative designs was linked to the desire to exhibit the creativity and practical skills of Italian fashion. For this reason, *Bellezza* featured "many garments whose 'drapery' lies in the extravagance of their shapes and materials and the way in which their justification must be 'brought' into a specialized aesthetic-technical field." But the fashion of the Italian people, in spite of the "French" eccentricities, must nevertheless "result in a costume" – in an aesthetic and moral "form."

In this sense, the war made its decisive contribution: evening dresses disappeared, along with inappropriate exhibitionism, skirts were shortened, fabrics were practical and durable, simple "Bedouin" hats and shoes with cork heels "triumphed." But it was not simply a matter of practicality because according to Ponti, one could glimpse in the creations of the finest fashion houses a nascent taste: an Italian *line* that despised bleached blondes and microscopic nineteenth-century hats attached to the forehead, distant echoes of a French fashion industry which had long since exhausted its ability to create modern clothing and which was still living off ideas borrowed from the equestrian circus and the nineteenth century. On the contrary, for Ponti, the novelties of Italian fashion were not borrowed but were the fruit of a conscious choice of both an aesthetic – "out of love for a straightforward, austere, rigorous and energetic line, that highlights healthy physical beauty, adhering to noble human elegance, active and sport-loving, which repudiates the weariness of idle and flaccid elegance" – and moral type. The prejudice that the elegant woman must be frivolous must be dispelled. In Ponti's vision, war was the "supreme episode of a social movement" destined to extend justice and civilization. That was why, in February 1943, he harshly criticized the magazine's cultural disengagement:

> That we should only praise it for its colours, or shapes, or charms, or the gracefulness of sleeves, cloths, skirts, for example in relation to summer,

this decisive summer and the coming seasons over which the fate of the world must develop, seems to me out of place, in too stark contrast with the wounds of blood and now of works of art (see Turin itself) that entail the salvation and triumph of our civilization.[101]

Ponti emphasised that *Bellezza* should utilise "the privileges of its existence for noble propaganda and representation of taste, culture, criticism, art, elevation, addressing with elevated and deeply serious commitment the sectors of Italian spiritual life, such as the theatre, cinema, literature, philosophical thought, music and the figurative arts." With this in mind:

> We must not imagine that the readers of *Bellezza* are stupid Italians: we can also bring them up to date on the phenomenon of hermeticism and existentialism, perhaps fighting them [...]. There are Italian figures of great importance to be noted, essential voices (from Ada Negri, to Papini, to Cecchi, to Bacchelli, and that of young writers and poets) to bring to Italian women, artists to be made known through the trichromies and the black pages in order to affirm a well-formulated and disciplined critical program, cultural events, beloved places, sovereign ancient works of art.[102]

With the worsening of the war, Ponti insisted that the dramatic moment was finally transforming Italian fashion into costume, or rather "into a personal care, into a moral and physical line, into a *dignitas*, an extended civilization of creatures who want to survive, in their civilization, the harshness of events."[103] And, according to him, this was what distinguished costume from fashion:

> If in fashion, which is work and fruit and reason for a great deal of work for many people, there is something artificially (as well as imaginatively) changeable, because *les affaires sont les affaires* (...) the 'costume' is today represented by that kind of trend that is ineluctably followed even in the variation and diversions or desertions or evasions of fashion.[104]

---

101 Gio Ponti to Oppo, letter of the 13th of February 1943, ivi.
102 *Ibid.*
103 Ponti, G., "Abbigliamento ed arredamento," *Bellezza*, n. 36, December 1943, p. 47-51.
104 *Ibid.*

In his opinion, never as then in Italy – "the last gasp before its disappearance?" – had there been a flourishing of the arts and art publications (*Chimera, Conchiglia*) and, in clothing, of refined evocations of places and events, like the Tyrolean ones inspired by the events in Salzburg, the Second Empire and the late nineteenth century: "'fashion is men's imagination: 'costume' is what is dictated by life and chains their imagination"[105]. Costume would therefore reject long skirts and strange patterns and instead join colours in the unity of the whole and the new waterproof fabrics: "humanity will create a costume where – let us repeat – neither luxury, money, nor eccentricity will allow one to prevail, but with distinction, self-care, bearing, civility, in a way of dressing that leaves the body increasingly free of hindrances." It was the same process gone through by furniture, where there was already a "style," "a costume," which means:

> [...] Simplicity, good craftsmanship, good materials, novelty of material and technique, clarity, precision. The conditions of today, and more those of tomorrow, determine in reality (life!) that style that has been preached so by modern architects and so little believed and loved. Historically, they were right; as the artists, who present and prevent, always are. Because of their insanity, the history of men reaches its ends alas, not by means of reasonable evolutions, but through violent and passionate convulsions. Those we are witnessing, however atrocious, will result in real civil progress. Not only will clothing adapt to this, but also furniture, and our entire way of life, simplified on the outside but enriched on the inside.[106]

Not everyone agreed with Ponti, and Countess Elena Celani wondered *"Will Fashion Turn Into Costume?"*[107] Her article was provoked by another article by Luca Beldì who, in the pages of *Stile*, had argued that costume should be understood as a uniform which was practical as opposed to fashionable. For Celani, though, costume could only depend on fashion: being the stylised version of it, it could not be opposed to it. If clothing reflected the way of life, fashion anticipated it. Even if fashion

---

105 *Ibid.*
106 *Ibid.*
107 Celani, E., "La moda si muterà in costume?," *Bellezza*, n. 39, March 1944, p. 43.

were to establish itself more as a costume than as a mode of individual expression, fashion and its manifestations of luxury, according to Celani, only increased their range of possibilities:

> So tomorrow concert-goers in evening dresses, perhaps low-cut, will travel from one city to another by aeroplane, departing and returning the same evening. ... No, fashion that hunts the new needs that arise from man's desire to relentlessly improve his conditions of existence cannot "change into costume." It is foolish to speak of the likelihood of the disappearance of fashion![108]

Beldì stood up against the "easy delights of bourgeois salons" and made it a question of caste. *Stile* did not fight, he wrote, for a civilisation of easy fantasy and capricious dressmaking, but for a civilization of taste and quality. Celani replied that tradition owed a great deal to fashion, to the elite and to the caste, and that in an age of well-being, if a person of taste could fantasise "we will see what wonders can emerge. [...] A fashion does not impose itself – it is summoned, and then followed. Just as the great merit of a magazine, as well as taste, is its 'intuition': *tomorrow*."[109] But for Ponti, never as in war had one seen in women "so much self-care, so much *true* elegance, no longer made up of flaunted wealth and luxury, but of style, of care, of a demeanour, of a sought-after and achieved *tenue* [...] the costume does not permit of certain of the latest evocations, certain extreme fantasies that so many tenaciously want to believe."[110]

The aesthetic tone of *Bellezza* was of an almost enchanted and enchanting stasis which was not made for hasty and distracted glances but rather invited contemplation. The beauty of fashion was understood as a "perfume of civilisation," an intangible but genuine atmosphere that mankind must "feel." From this perspective, it was synonymous with art, elegance, "race," health, and physical and spiritual life: "fashion in Italy is not frivolity but the expression of a custom, an atmosphere of art, of taste,

---

108 *Ibid.*
109 *Ibid.*
110 Ponti, G., "Abbigliamento ed arredamento," *Bellezza*, n. 36, December 1944, pp. 47-51.

of a way of life, but above all of our creative virtues and of the work of thousands of artisans and workers, and of the felicitous imagination of our artists."[111] In *Fashion Horoscopes*, an article with a prophetic tone, Ponti described, or perhaps it would be more accurate to say prescribed, the fashion to come: "they say that the age of the home and garden dress of striking, beautiful colours, full skirts, boldly adorned with many colours will come,"[112] turning women into large flowers, happy and majestic figures "where the fabric does not 'follow' the movement of the body but moves, swells and falls, 'accompanying' the movement of the body. [...]. The era of the 'beautifully hidden body' in large, colourful garments will dress the body with fabric in a, let us say, 'natural' way." It is the description of what Ponti defines as "fashion-art" as opposed to costumes for work and the street: practical, perfect, rigorous, as beautiful as a uniform for the "battle of motion, speed, crowd, work, social equality, sport."[113] Here the garment would be close to the body and its movements and colour would be "more severe, more 'resistant'." This modern style code was opposed to the pre-war one, which was dismissed as bogus, made up of borrowed forms, neither art nor

---

111 Vera, "Fashion and beauty", *Bellezza*, n. 1, January 1941, p. 5. In *Il libro del cortegiano*, Baldassarre Castiglione writes that costumes should never be "extreme," "too large" like the French or "too small" like the Germans, but "corrected and reduced to a better shape by the Italians." There is no compromise on one detail: black, or at least "tending to dark," is better in the "ordinary dress" while "open and cheerful colours" are preferable with weapons and for festive clothes; "tightness" always moderate and not feminine. Francesco Sansovino, in his *Venetia città nobilissima et singolare*, published in 1581, reiterates that the Italians "forgetting they were born in Italy" and following the "fashions from over the mountains," change their clothes with their thoughts, wanting to look French or Spanish. "Only this city has been confirmed in general to be less corrupt," despite the fact that it welcomes foreigners who are "used to introducing their customs into other people's homes". As for the noblewomen, he emphasizes that they love colours while covering themselves in the street with a black "Greek style" scarf, which makes them look even more pale and beautiful even though they are already "very white by nature". Dresses and whites, in silk or linen, are embroidered, "decorated, worked, streaked" with the needle and silky, gold and silver threads.
112 Ponti, G., "Oroscopi sulla moda," *Bellezza*, n. 1, January 1941, p. 32.
113 *Ibid.*

costume and which took the shape of oddities that could still be seen in hats that "bordered on the ridiculous." Ponti's fashion horoscope could be summed up in "a more lively and serene and I would say natural style on the one hand, and a more severe, brisker costume on the other."[114]

But the house dresses featured in the first issue are dark and austere tailoring. Of the two Ventura dresses made for donna Giusta Manca di Villahermosa, one is in black crepe "with an accent of particular severity" and drapes held in place by a dense motif of pearl embroidery and gold and silver sequins, while the other is a long black woollen garment, snugly fitting, with trimmings, a bolero cut and a very composed "Germanesque" hairstyle, for receiving at home. Next to a baroque shelf, the austere nobility of a classic Ventura column dress, worn by Donna Maria Teresa Saporiti, in black jersey with statuary pleats: "a pact to which Italian tailors will give their understanding collaboration"[115]. Having discarded the aggressive and insolent luxury of certain evening dresses, "this year, when the blackout dims the elegance of the theatre," the two photos mentioned illustrate a harmony of essential lines "softened by the grace of precious details" that remove geometric rigidity from the whole because "the beauty of the healthy and flourishing Italian woman is soft and feminine, breasts, waist and hips temper any dryness and geometry becomes eloquent." Long tight dresses, modest necklines, sleeves on the wrist and dark colours (black, plum, amaranth, midnight blue) were dotted with gold and silver or "enlivened by the quiet sparkle of sequins of the same tone in a play of glossy-opaque."[116] The beautiful Italian woman "is anti-Hollywood, rejecting the international model that owes its popularity to the cinema. The woman is landscape. Natural beauty. The expression of an architectural rhythm and hills. […] Here there are none of the sexless women from Paris or New York. Italian women are then related by a unity of style, which does not mean that high fashion is for everyone. The variety in

---

114 *Ibid.*
115 *Ibid.*
116 "Moda e bellezza," *Bellezza*, n. 1, January 1941, p. 5.

each region, between commoners and patricians, will be clear. Art and folklore competing to invent. Not blondes or brunettes but Italians."[117]

Photographed in an austere black velvet evening dress, singer Gianna Pederzini is "severe and very Italian," while a model whose face is frighteningly similar to Mussolini's wears a Biki evening dress studded with tiny gold laminas.[118] As evidence of *Bellezza*'s aesthetic approach, there is a section dedicated to fashion in Turin with comments by Elsa Robiola, which describes the atmosphere of the city as follows: "Innate sense of elegance, line, refinement of dress; very refined taste, intuitive grasp and spontaneous passion for everything connected with the currents of fashion."[119]

In Turin the showcase for fashion was Via Roma, where the major dressmakers were based: Trinelli, Gori, Robiolio, Gambino, Mattè and others. Turin's output was distinguished by a "sober taste, never flashy, aristocratic par excellence." The image that illustrated the article on fashion in Turin was a photo looking up at a draped evening model of classical inspiration parading in an atelier in front of a huge crystal chandelier. Turin's dresses were black and unadorned but the caption again emphasised the details of the workmanship, demonstrating the level of excellence achieved by Turin and Italy's dressmakers.[120] But the genuinely new way of interpreting the evening dress was represented by a short and very simple Biki dress in rich blue-silver laminate fabric, accessorized with a black and sea green sequinned bonnet by costume designer Maria Battaglia (fig. 17). Other garments were covered with oriental motifs: the kimono sleeve of a black fox fur by Beppina Gori and the oriental collar of an evening dress worn by Princess Sciarra.

Given the centrality of the family in the regime's politics and the glamorous fairy tale position that weddings occupied both

---

117 Calzini, R., "Bellezza immortale delle italiane," *Bellezza*, n. 1, January 1941, p. 11.
118 Ivi, p. 55.
119 Robiola, E., "Moda a Torino," *Bellezza*, n. 1, January 1941, p. 70.
120 *Ibid.*

during the regime's time in power and afterwards, it was natural that wedding dresses occupied an important place in the fashion *Bellezza* featured. In addition, wedding dress symbolised an immaculate synthesis of the tailoring and craftsmanship skills of Italian fashion houses placed at the service of the 'purest' and most political of goals: fertile marriage. Even the wedding dress must be austere and solemn, like the one by Fercioni which appeared in the first issue of *Bellezza*. The important thing was that it be very high-necked and have a very long train. The solemnity in Fercioni's model was provided by a cloak which was of a piece with the yoke, leading into a train several meters long and by the whiteness of the veil that surrounded the figure. A *Marca d'oro* Noberasko design was inspired by Sardinian costume, with silver embroidery and white pearls and a wimple-like headdress in the same fabric as the dress, while the bridesmaids' dress was in white Romanian crepe, embodying a new geography.

In the second issue of *Bellezza*, the ENM "proposed" a new line to dressmakers: the *1941 Line*. It was an attempt to lower the waist and make the shoulders round, in opposition to the Hollywood fashion for padded square shoulders and narrow waists. Elsa Robiola thought the 1941 Line highly questionable, but the change of direction was made necessary, so it was said, in view of the presentation of the collections internationally. Dressmakers went along cautiously, inserting into their collections some timid attempts at interpreting the new line that, in some cases, seemed to be made "with such tact as to suggest that it should not be discarded *a priori*."[121] From the 1941 Line came jackets tapered just below the waist and gathered in a wide band tight on the hips, which resembled windcheaters, while in the dresses it was represented by the absence of the belt on a waisted bodice that reached up to the beginning of the side where the skirt was attached. The point was always balance, the geometric values "in which our clothes, without discussion, must always be framed." Direct proof of the state style could be found

---

121 Robiola, E., "In questa primavera una linea più semplice, più sciolta?" *Bellezza*, n. 2, February 1941, p. 3.

in the *Marca d'oro* models, where there was the use of autarkic fabrics, the taste for colour, the use of patterned fabrics, knitwear and fur, a stripped-down line and no concession to seduction and coquetry. The proposal for daywear was

> suited to the present day, simple, almost spartan, but never low quality, for active, young, agile women, for women who go on foot or by tram, who must move easily and be ready quickly. Short wide skirts for quick walking, no unnecessary frills, zippers, low heels, large bags, easy-to-put on hats.

In addition to being practical and feminine (however hard it might be to tell from the black and white photos), it was a colourful, luxurious and sometimes even garrulous fashion, with afternoon dresses and cloaks trimmed with furs of Tuscan or Sardinian lamb and Somali leopard, but also silver fox, sable and ermine. All testament to "the vast technical resources and the ability of Italian furriers to handle all kinds of materials, from the richest to the most luxurious,"[122] as well as to the power of the Empire. The day and afternoon fashion consisted mostly of dresses and skirt-suits, some trimmed with fur and in black with white detailing. Fur was not recommended for the city, for obvious reasons – many women put away their furs for safekeeping until the war was over – and therefore it moved inside, as a lining. The skirt was always below the knee, jackets were waisted and feminine, capes were straight and very wide behind, and hats were always proportionate.

The *Bellezza* woman dedicated her free time to the consumption of beautiful things, to self-care and to making clothes for the soldiers at the front. Consequently, fashion models were photographed in the most elegant shops, busy weighing the artistic value of Ginori ceramics, leaving an Elizabeth Arden salon, in the living room knitting with other ladies or touring cities of art, or admiring and photographing statues and busts of imperial Rome. Women were invited to read, and to read "Italian," but the problem was that reading was seen as a waste of time and

---

122 *Bellezza*, n. 1, 1941, p. 65.

a cause of perdition: "I am speaking," wrote Antonella "to all those women [...] who are solely concerned of the practical side of life, inclined to consider 'dreams, ambitions and emotions of the spirit, diabolical and dangerous things."[123] And there was nothing wrong with confessing one's desire to seduce or one's aspiration to coquetry,[124] because not looking after one's physical appearance meant hindering one's ego. For Robiola, a longing for pleasure was the "natural law" of women. Indeed, the power of seduction was "women's only great strength," and was for all of them, thanks to "human intelligence, science, medicine and healthiness."

For the ENM, the "discourse" about sport was one of those which would most strongly influence Italian fashion: "What a flexible, statuesque, cinematographic vision that of the female students of the Orvieto Academy."[125] After the 1936 Olympics, where Ondina Valla had triumphed, athletes were no longer a mysterious, aristocratic phenomenon but media figures. The results were positive: "Women's athleticism, boosted marvellously by the regime's youth organisations, has made great strides this year. The advances particularly concern the masses, which is to say that there are a greater number of practitioners than in the past and that young athletes are making notable progress."[126] The female body in motion, though, was subject to censorship. In 1937 the Ministry of Popular Culture sent the following instructions to the press, signed by an official called Casini: "Refrain from publishing photographs of female athletes in action, and only publish portraits of winners or participants in competitions."[127] *Bellezza*'s sports and fashion photos never showed athletes in movement but only with their bodies in stiff, statue-like poses.

---

123 Antonella, "Consigli per leggere. Invito," ivi, p. 106.
124 Robiola, E., "Plasmare e proteggere la bellezza," ivi, pp. 98-99.
125 *Ibid.*
126 *La Gazzetta dello Sport*, 27 July 1937.
127 Telegram to prefects of the 29th of January 1937, ACS, Ministry of Popular Culture, Cabinet, Gabinetto, b. 3, fs. 175.

> It was easy in Italy to do away with the importation of the anaemic woman with a flat chest, hunched back and skinny legs – the gloomy – looking "fashionable" woman who looked tired, unhealthy, sad and gaunt. [...] The image of the healthy woman triumphed and imposed itself. And now other nations, including America, are competing for it, referring to Leonardo and the divine proportions of human beauty. [...] Make way then for the classic Italian beauty, with her colours, full rosy cheeks and well-defined eyebrows![128]

In accordance with the directives of the ENM, *Bellezza* favoured clothes with a "sporty feel" that was not directly connected with any sport itself but was instead a reflection of a modern lifestyle, in tune with the fascist era. The first issue of *Bellezza* was entirely dedicated to the Cortina Winter Olympics, the novelty being the use of the skirt instead of the Norwegian trousers. In an interview with *Grazia*, Gabriella de Bosdari of Robilant, the creator behind the Gabriellasport brand, explained her invention: since from a distance all the skiers looked alike, she wanted "a nimble, slender form" that would stand out in this crowd of anonymous and identical costumes, "that, while twirling on wooden skis, would let its wide, short skirt swirl from her waist, which would be like a revelation of grace."[129] Feminine beauty "here means vigour, grace, measure and balance"[130] and the ski skirt brought a "new note of harmony and feminine beauty even on the snow." Men's trousers were fine for the hotel after the competition, where Nordic stiffness was tempered "by colourful sweaters and sparkling jackets in jet or metal threads."

Much of the Italian social world was at Cortina 1941 and the mountains acted as white backdrop for the colours of the Italian ski costumes. The common thread for mountain costume too was classicism understood as "measure, balance and grace." "The dressmakers agree on a thin waist, broad shoulders and a free bust, but the hair is too long! Long hair is for bare shoulders, for evening wear." In Cortina, Celani wrote, a Vanna design in black

---

128 Robiola, E., "Plasmare e proteggere la bellezza," *op. cit.*
129 Di Robilant, G., "Perché ho creato la gonna da sci," *Grazia*, n. 2, January 1940, p. 6.
130 Elena (Elena Celani), "Cortina 1941," *Bellezza*, n.1, January 1941, p. 13-14, p. 13.

wool with flower and fruit embroideries was a hit. Countess Cicogna "her hands heavy with rings" dressed as a man and wore a waxed, transparent Biki jacket. There were also divas. Vivi Gioi in a "casual and therefore elegant" jumpsuit with strips of fur.[131] Cortina was also apparently invaded by a knitted Biki cap that framed the face like a balaclava. Countess Borletti and Princess Massimo wore gabardine hoods and Nicoletta Visconti di Modrone was elected as the model of "pure beauty of our race, simplicity made flesh: beauty made modest."[132] Altogether,

> and reasonably, given the current period, we are witnessing the triumph of the classics. Countess Borletti is all in steel gray gabardine [...]. Princess Massimo dresses in brown; herringbone jacket, an emerald-coloured knit blouse and a bright-coloured scarf liven up the dark ensemble. A white lamb fur coat, and once again the graceful fairytale hood [...]. She reminds one of a pearl diver.[133]

Gabriellasport proposed a light, elegant ensemble consisting of a white flannel gown with pockets and buttons and a wool and marmot coat, "for stays in the great hotels of Cortina, Sestriere and Madonna di Campiglio," which were considered genuine "showcases for winter sports." Showcases for the fur sports jackets whose colours and lines broke from Parisian orthodoxy in 1941, according to Celani, an expert connoisseur of French fashion who gave the example of a Gabriellasport rabbit fur jacket dyed cypress green.[134] Countess Cicogna instead chose from Biki "a jacket in a new, very Italian fabric, waterproof and at the same time waxed and transparent."[135]

For sport, *Bellezza* did not limit itself to proposing new looks but proposed an entirely new way of dressing: a versatile wardrobe, with knitted jackets that alternate "over the costumes, multiplying their effects." The embroidered sweaters by the artist Lea Galleani and the blouses by Emilia Bellini were considered sports accessories, as were painted scarves. A white Comolli

---

131 *Ibidem.*
132 *Ibidem.*
133 Ivi, p. 14.
134 Ivi, p. 17.
135 *Ibidem.*

belt of colonial inspiration with two pouches stood out for its originality while Vanna, for her part, offered the "Casentino" ski model, a "purely Italian" fabric whose bright colour went well with the white of the wool. Black and white – which recalled the colours of the uniforms of young Italians – were recurring choices, together with autarkic fabrics inspired by Italy's colonial, sporting and artistic exploits, producing visions of *Italianness*.

For the après-ski, the dominant note was imaginative and lively. As an emblem of "fashion-art" *Bellezza* selected some designs – illustrated by Federico Pallavicini – by Vanna, Matrigali and Gabriellasport. They all shared the use of polychromy and bright accents of sequins, metals, pearls and bows embroidered on velvet. The new Italian-made fabrics were described as having a "solid and sporty" character, made to last and "function with elegance" and presented in the form of collections in original collages signed by Pallavicini. For the winter of 1941 the proposed fabrics were albene shantung, checked wools and cotton and rayon velvets. But in the field of fabrics, *Bellezza* did not limit itself to showing what had already been done and encouraged Italian artists to submit prints for imaginary fabrics, like those of Germana Cattadori, defined as "imaginative art." Art was the tool for inventing new designs and shapes that could serve as nourishment for fashion, according to a method already proven for decades in Paris and Vienna. Printed fabrics were "assorted novelties": they balanced and animated simple lines, removed the Englishness of traditional wools, and gave character and elegance to the dress. Among the spring 1941 motifs were Roman medals, animals, chess pieces, toys, moons, celestial constellations, very large and small flowers, polka dots and views of Rome, in a "favourite" model by Vanna.[136] The idea was that, in times of war and scarcity of raw materials, printing could bestow artistic and fashionable value by upon even modest fabric, "and fashion is the liveliest of the decorative arts, as can be seen in the De Angeli-Frua factory in Milan."

---

136 *Bellezza*, n. 3, March 1941, p. 42.

Those "outside of fashion" were artisans who did not follow fashion but blazed their own solitary and personal artistic path.[137] "Outside of fashion" meant Gegia Bronzini,[138] whose creations were distinguished by their colours and the quality of the yarns. Her ski jackets were partly knitted, partly hand-loomed and very colourful: "Madonna blue, flame red, bright orange, golden yellow, jade green and black."

The modernity of the Italian woman was also reflected in the composition of her wartime wardrobe, the "basis" of which must be inspired by ideas of order, measure and discipline. First of all, it needed to rely on several quality garments that brooked no imperfections: a masculine-cut cloak or frock coat in plain, dark fabric, classic skirt-suits, one of which dark and "absolutely severe" and another of sporty fabric in resistant neutral colour, three blouses of which one white, one patterned and one smart, and soft and washable knitted blouses, a well cut skirt and fabric, a black dress – that international female uniform which can be personalised with accessories, gestures and immaculate underwear, "testimony to your vigilant attention." In the summer she would need to have silk dresses that could be folded in her suitcase without losing their freshness. Finally, a raincoat and a fur coat that, if worn, could become the lining of a cloak. As far as hats, all that was needed was one that could be folded and fit easily into a suitcase and a turban that could be slipped into a pocket. And then white handkerchiefs, a pair of sunglasses and a light and roomy suitcase. It was a wardrobe which answered the needs of a life made uncertain by the war and its displacements, and which took its example from the codification of the male

---

137 Genoni, R., "Arte e storia del costume. Rivendicazioni femminili nella moda", *Vita d'arte: rivista mensile illustrata d'arte antica e moderna*, II, 1908, fasc. 11, pp. 202-207.
138 In the early 1930s, a hand weaving business began near Venice on the initiative of Gegia Bronzini, a young woman with uncommon entrepreneurial energy. First as a weaving school and soon after as a production laboratory, the business grew and developed its own creative identity. Exhibitions followed one another, starting with one at the Loggetta Sansovino in Venice in 1936, followed by the opening of the first shop in Venice, then in Milan in 1939 and, finally, in Cortina d'Ampezzo.

wardrobe, made up of classic pieces that were immune to the whims of fashion.[139]

But it seemed that *Bellezza*'s suggestions went unheeded on the streets of Italy, where female figures were "disproportionate," "barbaric" hair hung loose on their shoulders weighing down figures "shortened by short skirts," the volume of their heads taking up half of their body and their legs climbing up from strange and ugly clogs with cork soles which were no good for walking in the city. *Bellezza* was obsessed with the harmony of the look as an aesthetic and moral quality: fashion objects and hairstyles were not valid in themselves but as part of this harmonious relationship they established with the rest of the body and its surroundings:

> Sumptuous and eccentric fashion pleases the eye but does not contribute to the formation of women's characters. This is why in recent years the concept that fashion is born not from and for an elite but is aimed rather at the entire community has been well-received for the way it responds to the social life of the day. [...] Fashion wants to make women appear the way we want them: lively, nimble, happy, in a healthy and disciplined body, animated by the desire to please.[140]

Summer was the ideal season for this "healthy and disciplined" body to show itself off in Viareggio, Forte dei Marmi, Venice, Capri, Ravello and Portofino. Italians "are given to vacationing in places blessed by nature" and the dressmakers "have worked imaginative wonders." 1941 was the year of "transformable" swimwear for the sea, of sun dresses hidden under jackets and *paltoncini* ("small coats"), of colourful striped skirts, of garden aprons. The dressmakers commented that modular garments had been popular with women, who had ordered them enthusiastically. The autarkic hemp and staple linen fabrics were "heavy but crease-resistant," with compact and deep colours. Nothing went wasted: dinner and evening dresses were short, the folds giving consistency to veils and muslin, the long sleeves closed like blouses. The transformable dresses reflected the dynamism of

---

139 "Educare l'occhio," *Bellezza*, n. 3, March 1941, p. 32.
140 "Il tatto e la vera eleganza," *Bellezza*, n. 3, March 1941, pp. 40-41.

the vision of modern spaces and clothes. The most successful model of the 1941 summer collections was "a skirt-suit with a blue canvas jacket that looked very composed but then revealed beneath it a swimsuit" which evoked, without rhetoric, the futurist idea of the "transformable dress" with "surprises, tricks and disappearances" theorised by Giacomo Balla in the 'Futurist Reconstruction of the Universe Manifesto.'[141]

Finally, in the September 1941 issue, *Bellezza* declared that Italian fashion was born and, using the gimmick of a waxed envelope, presented its readers with seventeen designs chosen from those destined for the international market. The selection gave an indication of which tailors were considered "compliant" and proclaimed in bellicose tones that "Italian fashion has begun its march through the world. Fashion gradually became an export industry and the now consolidated phenomenon began. Italian patents for new fibres were purchased, our fabrics spread to America and Europe, foreign dressmakers bought our designs." The dressmakers included were Barbieri, Binello, Botti, De Gaspari Zezza, Gabriellasport, Gambino, Gandini, Modelia, Moretti, Moschini, Noberasko, Tizzoni, Trinelli, Vanna, Ventura and Villa and the garments were characterised by embossed embroidery, high collars, slanting pockets, jackets at the hips or very long, military-style cloaks, velvet, Asian influences like raglan sleeves, original knitting, fur trimmings (marten and silver fox), an original collar that turned into a pair of pockets and a sporty cycling outfit with that "Italian favourite," the trouser-skirt.

Following the *Linea 1941*, the ENM launched the *anfora* (amphora) line: "a dangerous and fascinating line that requires first-rate technique. In one, the drapery is carried forward under the waist, so as to leave the side free, revealing itself in all its slenderness."[142] The amphora silhouette was a reference to the myth of classicism and a way of enhancing the "natural"

---

141 Crispolti, E., *Il Futurismo e la moda: Balla e gli altri*, Marsilio, Venice 1986, p. 25.
142 Rossi Lodomez, V., "Le signore hanno visto…," *Bellezza*, n. 10, October 1941, p. 5.

and maternal curves of the female body. Although the fashion proposed by *Bellezza* was "elegant" and "simple," the ENM offered women a look complete with hat, gloves and bag: the fashion "details" that allowed women to renew their look without having to change their dress. Thus, in the autumn of 1942 "they mostly wear small hats, very far forward or backward." But the Italian novelty was in the "hats that fall with draped flaps or wings of very soft felt down to the middle of the shoulders. Hats that frame the face and contribute a great deal to giving the figure of the 1942 Italian woman an unmistakable profile, very different from past seasons."[143] The image of this woman took shape in a Venus by Botticelli redesigned for the occasion by the painter Alessandrini.[144] *Bellezza* brought together a selection of images from the ancient and Renaissance Italian past with great refinement to create a myth of appearance that seduced its readers and influenced them in their fashion choices. From its pages, women or details of fashions emerge from paintings and theatrical and film costumes and are proposed for everyday life, the whole thing a show of fashion and an occasion for propaganda.

Fashion historian Valerie Steele has argued that Italian fashion played a less marginal role in the formation of international style than prevailing opinion admits, and invites scholars to make a collective effort to re-evaluate and explore it without prejudice. In contrast with the opulence and "constructedness" of the French fashion inaugurated by the New Look, post-war Italian fashion seduced America and the world with a taste that was described in fashion magazines as "sophisticated," "gay," and "artistic." She claims that as haute couture gains its legitimacy from and bases itself on the invention of a line by a couturier, Italian fashion has paid the price of its pre-eminence in the field of accessories, accessories being considered secondary to dresses.

---

143   *Ibid.*
144   *Ibid.*

3.3 "Behind Closed Shutters"

During the war, clothing in Italy was "subjected to instinctive and logical moral restraints, but also to real and unequivocal material restraints,"[145] a moral and material discipline which the ENM and *Bellezza* hoped would inform the "taste" of the nascent Italian fashion, inspired by principles of elegance and sobriety but, above all, by obedience to the directives of the organisation. Italy was the only country that, through the tool of the *Marca d'oro*, took the opportunity of the war to forge an ethical fashion subject to the control of a totalitarian state.

In the ten-point manifesto of wartime fashion[146] published in *Bellezza* in November 1941, it was established that the limitations of wartime were not actually such – as they were in England – but instead represented an opportunity "for a more personal expression of ourselves, of our taste, of our education and civilization." Paradoxically, the war was the occasion for the creation, "finally," of an Italian fashion: a crucible where the image of the new fascist woman would be forged. It was predicted that the Italian woman would find moral strength in her personality, in the distinction of her clothes, in ornamentation and in bearing. As absurd as it may seem, in this context the shortage of materials was welcomed because "difficulties have always refined and enhanced the resources of artists, limitations will sift the creators, putting them to the test of the essential motifs of line, colour and execution." The elegance of the Italian woman was not measured by the price or the exclusivity of her possessions, but by her way of choosing and wearing them:

> We will see styles full of ingenuity and skill, inspired combinations, imaginative designs and prints of fabrics, wonderful new uses of very new and very old fabrics, both urban and rural. We will see surprising uses of old and new ornaments. We will see the resurrection of beautiful things, and alongside our arts, which are the highest expression of the human spir-

---

145 "Risorse della moda secondo la disciplina dell'abbigliamento," *Bellezza*, n. 11, November 1941, p. 3.
146 Ivi, p. 7.

it in contemporary civilisation, we will see Italian costume affirm itself and dominate thanks to its virtues.[147]

One of the peculiarities of *Marca d'oro* war production was the return to the 'transformable' fashion of the 1930s, in which "the same accessory or dress changed for different uses: muff-handbags, fur cape-collars, double-sided dresses and cloaks, very long double sleeves to transform clothes, etc." Looks were transformable: "two-faced dresses and cloaks will reappear, adding or eliminating a piece to change the look and use of a skirt-suit, alternating blouses, a jacket-like dress that becomes a princess-style dress, a play of accessories"; above all thanks to the hats that were not limited by rationing "and will alternate on the same dress, adapting it to its various functions: stroll, afternoon, evening, visit, etc. Fashion will be managed to keep itself as alive as is required of it today."[148]

The "Italian costume" destined to rise again and "dominate" would not be distinguished by whims of the line and changing inspirations, as in Paris, because it would be wholly concentrated on the expression of the "costume" of the new Italian civilisation. In it the "very old" and the "very new" were no longer separate or "superficial reasons for inspiration," but were placed at the service of the myths of fascism:

> For the morning you will wear plain wool jackets or tight-fitting checks, small lapels, tightly buttoned at the neck. A scarf to match the wool or velvet hat in a bright tone. Long jackets. Fitted undershirts with *cannelloni* or folds. Hats, gloves and bag in a different colour from the rest, or if the same colour, look brightened up by the bold colour of the blouse: red on dark blue, light blue and orange on brown, cherry green, pink, purple on grey and dark blue. For the afternoon, dark velvet jackets and skirts with fox collars or fur appliqués. Few large, simple buttons, high closed collars that frame the face and protect from the cold, hats of one colour, small, low on the nose, trimmed with fur held in by veils or ribbons with golden pins. Gloves and dark shoes. Light and colourful morning blouses. Count on them to brighten your face and change the look of your clothes. Always high-necked but fanciful (the masculine shirt is dead and buried). Blouses

---

147 *Ibid.*
148 *Ibid.*

for the day in velvet, silk knit, laminate, wool knit, trimmed. Fur doublets under the jacket.[149]

Baroness Luciana De Reutern Aloisi suggested to her readers a wardrobe divided between day and afternoon, light and dark, with "very tight" jackets to highlight feminine forms, buttoned up high and tight to "frame the face." The combination of colours was important: the scarf must match the hat which, with gloves and accessories, must stand out from the ensemble. If it were the same colour, the shirt must "brighten up" the look. Under the jacket, fur doublets protected from the cold. Princess Marinetta Ruffo di Bagnara, president of the Hemp Propaganda Office, spoke about the "miracle" of hemp and the Milanese industrialists entrusted the Autartex[150] laboratories with the launch of hand-

---

149 Reutern Aloisi, L., "Le carte dicono che…," *Bellezza*, n. 11, November 1941, p. 18-19.
150 In 1940, Rava was entrusted with the coordination and preparation of the "Colonial Equipment Exhibition" at the VII Triennale in Milan. In this initiative he was assisted by architects Malchiodi, Pellegrini, D 'Angelo and Piccinato, who designed furniture and objects which were realised by various companies and craftsmen. Pellegrini was the only one of the three architects to design numerous accessories for the home, constructed by Libyan artisans, inspired by the techniques, shapes and colours of the local tradition. Among these artefacts were fabrics for furnishing and clothing in wool, silk and cotton; deep pile and short pile carpets; various types of mats; woven esparto grass items; two trellis screens of painted palm leaves; vases, basins and serving dishes in brass and copper and table accessories in leather. In particular there was "a type of set of earthenware tableware which will be presented in three series of different colours […]: these sets curated by Pellegrini are of particular interest as they renew the old techniques of the North African potters of Libya, of Tunisia and of the island of Djerba (which perpetuate an art inherited from conquering and civilizing Rome) creating, particularly in certain warm yellow and deep green tones, delightful harmonies in their genuine rustic flavor, which happily alternates the dense bright glazes with opaque tones of porous lands." in C. E. Rava, C.E, "Abitare e vivere in Colonia," in *Domus*, XIII, n. 145, gennaio 1940, p. 21. According to Rava, the two novel elements of the Milanese exhibition were the adoption of new materials and a special anti-folk tendency, visible above all in Pellegrini's work, which brought out an absolutely novel "Mediterranean" design, but also linked to the ancient techniques of craftsmanship of the colonial countries. In the first room the furniture of a bedroom designed by Rava and G.G. Sichirollo was exhibited. Completely disassembled and reassembled with a system of joints and enclosed in a single box, they ere

woven fabrics for clothing and furnishings, particularly suitable for life in the colonies. The aim, among other things, was to teach weaving and to give women who could not work outside the home a trade to help them survive the war. The jewellery was made of metal, which was considered more modern than precious jewellery, with Dalmatian necklaces used as an example. For *Bellezza* the value of the jewellery was sculptural and allegorical and did not reside in the intrinsic value of the materials used, like the copper and coloured stone jewellery made by Princess Marozia Borromeo. The technique was crude, almost primitive, but many elegant women from all countries, *Bellezza* assured, possessed jewellery of this type: "today more than ever the goldsmith's art applied to humble metals, the sobriety of the ornaments, the simple arrangement of the stones is in line with the linearity of fashion."[151]

The pages dedicated to jewellery and accessories were among the most original. The metaphysical compositions by Lucio Ridenti showcased the jewels, their theatrical staging enhancing their merits as art rather than as luxury. "Superior jewellery is not a luxury but an art that has a glorious tradition in Italy," reads the caption under Margherita's jewels in the first issue of *Bellezza*. Lucio Ridenti photographed the jewellery of Traglia and Riesla on plaster hands and fabric mannequins decorated with flowers specially made by Viora of Turin, as in a luxury shop window. The most famous jewellery creator, who was constantly featured in *Bellezza*, was Giuliano Fratti. Original belts were given relevance by being worn over sober, dark clothes. For the winter of 1941, *Bellezza* proposed a wide belt of Oriental inspiration in Bengal red suede with leather inlays, gold fringes and thin, articulated elastic belts in engraved metal. Handbags for the summer were made of cheap materials like a country-style scarf, straw and straw cloth, with a shoulder strap for cycling.

---

made of brushed oak and oxygen-bleached Faesite. The bed and the armchair were upholstered in Autartex hemp with pistachio green and lemon yellow stripes; in Santoianni, V., *Il Razionalismo nelle colonie italiane. La "nuova architettura" delle Terre d'Oltremare*, PhD thesis.
151 *Bellezza*, n. 11, November 1941.

A Zanollo straw hat bearing the *Marca d'oro* possessed the characteristic of "ingenious versatility," lending itself to various transformations: straw attached to a base made of the same fabric as the dress formed a pointed cap (fig. 1, 2, 3). If desired, the brim could be removed, leaving only the cloth cap. The cap had flaps that framed the face and which could be lowered in front or behind. Other hats were more extravagant, interpretations of Hollywood models which it was recommended be worn with extreme caution. Millinery occupied an important place in the regime's autarkic policy even though eccentric models, which the press condemned, continued to be seen on the streets and younger women did not seem enamoured of headgear. Journalist Vera Lodomez, in fact, lashed out against "this mania of going bareheaded, an expression of the desire to be young, only to then wear a huge hat to the theatre. A light hat protects from the cruel sun that exposes wrinkles."[152] Sometimes it was the fashion houses that tried their hand at the art of millinery, with original results. Two "bizarre" Biki models showed a Surrealist influence reminiscent of Schiaparelli and remarkable craftsmanship, the colonial influence visible in a double hat with a woollen scarf framing the oval of the face. Great importance was attached to the framed geometric face and in 1941 the wide-brimmed hat regained "a privileged position," for its ability to delicately frame the face[153] and to evoke "innocence." Furthermore, *Bellezza* spurred the creativity of milliners by asking them to reinterpret the Dalmatian cap.[154]

The use of leather was prohibited and the only shoes available on the market, before disappearing completely except in the pages of *Bellezza*, had a fabric upper. For the 1941 collection Matrigali, a shoemaker from Viareggio, offered sporty, flat shoes with extensive use of wool, which, however, was condemned in the caption: "A contradiction in this winter of war, and a trend in sharp contrast with the limiting directives which currently regulate some sectors of the clothing industry." These captions,

---

152 *Ibid.*
153 *Bellezza*, n. 1, January 1941.
154 *Bellezza*, n. 9, September 1941.

which all the evidence shows were added after the magazine was ready for print, highlight the tensions between the magazine's editors and the regime's directives. Fortunately, it went on, spring would sweep away this "weakness" for wool.

Blackouts in the cities, curfews and fear forced people to spend more time at home, so the "house dress" became a privileged item of the wartime wardrobe, even if it had already been indicated in Meano's 1938 *Commentario* as one of the ENM's "preferred" "discourses". The long dressing gowns and the "house dresses" were the typical clothing of the woman shut up in her home because even in private it was important that, "though absorbed in thoughts from which the frivolous is banished," she never forgot to "always appear harmoniously styled."[155]

Due to rationing, "the new year must begin with a logical elegance that renounces quantity in favour of quality, opulence in favour of sobriety." Four month "*quadrimestrí*" and "points": "new words in the language of fashion!"[156] A few months earlier, from the 25th to the 31st of August 1941, seventeen high fashion tailors had presented to foreign buyers their autumn-winter collections[157], of which *Bellezza* presented a selection in its September issue. The aim was to show that clothes rationing "did not mortify intellectual energies."[158]

For 1942, the ENM established that the line of clothes must be in tune with the current moment, both in terms of simplicity and in terms of their minimal use of fabric, with colours that, it assured, would leave no room for whims and eccentricity. For spring-summer the line was spindle-shaped and tapered at top and bottom – short tight skirts, elbow-length sleeves and tight bodices – but the economy of fabric must not mean dull, unadorned designs. The institution tried to differentiate fashion with the use of rounded shoulders and elaborate attachments, wide necklines, pleats, drapes, flounces and plain or printed fabrics to obviate the scarcity of skirts, very short sleeves and

---

155 «Risorse della moda», *Bellezza*, n. 11, November 1941, p. 5.
156 *Bellezza*, n. 12, December 1941.
157 *Bellezza*, n. 9, September 1941.
158 Ivi.

short, wide jackets. Naturally, it underlined that the fusiform line respected and "fits very well" the body of the Italian woman. Not very voluminous at the top, it was accentuated in the centre of the figure and narrowed at the bottom. The fusiform line was the opposite of the hourglass line, emphasising the belly and filling out the gaps, as motherhood does. For the shoulders, the advice was to create elaborate "crepe attachments, in small *tortiglioni*, with transversal bands inserted in the circle. Necklines must be rather wide: triangular or square, very pronounced." The smallness of the skirts was to be attenuated by trimmings at the bottom "which will make them graceful." And in the height of summer, there were to be no sleeves: "shoulder pads and detachable sleeves, with short wide jackets of clear Oriental inspiration"[159]. The predominant colours of the season were based around sand and orchid colours ranging from delicate to purple, alpine colours based around green and nocturnal colours going from light blue to blue. The novelties of spring-summer 1942 were expressed by capes, encrustations of embroidery, lace jackets, "again and always" polka dots, loose on the hips and large puffy lapels, tartan motifs, double fabrics, very short jackets, striped *bajadera* patterns, small capes, sleeveless dresses and pointed necklines. The garments showcased in *Bellezza* (selected according to aesthetic and moral principles, explained Ponti) were to be understood as a small fashion collection, where the flair displayed – a way to smuggle ideas from across the border – only served to demonstrate, even in wartime, the inspiration and the creative capacity of Italian fashion: "the fashion of a people like the Italians, of natural moderation, line and good taste, must lead to a costume – an aesthetic and moral shape." According to Ponti, the war was already determining a costume: "in the creations of the best Italian fashion houses, a line, a style of simplicity, of true taste, of the interpretation of today's life, is a prelude to a real Italian fashion that must possess this formula: excellence of line in a costume suited to modern social life."[160]

---

159 "La nuova linea primavera estate," *Bellezza*, n. 15, March 1942, p. 5.
160 Ponti, G., "Scelta di bellezza," *Bellezza*, n. 16, 1942, p. 2.

Ponti was in fact rather satisfied, because evening dresses – along with certain kinds of exhibitionism considered inappropriate – had disappeared, the values of quality, practicality and artistic workmanship had acquired the primacy over the luxury of raw materials, accessories had acquired a new importance, the fabrics were practical, durable and typified, the printed-patterned dresses compensated for the simplicity of fashion, and designers were experimenting with new materials and sporty new lines. In winter, simple Bedouin hats that wrapped and protected the neck and ears "triumph again," as, for autarkical and practical reasons, did shoes with cork-filled soles and heels, "a fashion born from the invention of a courageous creator": Salvatore Ferragamo.

Among the novelties of rationed fashion was printed tulle.[161] Printed fabrics in general utilised different patterns from the omnipresent flowers in textile catalogues from the nineteenth century onwards, with new and original ideas that defined an expressive fashion: "brand new" dark blue veiled in grey with a hint of violet, and a grey blue like a "restful horizon," the "Prayer" fabric where basilicas overlapped diagonally on a grey-black background, and "Fuga," with "jade" coloured palms and "duck blue" gates. The prints were dominated by small motifs: pen drawings on a plain background, arabesque landscapes inspired by semi-precious stones. All creations carried "like a veil that makes harmonies sweeter." Finally, the tulle was worked into jerseys. Belmoda launched the "Mondi" design, with shaded white and green geographic maps, the thin linear motifs on plain backgrounds "continue their success," like Tessital's rural and humorous scenes. Overall, *Bellezza* concluded, the collections of the season were extraordinary. According to *Bellezza*, it was precisely thanks to the war that Italy expressed its finest spiritual energies: "Let us therefore rejoice that the difficulties have served to stimulate our energies and improve them. Later they will contribute to increasing the prestige of Italian taste and work."[162]

---

161 Ivi, p. 4.
162 Labroca, M., "Valore delle stoffe stampate," *Bellezza*, n. 16, 1942, pp. 5, 61.

High quality production was flanked by the state-approved fabrics: the stripes and dots of Belmoda and Toninelli,[163] Toninelli's marbled designs that made the colours vibrate, those by De Angeli-Frua, again with dots and stripes, the creations of Dafmi – a De Angeli-Frua production exclusively for Belmoda – and the sporty, multicoloured stripes.[164] The aesthetics of wartime fashion can be summed up as "something new that doesn't stand out at first glance but at second," with wooden buttons in the shape of a jar, urn and amphora, in an "almost Franciscan" style. Among the accessories, one of the novelties was a "very high" belt in the shape of a corselet. For the afternoon, the detailing was enhanced thanks to the use of shiny metals, pearls and stones. Metallic effects were achieved even without the use of metal, simply by gilding and silvering the plastic materials with the galvanisation method. The coloured stones were not made of glass, since it was necessary to save coal, but of fabulous new materials like Pristal.[165]

In this year of the war, the ENM organised a tour abroad "from Bucharest to Budapest, from Stockholm to Zurich," with more than one hundred designs whose purpose, as well as propaganda, was to promote industrial heritage and the awareness that only through exportation "do the products of a country create that reputation for excellence which is consolidated over time." The fashion tour was a "caravan of beauty" meant to conquer wild places. With rhetorical emphasis, *Bellezza* decreed that its success was "absolute," so much so that a Stockholm newspaper apparently wrote: "We must ask ourselves if Italy will not be the dominant country of the future for fashion."[166] Among the models presented was a Japanese silk-patterned dress with bag in the same fabric by Ferrario, a jacket dress in coarse canvas by

---

163 A frequent feature of post-war cinema, for example Monica Vitti's polka dots and stripes in Antonioni's *L'avventura*.
164 "Sete stampate," *Bellezza*, n. 17, 1942, p. 39-41, p. 39.
165 Rossi Lodomez, V., "Importanza dei particolari," *Bellezza*, n. 17, 1942, p. 52-53.
166 C.M., "Presentazioni di modelli italiani all'estero," *Bellezza*, n. 19, July 1942, pp. 5-7, p. 5.

Vanna, a dress in fringed silk scarf-like fabric of Asian inspiration and one with large pockets by Noberasko.

On the eve of summer 1942, the greatest annoyance for wealthy women was having to understand "something which had previously been unthinkable": how to lighten their luggage for autarkic holidays. Elsa Robiola came to their rescue with the article *Reforming Holiday Luggage*. The ideal suitcase weighed twenty kilos and, given that rigid hat boxes were uncomfortable, Prada invented a type of hat box and handbag in very light moleskin, without a frame, which could be folded onto their base, the only rigid part. The formula, "twenty kilos for twenty days," Robiola assured, was a "model of discretion and practicality," both of which were essential during wartime.[167]

For the autumn-winter 1942-1943 fashion, *Bellezza*'s watchword to Italian creators, "unlike what happens in other countries where an exasperated desire for distraction from the disturbances of the time manifests itself in anachronistic forms of clothing," was always the same: fashion must be based on the needs and mood of present-day life, in contrast with the idea of a magazine transformed into a "dream for displaced people." Ponti refused the idea of fashion abstracting from the historical moment, insisting instead on finding resources in it. The fashion industry would have to work to raise the tone of afternoon and evening dresses, while milliners would have to avoid cliché, finding inspiration in Carlo Dolci hats, "with bonnets, caps and turbans that connect to paintings of that epoch." Many seemed convinced that due to its practical nature, no trace would remain of wartime fashion, which was called a fashion "without an era." Therefore, the truth of wartime fashion would be found in the ornaments and hats, in the smallest details and in the important accessories, "for the creation of which all the finest forces have been mobilised," which "will have the honour of going down in clothing history as a living testimony to the fruitfulness of the spirit and hard work of these troubled years."[168]

---

167 Robiola, E., "20 chili di bagaglio," *Bellezza*, n. 19, July 1942, p. 46-47.
168 Robiola, E., "Moda Autunno Inverno 1942-1943. Orientamento," *Bellezza*, n. 21, September 1942, p. 5.

Bellezza also dedicated space to mass produced clothes. Girls, "more than on the seamstress rely on the specialised warehouse where there are mass-produced dresses. Garments with a confident and characteristic cut that repeat without monotony and that meet the aspirations of youthful elegance with a simplicity like their own but that leave them the pleasure of choosing." The example *Bellezza* gave for young women was Hanska Vis, a singer by trade but, of course, also a good housewife who knew how to cook, who was photographed in austere clothes in a bohemian but very tidy apartment. Her favourite tailor was Caraceni, a men's tailor shop where she had a sports coat made, while she wore a jacket dress with blouses embroidered by herself.[169] Personalized embroidery was a recurring motif of wartime fashion, with women's magazines encouraging women to embroider their clothes to raise the tone, personalise them, and appear more "beautiful" and "cheery." In this look, mass produced garments, modern men's tailoring and handcrafted embroidery came together to form an original and cohesive image. Fairytale weddings retained their centrality and so *Bellezza* published a report on Marita Sanfelice di Monteforte's journey to Madrid to marry her future husband, a secretary at the Italian embassy. Among the guests were Princess Colonna di Belmonte and Virginia Agnelli. But the magazine also featured "beauty workers" like Dora Bruschi, whose work consisted of "giving beauty," and fashion designer Biki, who was "dynamism in human form," depicted for the occasion by Brunetta in her favourite dress of this period, a black and grey check skirt and a red blouse. Biki, Robiola wrote, was a complete woman because she had another source of strength to assist her: her five-year-old daughter Roberta.[170]

The repeated bombing of Milan and the worsening of the war situation prompted *Bellezza* to insist obsessively upon the idea

---

[169] *Bellezza*, n. 22, October 1942.
[170] Robiola, E., "Donne che lavorano," *Bellezza*, n. 23, November 1942, p. 56. In *Bellezza*'s first year, in the "Women who work" section, there were ladies knitting. In November 1942 the ladies had become beauty entrepreneurs, and *Bellezza* chose to speak about them.

of a single garment, which "is in some way grounded," and upon an emergency fashion. To evacuate, for example, you needed a suitcase inside which you put shoes, a skirt-suit, wool knitwear and some spare clothing which was not heavy, as you would have to carry the suitcase a long way, no rigid hats, and finally alcohol and gauze, because "you never know."[171] Those who could, evacuated to "mountains and valleys". The war "gets one used to the rural life" so that, even for the city, people would become used to dressing in practical skirts, sweaters and boots. But the violent air raids on Milan and Turin that started in the summer of 1943, about which poet Salvatore Quasimodo said of Milan that "the city is dead,"[172] made movement difficult and the situation of clothing dramatic:

> The postal interruption for a period of time and the precariousness of movement due to the violent air raids on Milan and Turin have paralysed our publishing for a few weeks. [...] The fashion sector in the cities most badly affected in fact endured almost complete stagnation until the last few days. Our most fraternal solidarity goes out to those who have suffered the loss of people, things, workshops, warehouses, materials [...] The life of the nation continues, as in every sector of work, clothing included. It might seem absurd to talk about fashion in this moment, but it is a necessity: not depriving workers of their jobs in these terrible times. How women's clothing is oriented towards the most modest and almost humble practicality can be better understood from this issue, even better than in all the previous ones over at least the last two years. It is no longer now a question of creating "admirable elegance"; women simply want to get dressed, since it is indispensable. And the advice to wear one garment instead of another, to resort to an alteration many women would not know how to come up with by themselves, to use the minimum necessary carefully to avoid waste, is the task of these pages of ours, which, even in less difficult moments, have always ignored eccentricities and oddities. In the minds of our artists, in the hands of our artisans, all committed to solving constant financial problems, we still have what it takes to give women that moment of joy that fashion, day by day, knows how to give and renew. And we, with our magazine, will continue to promote the best, to encourage so that with the least we do more and more, even the impossible.[173]

---

171 "È pronta la valigia per sfollare," *Bellezza*, n. 25-26, January-February 1943, pp. 8-9.
172 Quasimodo, S., "Milano, agosto 1943," in *Giorno dopo giorno*, Mondadori, Milan 1947.
173 *Bellezza*, n. 33-34, September-October 1943, p. 3.

At this point it was not a matter of creating elegance, but of surviving: "There are no fabrics; it's practically impossible to get any special colours in the dyeing shop; there are no female workers; we are without electricity and without energy (metaphorically and literally). In these conditions it is impossible to speak of collections."[174] But Robiola was convinced that "behind the closed shutters" something was "taking shape." Among the sketches and drawings there was "the elusive line of the jackets, motifs of steering wheels and handwheels, drapery pulled all to one side."[175] In fact, *Bellezza* insisted on promoting a core of collections for autumn-winter 1943-1944 based on exports to Switzerland and other unspecified countries. There were no examples to photograph so the editorial team strived to show how the designs had come about by showing sketches and samples of fabric. The mission of keeping Italian fashion alive took on mystical nuances: in one editorial even the forgiveness of the Madonna was invoked for having lost "the faith." Even in those dramatic months, there was no trace of the war, of the rubble or of the German occupation in the photographs, but the names of the advertisements and tailors had changed. Favro was a dressmaker's known in Milan for its frequent shows that distinguished itself by its "completely white, modern headquarters whose linear architecture has the merit – and her owner's taste – of not looking like a traditional *maison*, with sofas along the walls for the seasonal presentations."[176] And in Turin, numerous boutiques specialising in sportswear had sprung up on the model of Aprato, among them Maria Cristina and Voga Torino, sheltered by patched up arcades[177] with plywood in place of glass:

---

174 E.r., *A battenti chiusi, Bellezza*, n. 48, December-January 1944, p. 3.
175 Ivi.
176 *Bellezza*, n. 47, November-December 1944, p. 2.
177 Robiola, E., "Carattere e ripresa delle attività torinesi," *Bellezza*, n. 47, November-December 1944.

Turin. Along the endless line of shops under the arcades, rebuilt or patched up as well as possible depending on the damage, we unconsciously sought something that seemed to be missing.[178]

Signora San Lorenzo was in a house that bore the signs of one of the countless bombing raids: "Since the furniture, mirrors, paintings have been displaced, the rooms have been arranged as well as possible, without worrying about how they look."[179] In her latest collection, her dresses were of "exemplary sobriety, refined in every detail, irreproachable in execution." From Gambino there was a "sense of order," faithful to the tendencies of balance and refinement of ideas appreciated in "happy years, just as in these black years full of nightmares," and the same "atmosphere of war" permeated Binello, where the spirit of the late Maria Rosa Binello and of afternoon elegance hung in the vast half-empty undamaged rooms, "the silver fox trimmings, the quick and youthful cut with the soft pleated skirt, all in tune with the black" stood out for their simplicity. The shop windows of Aprato "are inviting with twinsets in all colours, tartan skirts, together with a knit and suede jacket, fur-lined coats, a range of classic sporty models."

Among the novelties of 1944, *Bellezza* praised the use of white lambskin for the inside of coats (being extremely elegant without being noticed "is the indispensable criterion for life today"[180]), wool and velvet dresses photographed in the Borromini Gallery in Como[181] and various patriotic designs that combined the red and green of the Italian flag.[182] Among the advertised novelties there was the beauty brand Chita-Corday Budapest-Turin, which

---

178 *Ibid.*
179 *Ibid.*
180 Ivi, p. 13.
181 Guido Le Noci began his career as an art dealer in 1943 with the Borromini Gallery in Como. After the war, in 1946 he moved the Gallery to via Brera n. 4 in Milan and began his activity with exhibitions of paintings and drawings by, among others, Russolo, Sassu, Modigliani, Savinio and Soldati. In 1954 the gallery changed its name to Galleria Apollinaire and was inaugurated with a collective exhibition held on December 17, 1954, with works by Modigliani, Morandi, De Chirico, Savinio and others.
182 Ivi, p. 20.

presented a stylised figure in folk costume, Borsalino with a puppet of a Japanese woman, Italviscosa rayon that gave "instant elegance," hemp fabrics, the perfume *Mormorio nel bosco* inspired by the novel of the same name by Austrian Felix Salten, released in 1944, and the Tauro pocket torch for blackouts.[183] Valstar and Contex raincoats, garments of "real utility" for working women – "and almost all women work today" – and umbrellas for women also gained visibility:[184]

> A 1943-44 "collection" which will certainly go down in the annals of clothing. And the memory of it will increase in wonder when we think that the clothes were born in makeshift workshops, in temporary displacement sites. [...] It is well known that every generation has its own fashion (in fact, we only need browse a collection of old fashion plates to realise this particular aspect of the evolution of peoples), but the fashion of these "war years" will one day certainly succeed in bringing his contribution of experiences to the new generations who work with clothing, since these "collections" are above all a triumph of the imagination; made with little, yet bearing the unmistakable mark of imagination and taste."[185]

At that time people spoke "always about the cold and food" but in the chaos, it was reiterated, a "new order" was born. Celani, who went to visit Vanna's atelier in Corso Venezia and private residence in Porta Nuova, Milan, in an apartment on the fifth floor with blue cardboard instead of glass in the windows, which offered asylum to her associates, noted that Vanna was already thinking about the post-war period and that Signora Valente was "overcome by the desire to have work to offer her employees." For his part, Ferrario, in the devastated Via Montenapoleone, "was lucky, suffering only minor damage, and presented a small collection in October and even sent invitations." Damaged or not, other houses – Tizzoni, Primalba, Villa – had moved. The milliner Proietti, who lost everything, was a guest of another tailor's shop and took his collection to lake Como. The associates of the fashion houses attempted to reach their customers scattered all over the world with the motto: "Women shall not

---

183 *Bellezza*, n. 37, January 1944.
184 "Ombrelli," *Bellezza*, n. 33-34, September-October 1943, p. 37.
185 *Bellezza*, n. 35, November 1943, p. 2.

become savages." The evacuated Villa held out in its hermitage, a village on the outskirts of Milan "feudally gathered" around Villa Greppi, which housed the company, and in Milan Primalba, which had remained intact, "has dealt with the theme of the transformation of the sleeves." Vanna, haunted by bad luck, was again a victim of a nocturnal bombing run, and Tizzoni was displaced to Como. The success of the season seemed to be the Rina collection "which leaps to the fore with designs that are easy to wear, of linear simplicity, perfect execution and variety."

Unlike in France, where the issue of occupation fashion has been widely debated, there are no studies of fashion in the Italian Social Republic, the German puppet state whose capital was the small town of Salò. The photos in *Bellezza* show the great salons of the tailors turned upside down, burnt and deserted – "one would have to stop thinking and only work continuously to stand it" – and "cutting and sewing" in villages "whose existence had been unknown."[186] Not working meant deserting: "You have to live with all your strength, not doing so is desertion. It feels as if the ground is missing beneath your feet at every step, and what with taking trams and having to walk everywhere there's never any time...In the meantime, you live."[187] In those terrible years, new fashion houses somehow appeared. Cerri, Pascali, who from fashion designer became creator, "avant-garde seamstress" Lionella, the "highly remarkable" Guillermaz and Lilly Mode:[188] names that have fallen into oblivion. In Como, exhibitions and competitions were organized, such as the one for printed fabrics, considered the symbol of the time,[189] which were held at the Borromini gallery.

There was an awareness that the post-war period would have to dress the Italian people with mass-produced clothes:

---

[186] Elena, "Bilancio delle attività della moda," *Bellezza*, n. 36, December 1943, p. 7-9.
[187] Celani, E., "Valore del presente," *Bellezza*, n. 44, August 1944, p. 3.
[188] Robiola, E., "Malgrado tutto," *Bellezza*, n. 46, 15 October-15 November 1944, pp. 3-4.
[189] Carozzi, D., "L'arte decorativa dei tessuti stampati," ivi, p. 18-21.

High fashion, the pride of Italian dressmakers, may survive. But it will be required to supply a mass-produced fashion that answers the needs of the masses. So far, Italian women have preferred to let the local seamstress impose her taste, even if her taste is bad. It is difficult for the kind of mass-production which has been in use for years elsewhere to work here. Difficult but not impossible, as evidenced by the visit to a factory destroyed in August 1943 which was miraculously resurrected 15 days later in a temporary location.

Starting from the "Italian" mentality, the company found a solution to the uniformity and coarseness of mass-produced clothing through an unusual attention to detail and stitches: "this is how luxury mass production is achieved. This is the solution to the post-war clothing problem. There will be many new poor women who will want to dress well."[190]

There would be many women who, rather than dressing well, would simply want to dress. Publication of *Bellezza* ceased definitively in February 1945, and in the first issue of the new series directed by Michelangelo Testa the "return of femininity" was proclaimed. The rubble and the passers-by now appeared in the photos, along with the French words in the text, but *Bellezza*'s values did not change: "Elegance, we will never cease to say, is quality. You do not know how to live if you do not introduce a sign of moral elegance, whose appeal is inverse to its effect. [...] We will start again by resuming contacts with abroad, to value our characteristics of Italian beauty."[191] Brunetta said she was happy because "we are no longer harassed by our photo shoots being interrupted by sirens over the roar of the bombers. A world of troubles getting across the city. Transportation, postal services that don't exist, electricity coming and going, paper hunting, inflation." Now, "with a slightly out-of-phase fashion, [Paris] wants to revive forgotten sensations, and states that there is no upheaval that is not followed by a new fashion." Italy could not compete, everything had been destroyed, but for Brunetta "the uniqueness of some of our artisan production can play a role in

---

190 Vera, "Necessità di domani: le confezioni in serie," ivi, pp. 42-43.
191 Celani, E., "Ritorno alla femminilità," *Bellezza*, n. 1 (new series), November 1945, p. 3.

world fashion, the quality of printed silk fabrics testifying to the maturity of our artistic sense," and she entrusted "to a dignified diplomacy the fortune of our fashion initiatives, the success of a sum of work which is one of the very few fortunes we have left."[192]

---

[192] Robiola, E., «Dall'album di Brunetta: atto di fede», ivi, pp. 4-13.

4
"WILL ALL WOMEN WEAR LACE COLLARS?"

4.1 *Cinematic Venuses*

> It was necessary, link by link, to forge the chain: from the fabric designer to the weaver, from the weaver to the illustrator whose job it is to create a drawing capable of capturing women's attention, from the illustrator to the grand dressmaker who, with a simple watercolour sketch, is able to envision the final garment as it will be in real life and create it, just as the great actor creates the part, written in the script, and so on gradually right up to the fashion model, who is not a self-propelled puppet but an artist in her field who must inhabit that dress and bring it to life and, finally, to the photographer, to the fashion magazine, to the elegant lady who buys the garment at a high price or, to mass production, to the general public.[1]

Although not mentioned, among the links of this fashion chain there was cinema, that unparalleled means of communication for propagating fascist state's new tastes, ideals of beauty and fashion textiles to the widest possible audience and thus remedying their inevitable fragmentation. Exhibitions, films, magazines, shop windows and the seduction of opulent and modern atmospheres were all to serve the cause of the fascist beauty revolution. Alongside the widespread distribution of American films, Italian cinema acquired a new centrality during the 1930s with the 1937 foundation of Cinecittà and of the Centro Sperimentale di Cinematografia ("Experimental Cinematography Centre")[2]. As famous critic Irene Brin has pointed out – not without a hint

---

1 Gentile, E., *The Struggle for Modernity, op. cit.*, p. 111.
2 Savio, F., *Ma l'amore no. Realismo, formalismo, propaganda e telefoni bianchi nel cinema italiano di regime (1930-1943)*, Sonzogno, Milan 1975; Savio, F., *Cinecittà anni Trenta. Parlano 116 protagonisti del secondo cinema italiano (1930-1943)*, 2 vol., Bulzoni, Rome 2021; Brunetta, Gian Piero, *Buio in sala: 100 anni di passione dello spettatore cinematografico*,

of sarcasm – female audiences loved American stars like Greta Garbo, Joan Crawford and Marlene Dietrich, and the ideals of beauty and elegance that America's stars exported to the rest of the world had, obviously, a far greater hold on the imagination of the Italian public than did those domestic actresses who were forced to imitate them, though a serious study of the phenomenon is still lacking.

From 1932, Luigi Freddi – head of the General Directorate of Cinematography – had invited Italian directors to study the sophisticated Hollywood comedies and musicals, encouraging a debate on cinematographic costume, fashion and production design which took place in the architecture, cinema and fashion magazines and which was reflected in films such as *Contessa di Parma* (*The Countess of Parma*, Alessandro Blasetti, 1937), a fashion movie featuring fashion house Mattè[3] which can be seen as a document of the politics of fascism in the field of women's fashion in relation to sport and the development of new cultural models. In this film, the idea – of French origin – of the "individual genius" of the couturier is an object of ridicule and couturiers are looked upon as inventors of equivocal, questionable and bizarre styles. French fashion is depicted as a ridiculous farce and for Marcella – the lead fashion model, played by actress Elena Cegani – the fashion show held in Sestriere is an opportunity to finally cast aside its absurd tenets.[4] The spectacle of fashion in the film, embodied in a fashion show featuring twelve Italian designs, aimed less to promote the individual creative genius of the dressmaker capable of awakening female desire and rather to exhibit fashion as a spectacle which marked the stages in the life of the new Italian woman, from courtship to marriage. State

---

Marsilio, Venezia 1989; Hay, J., *Popular Film Culture in Fascist Italy: The Passing of the Rex*, Indiana UP, Bloomington 1986.

3   Mary Mattè had registered the first trademark, representing a woman wrapped in a luxurious drape in a dance pose from antiquity, in 1927. In 1937, she opened her own atelier, a meeting point for the best of Piedmontese society, in the renovated historical and commercial heart of Turin, Via Roma.

4   For the motif of "the mask" see Fitzpatrick, Sheila, *Tear Off the Masks! Identity and Imposture in Twentieth-Century Russia*, Princeton UP, Princeton and Oxford 2005.

fashion, unlike the "xenophilic" and "depraved" conception of the effeminate caricature of Commendatore Carrani, must be *for men*, and aimed at the roles of wife and mother that women must play in fascist society. The final show, where Marcella wears a wedding dress, allows her – after a series of misunderstandings – to "reveal" her "true" identity as an honest and simple girl of the people who aspires to nothing more than marriage: the world of the catwalks risked being barren and dangerous if it was not brought back within the canons of the "fascist procreation policy."[5]

In *Contessa di Parma*, the spokesperson for *fascistifying* values, through an idea of Italianness understood as "authenticity," is the dynamic and unkempt Marta Rossi, the new owner of the *Primavera* fashion house in Turin. The fashion show in Sestriere is the climax of the film, where Rossi teaches a valuable lesson to the protagonists, particularly to Commendatore Carrani, who is unwilling to end the fashion show with a wedding dress, insisting that a wedding dress cannot be the highlight of such an event. The cutting riposte comes immediately:

> The wedding dress which you, a parasite of society, have been refusing for twenty years – and that is precisely the reason why I put it at the end of the show, so that men can see them (women) dressed this way and that, elegant and low-necked, but get it through their heads that they need to marry them. All of them. Only then will fashion have a meaning and a purpose.

Films as showcases for Italian fashion were one of the many interests of *Bellezza* which, from its third issue onwards, hosted the fashion critic column *La sensazione cinematografica* ("The Cinematographic Sensation"). The first two issues – edited by

---

[5] Eugeni, R., "Modelli, figure e ideologie della rappresentazione in *Contessa di Parma*," in Prono, F., Della Casa, S., (edited by), *Contessa di Parma. La modernità a Torino negli anni Trenta*, Fondazione archivi del Novecento, Rome 2006, p. 34. For an interpretation of *Contessa di Parma* see also Paulicelli, E., "From Hollywood to France. From France to Italy: Alessandro Blasetti's *Contessa di Parma*," in *op. cit.*, pp. 87-98; and "*Contessa di Parma*: A Manifesto for the Promotion of Italian fashion and Turin as a fashion city," in Paulicelli, E., *Italian Style. Fashion & Film from Early Cinema to the Digital Age*, Bloomsbury, New York-London 2016, pp. 91-100.

Gio Ponti without the stringent supervision of ENM and printed in Milan – focused on theatre, which was perhaps considered more suitable for *Bellezza*'s refined readership. In the first issue, theatre actress Evi Maltagliati, in a nineteenth-century-style costume created by fashion house Ventura, is spoken of as an example of "spiritual gracefulness,"[6] while in another black and white photo a "young actress" wears an organdie evening gown that the caption describes as an imaginary "stage costume":

> Ventura designed this diaphanous white organdie dress with small frills of silver sequins for a young actress imagined on the stage as in a painting, in the setting of an Imperial house.[7]

In the play *Una famiglia di Filadelfia (*A Family from Philadelphia), fashion designer Biki contributed "to the spiritual grace of Laura Adani" with a white dress with a two-colour sash and a pair of the famously forbidden trousers. Collaboration between fashion and theatre was encouraged and welcomed because "the climate of taste is measured by the amount of collaboration between creative forces."[8] *Bellezza*'s vision of fashion as a "perfume of civilization" can be found in the integral fusion of dress, model and furnishings. Among other things, *Bellezza* focused on "theatre" styles to smuggle through spectacular designs for its readers, since luxury and extravagance were officially forbidden in wartime and the separation between everyday and party clothes was painfully clear.

From the columns of *La Sensazione Cinematografica*, Eugenio Giovannetti – a fine writer and film critic – spoke in dismissive and contemptuous tones about the looks of Italian divas, propagandising for ideas of dress and body coherent with the directives of the ENM. In the first issue, for example, the critic complained about the lack of elegance and fashions on the screens of Italian films and Italian divas' lack of interest in their image:

---

6   *Bellezza*, n. 1, 1941, p. 33.
7   Ivi, p. 79.
8   "Interpretazioni eleganti per il teatro," *Bellezza*, n. 2, 1941, p. 46.

> Recent films possess little in the way of elegance and fashion. A film actress should at the very least ask herself which hairstyle suits her. A question which, judging by the ugly hairstyle she wears in *Alessandro sei grande*, Vivi Gioi, the great white hope of Italian cinema has apparently not yet asked herself. Only one actress strikes me for the simple grace of her hairstyle, for her sensitive naturalness, for her candour - Beatrice Mancini in *Caravaggio*.[9]

In addition to criticizing the image of the divas, Giovannetti outlined an aesthetic theory of cinematic fashion in his description of Merle Oberon's "magical" dress in William Wyler's 1939 *Wuthering Heights* as "revelation and metamorphosis"; because when the dress lives and adheres to the character "one would swear one could smell the speaker's scent":[10]

> What light [...] from that early nineteenth-century dress! The nineteenth century knew the joy of dressing like few other centuries. For me it knew better the joy of living. Bourgeois in tone but fervent with ideas. The twentieth century loved vitalism, the nineteenth century loved life. Even in terms of fashions, how much secret nostalgia, through our geometrized impassiveness, for that great romantic blaze![11]

The nineteenth-century costume drama, with its fairytale atmosphere, seemed to be a favourite of Italian cinema during wartime, at least until the collapse of the regime. In 1943, in a speech to the legislative committees of the Senate, the Minister of Popular Culture Gaetano Polverelli[12] had in fact declared that "the return to the works of the nineteenth century and in general to the works of the past, can only be justified for the masterpieces."[13] The magical theory of the film costume coming to life and emerging from the screen recalls Elizabeth Wilson's definition of fashion, according to which fashion is magic at work: "Fashion is a magical system, and what we see as we

---

9 Giovannetti, E., "La sensazione cinematografica," *Bellezza*, n. 3, 1941, p. 74.
10 Ivi.
11 "La sensazione cinematografica," *Bellezza*, n.1, 1941.
12 Gaetano Polverelli was Minister for Popular Culture in the Kingdom of Italy from the 6th of February 1943 to the 25th of July 1943.
13 "Punti fermi," *Si gira*, n. 15, June 1943, p. 1.

leaf through glossy magazines is 'the look'."[14] A theory that would seem to be in tension with the more common approach of "invisibility," whose most fervent supporter is costume designer and scholar Deborah Nadoolman Landis.[15] Landis' philosophy notwithstanding, movies offered unprecedented possibilities for advertising products, brands and looks – eager to become "visible" and desirable – to a large audience. Even the most artistic films could be showcases for everything that they contained, the actresses living mannequins immersed in fetishistically designed settings of emotion and music. Viewed from this perspective, all the films were, at least in part, fashion films which promoted aesthetic and moral ideals through the creation of a look.[16]

Like those promoted by Giovannetti, who in the pages of *Bellezza* promoted the female "fashion of beauty" that Italian cinema should pursue. According to the critic, the cinematic Venus should not aspire to classical beauty nor to the beauty of the common woman, but to an ideal that united art with sport: "More than an ideal, a composite and ephemeral fashion for beauty"[17] as in a modernist collage. On the silver screen, sport gave rise to masculine garments, "very becoming on a florid, lively nude," while art made us dream of "an exotic beauty, of a Maori Venus" with a tubular body shape implying light, pale garments and multicoloured necklaces. The Italian "1941 beauty," on the other hand, must be eclectic and syncretic, a synthesis of Memphis, Siena and Tahiti:

> For us the leg is tapered and not (with derision) like a piano, a column. Reconciliation. I saw a photo yesterday of an American sportswoman that reflects the aesthetic eclecticism of our days. It showed how much our cult tends towards ornament, towards gracefulness. A trend corrected by a new taste for vivid and powerful architectures of the body. The girl was indeed a statuette, a small bronze, but she evoked the florid bronzes of Memphis, the ultra-vivid squaring of those figurines in which limbs and fabrics possess the same expressive and incisive rigour. It was as if primitive Egyp-

---

14 Wilson, E., *Adorned in Dreams*, op.cit, p. 4.
15 Landis, Deborah, *Hollywood Costume*, V&A Publications, London 2013.
16 See Munich, A., *Fashion in Film*, Indiana UP, Bloomington 2011, p. 3.
17 Giovannetti, E., "La moda nell'estetica. Menfi, Siena, Tahiti," *Bellezza*, n. 4, 1941, p. 56-57, p. 56.

tian architectural sculpture had warmed in the Tuscan sun. In those limbs shone the joy of fullness remarried in its magnificence that makes a body shaped by Jacopo della Quercia recognisable among a thousand... The beauty of the oceanic paradise emanated in unthinkable ways from the Mediterranean paradise. And how much of Italy there is at the centre of this oceanic wandering![18]

The Memphis-Siena-Tahiti triad deserves serious consideration, the mention of "those figurines in which limbs and fabrics possess the same expressive and incisive rigour" being in fact a reference to a modernity which aspired to look as exotic as the beaches of Tahiti, consistent with the philosophy of costume expressed elsewhere by Gio Ponti in the pages of *Bellezza*. The same exotic miscellanea was to be found in *Are Clothes Modern?*, Bernard Rudofsky's first book on clothes[19] which was published in 1947. The book was essentially an expansion of an exhibition catalogue for a show of the same name that Rudofsky – a friend of Ponti who wrote regularly for *Stile* – had curated at the Museum of Modern Art of New York in 1944.

Here viewers were treated to unfamiliar sights, among them the paired pictures of a woman in a fashionable 1880's bustle and a naked Hottentot woman with huge buttocks. The show and the book together had a message and an agenda: our way of dressing is foolish and we should learn from more enlightened cultures, chiefly the ancient Greeks. A message not dissimilar from that of Giovannetti's article. Instead of the ancient Greeks, Giovannetti referenced ancient Egypt and its love of stylisation; a love shared by Achille Starace's far from frivolous obsession with style. The behaviour of free-flowing fabric did not appeal much either to the early Egyptians – whose use of it in art was always stylised[20] – or to the fascists. Just as the dialectic of cloth and body, which must fuse to become one, was key for the ancient Egyptians, so it was for fascist costume, something which we might link with an interpretation of fascism as a political religion, though that might

---

18 Ivi, p. 57.
19 Rudofsky, B., *Are Clothes Modern?*, P. Theobold, New York 1947.
20 Hollander, A., *Seeing Through Clothes*, University of California Press, Los Angeles 1993, p. 5.

be taking things a step too far. With the help of art and sport, *Bellezza*'s fashion aesthetic aspired to an "artistic rightness" of nakedness and cloth together:

> The hidden archaic female body, on the other hand, a more static and simplified shape, was inseparable from its formal garments, somehow incapable of energy without the drapery.[21]

The ideal manner of walking for the "1941 Venus" was rhythmic and graceful, like that of Spanish actress and dancer Conchita Montenegro in *L'uomo del romanzo* (*The man of the novel*, Mario Bonnard, 1940): "If you have seen her running in *Giuliano de' Medici* you have seen a figure from a Botticelli running"; it was a film that "marks an era."[22] Even though "the fashions of today" had "abolished decoration by giving us back copious fabrics and plain jewellery,"[23] the critic was convinced that the ridiculous nineteenth-century bustles looked "appetising," and pointed out dresses with "exquisite handwork and luxurious applications." For "pure nineteenth century costume," the article cited Alida Valli in the final shot of *Piccolo Mondo Antico* (Mario Soldati, 1941), an ensemble worn by Carole Lombard in *Made for Each Other* (John Cromwell, 1939) for its exquisitely simple garments ("The costume in which she goes to the New Year's dinner? A very simple and flawless cut") and a look worn by Marie Dea in *Personal Column* (Robert Siodmak, 1939), with the usual dark silver fox fur, no low neckline and with very long sleeves and skirt.

According to critic Lucio Ridenti, fashion could add new interest to modern films if the public were aware that the costumes worn by the divas were a foretaste of the season's collections.[24] This was the case with Isa Miranda, protagonist of *È caduta una donna* (*A Woman Has Fallen*, Alfredo Guarini, 1941), who wore a Dragoni dress designed by Bilinsky, and with Vera Bergman's

---

21 Hollander, A., *op. cit.*, p. 5.
22 Giovannetti, E., "La sensazione cinematografica," *Bellezza*, n. 5, 1941, p. 69.
23 Ivi.
24 Ridenti, L., "La moda e il cinema," *Bellezza*, n. 5, 1941, pp. 70-71.

wearing of Zecca[25] clothes. Although the problem "posed by the ENM" was widely debated in the press at the time, a satisfactory solution had not yet been found, according to Ridenti. The biggest difficulty lay in the time factor, because planning the fashion in a film several months in advance of its release was a challenge, meaning it was therefore necessary to establish collaborative relationships between producers, directors and dressmakers so that the stars never wore everyday clothes and thus anticipated fashion. The stimulus to create new models for the era in which the film was set, wrote Ridenti, should come from the actresses themselves, otherwise, the film would remain distant from fashion, unlike in other countries where similar relationships had been in place for some time and where entire films dedicated to it, such as William A. Seiter's 1935 *Roberta*, could be seen.

4.2 *Desiring Fascism: The Garment as Spectacle*

Giovannetti also opined on the fashions of the Venice Film Festival of 1941. The fashions he discussed were the ones exhibited in Swiss and German films which, according to him, celebrated "the joy of soaring," a passion for the figure skating of which Mussolini was an ardent fan.[26] Popular films could and should also inspire fashion, Giovannetti argued. *I promessi sposi* (*The Betrothed*, Mario Camerini, 1941) was described as a "costume party" where Gino Sensani's "magnificent and picturesque" costumes should inspire Italian fashion designers: the "Brianza-style" look of Lucia's face, hair and headdress, the evening dress "of exquisite simplicity,"[27] the "vivid" originality of the folkloric motif of the halo crown, or the modest green hairnets worn by the girls.

---

25 Ivi.
26 Freddi, L., *Il cinema, L'arnia*, Roma 1949, cit. in Faldini, F., Fofi, G., *L'avventurosa storia del cinema italiano 1935-1959*, Feltrinelli, Milan 1979, pp. 22-23.
27 Giovannetti, E., "I Promessi sposi come festa del costume," *Bellezza*, n. 11, 1941, pp. 69-71, p. 69.

Unlike Ridenti, Nicola Benois – the main set designer of the Scala theatre – thought that the real problem lay in the fact that the Italian fashion plate was an end in itself, a mere expression of the artist's sentiment, imbued with intolerable bourgeois romanticism. For Benois, the real task of the illustrator was to enhance women both in theatre and in life. But what did Benois mean by "enhancing women"? Apparently, that the fashion illustrator should aim to eliminate any dissonance in order to achieve a level of elegance that would favour harmony between the spirit of the character and the person of the diva, in order to achieve

> integrated and perfect visions of beauty. Costume, dance and aspiration to the incorporeal. Agile figures freed from physical function, the costume helping the linear momentum, transforming them into figurative abstractions resulting from the participating arts, not from individual fantasy."[28]

Other articles in *Bellezza* turned the fashion spotlight onto the *rivista* show, interesting documents of an ephemeral genre of which much has been lost. For fashion houses, collaborations with theatre and cinema were also a way to survive the shortages of war, as well as an effective propaganda tool. For a new *rivista* by Michele Galdieri, Biki had created a turquoise and coral pink crepe dress with a draped skirt for the "Quadro dei coralli" ("Corals' Sketch"), while for the painting "La vetrina" ("The Shop Window's Sketch") she had sewn a black China crepe dress with emerald green sequinned panels and a large white Moroccan crepe dress with a bustier of metal, gold and green stones. In the article *I tre volti di Rosetta Tofano* ("The three faces of Rosetta Tofano") there was a sympathetic portrait of costume designer and film star Rosetta Tofano in the role of Pasqualina in Sergio Tofano's film *Cenerentola e il signor Bonaventura* (*Princess Cinderella*, 1942), the first Italian film to be based on the highly successful comic strip *Signor Bonaventura*. The author argued that the theatre, "consisting in its essence and in its exterior, as

---

28 Benois, N., "Attualità del costume teatrale," *Bellezza*, n. 12, 1941, pp. 60-61, 93-94, p. 94.

a representation, of constant change,"[29] was the ideal place for unveiling new fashion. Given that the phrase risked making the shows' main role sound like that of a launchpad for clothes, to avoid any ambiguity Corsi pointed out that he had not intended to say

> that it is the theatre that creates fashion and that the stage can be considered the forge from which the imaginative prodigies of eternally new styles of women's and men's clothes spring. Not that. Fashion is a genuine phenomenon, social in its purpose and artistic in its origin, which Taine rightly considers as forming in the moral atmosphere of an era and determined by race, climate and historical moment, with its practical, moral and aesthetic needs.[30]

It must be recognized however that the theatre, in particular the prose theatre, played an important role in the "devouring life of fashion," meaning that it could be its best and most eye-catching showcase. From this perspective, the actors

> end up becoming, more than any other social category, the promoters of the new styles of dress and contribute to imparting to fashion a given physiognomy, short or long lasting, of greater or lesser influence outside the scene, and therefore collaborate effectively in the expression and to the classification of collective taste and mentality.[31]

In the Italian theatre, Rosetta Tofano was considered one of the actresses who had the "gift" and the "privilege" of being a symbol and populariser of fashion. Described as a creature of "immense shyness" out of the limelight, she embodied the personalities of an actress, painter and creator of feminine fashions. Following her marriage to Sergio Tofano, said the author, Rosetta "spent her days alone, at home" and in order not to make it seem as if she were bored to death, she began drawing caricatures of her husband before moving on to drawing fashion sketches. Tofano's slender figures were extremely graceful and vivid, and the author considered her a profoundly modern illustrator because

---

29   Corsi, M., "I tre volti di Rosetta Tofano," *Bellezza*, n. 13, 1942, pp. 44-47, p. 44.
30   Ivi.
31   Ivi.

she knows how to make clothes that render the quality and diversity of the subject with a felicitous touch and with palatable sobriety of colours. She knows how to combine the sharpness and elegance of the drawing and the novelty of the ornament and the harmony and general sympathy of colour with a remarkable study of expression and concept. She does not follow fashion: she creates it."[32]

The article included some of her sketches for nineteenth-century looks for the actress Giuditta Rissone and for herself in Richard B. Sheridan's *La scuola della maldicenza* (*The School for Scandal*) which highlight the illustration of the actress, who was a skilled creator of her own theatrical looks. On the opposite page, the photo of actress Andreina Pagnani in *Fedora*, wearing a Belle Époque dress by Fercioni in ivory satin and "Barolo-coloured" velvet ribbons designed by set- and costume-designer Veniero Colasanti, stands out. In the same issue, *La sensazione cinematografica* column promoted the simple taste of a Joan Fontaine dress in the film *Rebecca* (Alfred Hitchcock, 1940); its simplicity highlighted by the contrast with the "vulgar" evening fashions of the film, "not surprisingly" inspired by an American fashion magazine: "A bad joke that *Bellezza*, with its living models and far from overly Olympian abstractions, will never play on you."[33] A dress which was considered "unforgettable" was the one worn by Clara Calamai – "who must be seen in evening dresses or in costume" – in the film *L'avventuriera del piano di sopra* (*The Adventuress from the Floor Above*, Raffaello Matarazzo, 1941),[34] while the author pointed milliners to the bizarre top hat worn with a large silver buckle in the centre by Assia Noris in the film *Un colpo di pistola* (*A Pistol Shot*, R. Castellani, 1942) as a "novelty" they should promote (fig. 29). For sports fashion, Mariella Lotti in *Disturbance* (Guido Brignone, 1942) was mentioned as a happy inspiration for spring collections.

---

32   Ivi, p. 47.
33   Giovannetti, E., "La sensazione cinematografica," *Bellezza*, n. 13, 1942, p. 74.
34   Ivi.

Since its foundation, the ENM had set itself the problem of creating collaborative relationships – "for mutual benefit" – between the fashion industry and the film industry, because "what better 'showcase' exists and is exposed to attention of the masses than the cinema"?[35]. The silver screen attracted a mass audience, without distinction of social class, upon which it imposed itself with the full force of its expressive means – including fashion – which, especially in comedies with bourgeois settings, aroused the greatest interest in the public. According to the anonymous author of the article, it was thanks to the war "that Italian fashion has imposed itself on all European markets" and the time for a closer collaboration between ENM and cinema was now ripe:

> With a reasoned spirit of foresight, even in the current wartime years, this industry of ours has persevered in its efforts while remaining perfectly faithful to the moral and material restraints imposed by the situation.[36]

The anonymous author was very clear-eyed about the connection between cinema, fashion and commercial culture that Hollywood had managed to forge and which Italy would have to imitate if it wanted to impose its own fashion on the scene. But at this juncture an artistic and industrial problem arose, because film costumes were not everyday clothes and film producers must take into account the needs of a genre of clothing destined to be seen in an industrial, artistic and spectacular setting. In fact, even in films with realistic settings, the costumes must be 'spectacular' in their own way, reconciling the need to represent everyday clothing with the needs of film costume, subjecting it to an aesthetic transformation that reinforced its expressiveness and character. This was a problem that Hollywood had solved with the specialised work of the costume designer, after various attempts to import French couturiers, including Coco Chanel, to Los Angeles had met with failure. In Italy

---

35   C.M., "Moda e cinema," *Bellezza*, n. 24, 1942, p. 32, 70, p. 32. The article makes reference to a plan of action of the ENM which was approved by the General Directorate of Cinema.
36   Ivi, p. 32.

> It is therefore necessary to create a new relationship between artists and specialized technicians, [...] and our best fashion creators, or, rather, those few, among our best, who are truly able to "feel" the dress not only as a supervised product of taste, but even as a creation of art.[37]

As the official voice of the ENM, *Bellezza* hosted several illustrations for "spectacular" dresses by Brunetta and Pallavicini which wittily evoked the divas Alida Valli, Clara Calamai and Doris Duranti (fig. 30).[38] The idea behind the editorial was that women's public life was like a "huge and permanent" beauty contest, where the participants cultivated their physical appearance to facilitate mutual selection in social relationships or to create a desired illusion. Add to this that everyone was aiming to physically express "the intimate characteristics of their nature and we arrive at the "person as material for the spectacle,"[39] so that every woman can be called an actress in a society that is no longer "naïve." On the silver screen, the body is transfigured into dress and face, and while the face acts as a "mask," the dress becomes an essential tool for creating the setting and the atmosphere. When there is an actress in the place of the everyday woman, the problem of spectacularization becomes complicated because, in the manner of Pirandello, the actress is all that she can and must be. And in this case, the garment as spectacle – of which the drawings of the Brunetta and Pallavicini designs of three women, three actresses, three types, three "shows," are emblematic – triumphs. For Marinucci, Alida Valli's spectacle consisted of a series of aesthetic contrasts: worldliness versus dramatic thoughtfulness, her modernity arising precisely from this tension. Nobody knew how to dress Alida Valli because the essence of her spectacle was the actress herself. On the other hand, Duranti and Calamai were "all spectacle." Clara Calamai was the diva-mannequin – a fashion icon par excellence. Dressing her was a "joyful and exciting" task, even if Giovannetti thought Calamai lacked the

---

37   Ivi.
38   Marinucci, V., "L'abito come spettacolo," *Bellezza*, n. 27, 1943, pp. 62-63.
39   Ivi, p. 63.

physical line that "magnetizes a dress" because her body stank of its bourgeois interior. Marinucci instead would have liked to have seen her the prisoner of her charm while she tried to demean and trample it, as had already been the case in *Ossessione*. Clara Calamai was considered to be the perfect actress for displaying the spectacle of Italian fashion on the silver screen, because she was perfectly capable of holding her own against the absurdity of over-the-top costumes. But unfortunately, the author complained, the maximum flamboyance was reserved for Doris Duranti. Film fashion, promoted through the styles of the stars and the "elegant" wardrobes of the actresses, testified to the regime's intention to exploit cinema and its female stars as a propaganda tool for eclectic ideals of beauty accessible to a mass audience.

From 1943, *Bellezza* would deal increasingly with fashion, cinema and theatre – all in the service of wartime propaganda – with examples of spectacular fashions. Among these, the typical wardrobe of "elegant actress" Diana Torrieri, whose style "always reveals itself to be coherent with the character, both in the costumes and in the stage clothes,"[40] even if for her personal wardrobe she "prefers simplicity of line and the refinement of details," according to the guidelines of ENM. The actress was photographed in the costumes for Céchov's *Uncle Vania*, made by Piera Filippini, one in "yellow muslin with a velvet belt and knot" and another in "white with lace trimmings and black velvet ribbons," in various Alma day-dresses and in several evening dresses worn with Schettini furs. In the editorial, stage clothes were treated as being on the same level as everyday clothes, part of an ideal wardrobe where the elegance of the actress adhered to the character, on and off the screen, thus cancelling the distinction between dressing for the stage and dressing for everyday life, between actress and role. The stage clothes were offered as part of a "real" and credible wardrobe, for example in the case of actress Lia Zoppelli who "brought on the scene" a sumptuous Schettini sable cloak over a black evening dress by Fercioni. The

---

40 "Eleganze delle attrici," *Bellezza*, n. 44, 1944, pp. 46-49, p. 46.

emphasis was placed on the "type" and the "line" of the actress, so the clothes she wore must always be "in character" in order to achieve a harmonious effect: an interpretation of Rovescalli's black pony coat was "in character" with the 'type' of Lina Bacci. And finally, there was actress "Wanda Osiri," who bestowed upon the *rivista* "greater dignity, made up not only of skill but of taste and elegance."[41] Bevilacqua's comedy *Monica* also featured some of Lionella's haute couture models with evocative names: the *Questa sera si recita* ("Tonight We Act") dress, a sapphire velvet jacket with flared basque and silver frogs with an amphora draped skirt of gray silk knit; and *Pavone azzurro* ("Blue Peacock"), in black crepe with a deep V-neckline, a rigid basque, set far from the hips and held in place by ruby velvet knots. To these was added a laminated gold dressing gown designed by the actress Sara Ferrati for Gabriele D'annunzio's *La Gioconda*. In Vazsari's *Ho sposato un angelo* ("I Married an Angel"), Sara Ferrati, with a covered head, wore two evening dresses by Fercioni, one of which was distinguished by panels that began from the hem of the dress to form a single scarf to be worn over the garment.[42] Elsewhere, actress Fanni Marchiò modelled the costumes she had designed for the comedy *La regina di Biarritz*[43] (The Queen of Biarritz), "having above all a personal concept of stage elegance in relation to the various comedies, by age and environment, she suggests her ideas and indicates the plans."[44] Also for theatre, the actress Margherita Carosio had a stage dress made with jewels by Alda, both dress and jewellery based on designs by fashion illustrator Edina Altara. An awareness of the need to outline a serial, individual image for theatrical and cinematographic actresses through the arts of appearance took shape, a task entrusted, strangely, not so much to the producer or costume designer as to the actresses themselves, in line with an older Hollywood practice.

---

41 Ivi, p. 49.
42 "Questa sera si recita," *Bellezza*, n. 48, 1945, pp. 22-24, p. 23.
43 Ivi, p. 24.
44 Ivi, p. 24.

In light of the above, Stephen Gundle's statement that "the fascist regime did not actively promote private consumption since it preferred public investment in industry and infrastructure"[45] seems questionable. Gundle shares Gaudenzi's point of view – centred around the figure of Mussolini – according to which "hostility to consumption was never translated into outright repression since 'Mussolini entertained fundamental connections [...] with Italian big business and the middle classes, which strove for that same 'comfortable life.'"[46] In his work on fascist stardom, Gundle undertakes to look at Italian cinema during fascism as one of those areas of cultural production in which the regime's aims of control were either defeated or struggling against the interests of private, commercial players; a position that contrasts particularly with what Emilio Gentile has asserted on the pervasiveness of fascism as a political religion.[47] The fascist regime never wished to oppose or repress commercial culture per se – quite the opposite, in fact. Rather, it was frantically involved in the metamorphosis of pluralistic private consumption into a pervasive consumption of the fascist state, trying to turn private desires into a desire for the regime through the fabrications of attractive modern images and bodies. The fascists understood that costume and set design – the *fabric* of film – must also "act" on set and that their "acting" qualities could not only boost fascism's success in an international economy but also help to define a modern Italian identity. The eclecticism of fascism's stance on film style – and fashion – is perhaps the reason why scholars and media have so far failed to grasp what exactly defines the aesthetic essence of the so called "Italian look". According to Valerie Steele

> Italian style occupies a special place in the international fashion system. Yet the precise nature of the Italian contribution to international style remains elusive. Is it simply that Italian craftsmanship is superior?

---

45 Gundle, S., *Mussolini's Dream Factory. Film Stardom in Fascist Italy*, Berghan, New York & Oxford 2013, p. 67.
46 Ivi.
47 Gentile, E., *Il culto del littorio. La sacralizzazione della politica nell'Italia fascista*, Laterza, Bari 2003.

Is there something unique about Italian culture with which people around the world want to identify? Is it that the Italian Look of easy elegance has become the quintessential modern style?[48]

It is striking how similar the adjectives generally used to describe Italian fashion are to those that shaped *Bellezza*'s multifaceted vision of what fashion should be. Giannino Malossi for example writes that for Italians, "Italy is the country of elegance" or, as Steele convincingly suggests, it has "perhaps, a special feeling for elegance and sensuality."[49] In contrast to these essentialist views, it should be stressed that during the *Ventennio* – the twenty years in which fascism was in power – the "birth" of Italian fashion as an embodiment of the state's "will to power" always took place under the guiding light of the radical politicisation of fashion.

In addition to a peculiar attitude towards fashion, an analysis of *Bellezza* during wartime reveals not only evidence of the existence of "commercial motivations" in Italian fascist cinema – the opulent mood of the "white telephone" comedies, the fabulous historical styles to be copied –, but also that the "commercial motivations" cannot be separated from the "political motivations." While fashion and film magazines and credits give us some evidence of more or less successful product placement and tie-in experiments,[50] unfortunately – as Gundle has pointed out – the study of fascist cinema has often ignored the contribution of extra-textual factors.[51]

Ignorance of extra-textual factors and an ideological approach have meant that the so-called "white telephone" films are a neglected chapter in the history of Italian cinema. Their breezy and, for some, essentially apolitical character has been negatively compared to the rawness and commitment of the neorealist style that followed the collapse of the fascist regime in Italy; but the

---

48 Steele, V., *Fashion, Italian Style*, Yale University Press, New Haven & London 2003, p. 2.
49 Ivi.
50 The use of mannequins from the Rosa di Milano company in the film *I grandi magazzini* (Mario Camerini, 1939) for example.
51 Gundle, S., *op. cit.*, p. 72.

escapist fantasies of these films, however far removed from the realities of wartime, shed light on the fact that Italian culture was not as insular, provincial and backwards as might be imagined. Their modernist fashions and sets reveal that even in the darkest days of fascism, workers in the film and fashion industry were fully aware of and drew inspiration from European aesthetics, the Bauhaus and the International Style.

Set designers such as Gastone Medin were keen to present the kind of modern and glamorous image of Italian society we more usually associate with the 1960s. If we look at extra-textual sources, for example, we see how in October 1931 *Casabella* dedicated fourteen pages to the film *Patatrac* (Gennaro Righelli, 1931), commenting that the work of Levi and Paolucci was both cinematographic and interior design, and describing it as a lesson in how to create domestic environments. According to *Casabella*, the importance of this work in the development of Italian cinema was fundamental because it represented the first time that a modern vocabulary had been applied to set design. A month later *Domus* published a two-page article on the film, contrasting the photos of the fictional restaurant and jewellery with the "bad taste" house full of fake antiques and kitschy decor.[52] While according to Gundle "there is little evidence of explicit product placement" in 1930s Italian movies while their "feel of opulence was informed by modernist interiors and furniture of elite design magazines like *Casabella* and *Domus*,"[53] it must be stressed that the relationship between film and architecture was not a one-way street from elite magazines to cinema since, as *Casabella* pointed out, Giuseppe Capponi's film architecture for *La voce lontana* (Guido Brignone, 1933) could easily be translated into real interiors: "While old cinema required a pure set designer, we require a pure architect."[54] Furthermore, a number of professional architects, including Giuseppe Capponi and Guido Fiorini,

---

52 "Arredamento di un film," *Casabella*, October 1931, p. 22-36; "Cinema e ambiente moderno," *Domus*, November 1931, pp. 70-71.
53 Gundle, S., *op. cit.* p. 71.
54 Giovannetti, E., "Architettura cinematografica: G. Capponi per *La voce lontana*," *Casabella*, February 1933, p. 41.

worked in Italian cinema also because it allowed them greater freedom of expression and the possibility of experimenting with new ideas. It is perhaps no coincidence that the opening credits of *I grandi magazzini* (Mario Camerini, 1939) chose to use the expressions "architecture" and "clothing" instead of "scenery design" and "costumes."

Unlike cinema historian Brunetta, according to whom the comedies pushed Italians in a direction incompatible with fascism,[55] many scholars – in particular scholars of Nazi cinema – have embraced what Gundle, using a sartorial metaphor, calls the "fold-back hypothesis."[56] In his discussion of *I grandi magazzini*, James Hay states that the film promotes the fascist ideology of corporatism,[57] according to which, films of this genre did not clash with the dominant system of values but rather presented a spectacle of consumption that captured the wishes of the public and folded them back into the fascist project. Some cinematic objects – cars, fashion, furnishings, advertising signs – symbolised totalitarian modernity, but at the same time, luxury consumers were reviled as criminals, a moral condemnation consistent with the anti-luxury campaigns undertaken during the war.

While we will not delve into the business history of the connection between Cinecittà and Italian cultures of consumption in this book, what emerges very clearly from my research is an interpretation of Italian cinema from at the latest the second half of the 1930s as a showcase of autarkic fashion, i.e. as something to be leafed through like a fashion magazine:

> A magnificent dressing gown, a beautiful evening dress, a gracious and original sports outfit, worn with verve and grace, can lift the tone of an entire scene and complete it; fine underwear, particular touches, that elevate and perfect the overall effect of an outfit have the effect of making an artist more attractive and appealing to the audience. Even in the most modest films, the female wardrobe must always be considered with every

---

55 Brunetta, G., *Buio in sala*, Marsilio, Venice 2001.
56 Gundle, S., *op. cit.*, p. 72.
57 Hay, J., *Popular Film Culture in Fascist Italy: The Passing of the Rex*, Indiana UP, Bloomington 1987.

care and always be perfectly in tune with the context and the personality of the artist.[58]

Inelegance must be avoided: "Certain absurd little hats, certain banal frills, certain operetta eccentricities that give the impression of poverty, neglect."[59] Cinema was considered an effective means of promoting Italian products, textiles and values, as was evident from magazines such as *Lo schermo*, where a certain 'Marta' wrote that film actresses were referees of elegance capable of revitalising the Italian fashion industry. For this purpose, the Istituto Luce organised the production of fashion films to be screened in cinemas. *Lo schermo* had a regular feature entitled *Il cinema e la moda* that explored various aspects of their collaboration, and even in the midst of the war, the ENM commissioned a lavishly illustrated volume entitled *Moda e cinema*.[60] The first costume designers to ensure artistic quality in Italian cinema were Nino Novarese and Gino Sensani, founder of the costume chair at the Centro Sperimentale di Cinematografia and initiator of the so-called "Italian school" of costume design.

Certainly, the Italian film industry and Italian commercial culture in general looked rather backward when compared to Hollywood, and calls for cinematic elegance were often ignored, but from the second half of the Thirties the first fashion tie-ins began to appear – the racist *Harlem*'s (Carmine Gallone, 1943) female wardrobe was created by Noberasko, whose name appeared in huge letters in the opening titles[61] – together with attempts by dressmakers to forge links with Italian celebrities who were aiming to build a public image of themselves through

---

58 Roffi, "La moda per le attrici cinematografiche italiane," *Lo schermo*, Dicembre 1938, p. 41, in Gundle, S., *op. cit.*, p. 77.
59 Ivi.
60 "Moda e cinema," *Documento Moda*, n. 3, 1943.
61 I had a one-of-a-kind opportunity to watch *Harlem* in the context of the seminar *Il fascismo. Un ventennio di immagini*, organized by Fondazione Archivio Audiovisivo del Movimento Operaio at Casa del cinema in Rome, in November 2022, where it was projected for the first time in its full and uncensored version.

fashion: Madame Anna for Edda Ciano, or Gori for Marisa Merlini. But it was with Luchino Visconti's *Ossessione* that the carnal body and eroticism burst into Italian cinema – in part thanks to the vampish glamour of Clara Calamai – and determined its condemnation, even before it was distributed in theatres:

> A film completely lacking in depth. The director has mistaken a morbid story and a crowd of details for the construction of a setting, which has instead remained only an intention. The protagonist's legs, the protagonist's dirty slip, the bed where two men sleep, the series of urinals, and crime and death, fail to give a sense of morbidness but only a sense of stink.[62]

The new focus on film fashion may have been linked to the feminisation of public space and film audiences during the war, but it was nevertheless consistent with the regime's totalitarian politics. The question "Will all women wear lace collars because Isa Miranda wore one in *Malombra*?"[63] (as Vivi Gioi in *Harlem*) that *Cinema* magazine asked itself in 1942 was relevant not only from a commercial point of view but also and above all from a political perspective. In fact, if *Bellezza* enjoyed the attentions of an elite audience, cinema could reach and seduce a mass audience, both urban and rural. The problem of how and with what production and aesthetic means to seduce it was the subject of heated debates that took place in the pages of the most relevant magazines but above all in the editorial offices, in the corridors of Cinecittà studios and in the city prefectures, at the cost of prison and exile. Considerations that deserve to be explored and which open up exciting new fields of research.

---

62 *Si gira*, June 1943, p. 1.
63 Gundle, S., *op. cit.*, p. 78.

REFERENCES

«Anticipazioni sulle nuove fogge dei cappelli invernali delle signore», *La Stampa*, 9 September 1940, p. 2.
"Arredamento di un film," *Casabella*, October 1931, p. 22-36.
«Blockade Injustice Disputed by France», *New York Times*, 13 May 1940, p. 4.
"Cinema e ambiente moderno," *Domus,* November 1931, pp. 70-71.
«Colori nuovi e sfumature inedite», *Stampa Sera*, 7 December 1940, p. 2.
«Convegni d'eccezione al Palazzo della moda», *Torino. Rassegna della città*, n. 2, February 1941, p. 45-50.
«Dalle manifestazioni del "centro" di Torino si irradierà un'azione tesa al raggiungimento dell'autarchia», *La Stampa*, 27 November 1937, p. 4.
Documento Moda, n. 1, ENM, Torino 1941.
Documento Moda, n. 2, ENM, Torino 1942.
Documento Moda, n. 3, ENM, Torino 1943.
«È pronta la valigia per sfollare», *Bellezza*, n. 25-26, January-February 1943, pp. 8-9.
«Edda Ciano Remarried to Wealthy Florentine», *New York Times*, 4 December 1944, p. 8.
«Educare l'occhio», *Bellezza*, n. 3, March 1941, p. 32.
"Eleganze delle attrici," *Bellezza*, n. 44, 1944, pp. 46-49.
«Esempi di produzione italiana», *Domus*, n. 148, April 1940, p. 92.
«February Fashions», *Picture Post*, 3 February 1940, pp. 44-5.
«Gli aumenti sui prodotti negli ultimi quattro mesi», *La Stampa*, 13 January 1940, p. 5.
«Gli ebrei nell'industria», *Il Corriere della Sera*, 6 September 1938, in Melograni, P., (edited by), *Corriere della Sera 1919-1943*, Cappelli Editore, Bologna 1965.
«Goering's Wife got Final Paris Outfits», *New York Times*, 1 September 1944, p. 10.
«Guerra e moda», *Rassegna dell'Ente nazionale della moda*, 15-31 October 1939.
«I littoriali femminili. Gusti e tendenze nell'arte, nelle lettere, nella moda», *La Stampa*, 15 April 1940, p. 2.
«Il Salone permanente della moda», *La Stampa*, 19 June 1932, p. 6.
«Il Segretario del partito presiede la Consulta centrale dei Fasci femminili», *La donna fascista*, n. 5, 30 December 1941, p. 2.

«Il tatto e la vera eleganza», *Bellezza*, n. 3, March 1941, pp. 40-1.
«Il testo del disegno di legge con la relazione del Duce», *Stampa Sera*, 26-27 November 1932, p. 1.
«Illecito traffico di un negoziante», *La Stampa*, 14 March 1942, p. 2.
«In un laboratorio di creature finte...», *Stampa Sera*, 28 May 1940, p. 4.
"Interpretazioni eleganti per il teatro," *Bellezza*, n. 2, 1941, pp. 46-47.
«Italy Aids Women to Keep Looks while Nazis Impose Dowdiness», *The New York Times*, 3 June 1942, p. 19.
«L'alta moda italiana nel quadro della nuova disciplina valorizzatrice: la "Marca d'oro"», *Rassegna dell'Ente nazionale della moda*, 20 June 1941, pp. 22-25.
«L'Ente della moda avrà più vasti compiti», *La Stampa*, 18 May 1935, p. 7.
«L'organizzazione del Salone della moda», *La Stampa*, 15 October 1932, p. 7.
«La delegazione germanica alle nostre case di moda», *La Stampa*, 5 February 1941, p. 5.
«La nostra guerra», *La donna fascista*, n. 1, 30 October 1941, p. 3.
«La nuova linea primavera estate», *Bellezza*, n. 15, March 1942, p. 5.
«Le modiste all'Ente della moda», *Torino. Rassegna mensile della città*, n. 10, October 1940, pp. 61-2.
«Maria di Piemonte presidente onoraria dei comitati dell'Ente Moda», *La Stampa*, 20 February 1940, p. 6.
«Mirabile varietà di prodotti», *Stampa Sera*, 10 May 1940, p. 2.
«Mode in der Zeitenwende», *Die Mode*, n. 1, 1941, p. 19.
«Nel mondo degli incantesimi per la bellezza delle signore», *Stampa Sera*, 12 February 1940, p. 2.
«Nuove linee della moda estiva», *Torino. Rassegna mensile della città*, n. 8, March 1941, p. 60.
«Oggi si inaugura il Centro», *La Stampa*, 11 May 1940, p. 5.
«Ombrelli», *Bellezza*, n. 33-34, September-October 1943, p. 37.
«On Fashion and Power», *Vestoj*, n. 4, autunno 2013.
«Orientamenti della moda», *Torino. Rassegna mensile della città*, n. 12, December 1940, pp. 46-8.
«Precisazioni per la vendita dei prodotti di abbigliamento», *La Stampa*, 10 November 1941, p. 5.
«Prepariamoci ad affrontare l'inverno», *La Famiglia Rinascente-Upim*, July-September 1942, p. 17-20.
"Punti fermi," *Si gira*, n. 15, June 1943, p. 1.
"Questa sera si recita," *Bellezza*, n. 48, 1945, pp. 22-24.
«Rassegna della stampa riguardante la vita femminile», *La donna fascista*, n. 1, 30 November 1941, p. 12.
«Risorse della moda secondo la disciplina dell'abbigliamento», *Bellezza*, n. 11, November 1941, p. 3.
«Risorse della moda», *Bellezza*, n. 11, November 1941, pp. 3-5.
«Sete stampate», *Bellezza*, n. 17, May 1942, pp. 39-41.
«Si crea nella disciplina una nuova mentalità», *La Stampa*, 15 February 1940, p. 5.
«Spettacoloso successo della festa mascherata al Teatro Carignano», *La Stampa*, 3 February 1940, p. 5.

«Tessuti di alta moda e possibilità di produzione autarchica», *Torino. Rassegna mensile della città*, n. 3, March 1941, pp. 55-9.
«Ultime notizie», *La Stampa*, 23 March 1942, p. 4.
«US urged as World Fashion Hub; Experts Say It Can Replace Paris», *New York Times*, 12 July 1940, p. 17.
1873-1903. Primo trentennio della Società Ceramica Richard Ginori, Stab. E. Bonetti, Milano 1903.
Adams, M., «Westward the Course of Fashion», *New York Times*, 19 January 1940, p. 12.
Adamson, W. L., «Fascism and Culture: Avant-Gardes and Secular Religion in the Italian Case», *Journal of Contemporary History*, 24, n. 3, July 1989, pp. 411-435.
Addis Saba, M., *La corporazione delle donne. Ricerche e studi sui modelli femminili nel ventennio fascista*, Vallecchi, Firenze 1988.
Ady, P., «Utility Goods», *Bullettin*, IV, n. 15, 31 October 1942, p. 359.
Agamben, G., *Che cos'è il contemporaneo?*, Nottetempo, Milano 2008.
Aglan, A., Frank, R., (edited by), *La guerra-mondo 1937-1947*, Einaudi, Torino 2018.
Airoldi, A., «Verso un mondo nuovo», *Critica fascista*, n. 1, 1 November 1939, pp. 4-6.
Alberti, M., *Senza lavoro: la disoccupazione in Italia dall'Unità a oggi*, Laterza, Roma-Bari 2016.
Alessandri, G. G., «Orientamento per le giovani lavoratrici. La dattilografia», *La donna fascista*, n. 10, 21 April 1940, p. 5.
Alfieri, G., «'Fare le italiane'. Il romanzo come testo modellizzante tra Otto e Novecento», *The Italianist*, 38, n. 3, pp. 384-401.
Alimenti, C., (edited by, for PNF's Ufficio propaganda), *Guerra allo spreco*, S. A. poligrafici Il Resto del Carlino, Bologna 1941.
Alpers, S., *Arte del descrivere: scienza e pittura nel Seicento olandese*, Bollati Boringhieri, Torino 1999.
Aragno, B. G., (edited by), *Il disegno dell'alta moda italiana, 1940-1970*, De Luca, Roma 1982.
Argentieri, M., *L'occhio del regime. Informazione e propaganda nel cinema del fascismo*, Vallecchi, Firenze 1979.
Argnani, L. M., «Il laboratorio 9 May (Federazione dei Fasci femminili dell'Urbe)», *La donna fascista*, n. 3, 30 November 1941, p. 5.
Arital (Gio Ponti), «La foggia italiana», *Aria d'Italia*, n. 3, estate 1940, pp. 59-60.
- «Moda», *Aria d'Italia*, n. 4, Autumn 1940, p. 74.
Arnaldi, E., «Minuscoli piedini in scarpe mastodontiche», *Stampa Sera*, 22 February 1940, p. 2.
- «Accettiamo le gonne corte ma non le tasche da canguro», *Stampa Sera*, 30 March 1940, p. 2.
Arnold, R., *The American Look. Fashion, Sportswear and the Image of Women in 1930s and 1940s New York*, I. B. Tauris, London-New York 2009.
- «Fashion in Ruins: Photography, Luxury and Dereliction in 1940s London», *Fashion Theory*, 21, n. 4, 2016, pp. 341-363.

Arrigoni, A. L., *Atti del 1. Convegno Nazionale di studi autarchici*, Milano 1939.
Artom, E., *Diari. Gennaio 1940-febbraio 1944*, Centro di documentazione ebraica contemporanea, Milano 1966.
Ash, J., Wilson, E., (edited by), *Cheap Thrills*, University of California Press, Berkley 1993.
Aspesi, N., Ricci, S., (edited by), *Lusso & autarchia 1935-1945: Salvatore Ferragamo e gli altri calzolai italiani*, Sillabe, Livorno 2005.
Associazione Italiana Industriali Abbigliamento, *Guida della confezione*, Aurelio Canevari Editore, Milano 1961.
Baker, D., «The Political Economy of Fascism: Myth *or* Reality, or Myth *and* Reality?», *New Political Economy*, 11, n. 2, 2006, pp. 227-250.
Baldini, A., *Beato fra le donne*, Mondadori, Milano 1940.
Ballario, P., «Clima duro», *La donna fascista*, n. 1, 30 October 1941, p. 5.
Balli, A., *La mostra del tessile nazionale*, Cesari, Ascoli Piceno 1937.
Banca d'Italia, *Fine dell'autarchia e miracolo economico 1946-1959*, Janus, Roma 1960.
Bandini, F., *Claretta*, Longanesi & C., Milano 1969.
Barnard, M., (edited by), *Fashion Theory. A Reader*, Routledge, Oxon-New York 2007.
Barrella, N., Cioffi, R., (edited by), *La consistenza dell'effimero. Riviste d'arte tra Ottocento e Novecento*, Luciano Editore, Napoli 2013.
Barry Katz, M., «The Women of Futurism», *Woman's Art Journal*, 7, n. 2, 1987, pp. 3-13.
Barthes, R., *The Fashion System*, Hill & Wang, New York 1983.
Bartoloni, S., *Il fascismo e le donne nella «Rassegna femminile italiana» 1925-30*, Biblink, Roma 2012.
Bassignana, P. L., *Torino in guerra. La vita quotidiana dei torinesi al tempo delle bombe*, Edizioni del Capricorno, Torino 2013.
Baudot, F., *Elsa Schiaparelli*, Octavo, Firenze 1998.
Belfanti, C. M., *Civiltà della moda*, Il Mulino, Bologna 2008.
Belfanti, C. M., Giusberti, F. (edited by), *Storia d'Italia. Annali 19: La moda*, Einaudi, Torino 2003.
Belmonte, C., «La Sapienza, il fascismo, una mostra. Snodi critici nella ricezione dell'arte del Ventennio negli anni Ottanta», *Studi di Memofonte*, n. 24, Firenze 2020.
Ben-Ghiat, R., *La cultura fascista*, Il Mulino, Bologna 2000.
Benadusi, L., «Storia del fascismo e questioni di genere», *Studi Storici*, 55, n. 1, January-March 2014, pp. 183-196.
Benois, N., "Attualità del costume teatrale," *Bellezza*, n. 12, 1941, pp. 60-61.
Benzi, F., *Liberty e Decò: mezzo secolo di stile italiano (1890-1940)*, 24 Ore Cultura, Milano 2007.
- «Arte di Stato durante il regime fascista: una storia di fallimenti nel segno dei meccanismi del "consenso"», *Arti e culture visive*, 3, n. 1, 2019, pp. 162-185.
Berezin., M., *Making the Fascist Self: The Political Culture of Interwar Italy*, Cornell UP, Ithaca-New York 1997.
Berman, M., *L'esperienza della modernità*, Il Mulino, Bologna 1985.

Bernabò, M., *Ossessioni bizantine e cultura artistica in Italia. Tra D'Annunzio, fascismo e dopoguerra*, Liguori Editore, Napoli 2003.
Bertini, V., Foggi, F., (edited by), *Il pappagallo giallo. La pelle nella moda, nelle arti minori, nell'industrial design (1900-1940)*, Alinea, Firenze 1986.
Bianchino, G., Butazzi, G., Mottola Molfino, A., Carlo Quintavalle, A., (edited by), *La moda italiana. Le origini dell'alta moda e la maglieria*, I, Electa, Milan 1985.
Biddle-Perry, G., *Dressing for Austerity. Aspiration, Leisure and Fashion in Postwar Britain*, I.B. Tauris, London-New York 2017.
Bignami, S., *"Aria d'Italia" di Daria Guarnati. L'arte della rivista intorno al 1940*, Skira, Milano 2008.
Biribanti, P., *Boccasile: la Signorina Grandi Firme e altri mondi*, Castelvecchi, Roma 2009.
Blackman, K., *100 Years of Fashion Illustration*, Laurence King, London 2007.
Blignaut, H., *La scala di vetro. Il romanzo della vita di Biki*, Rusconi, Milano 1995.
Bloch, M., *Apologia della storia o mestiere di storico*, Einaudi, Torino 2009.
Boccalatte, L., Giovanni De Luna, G., Bruno Maida, B., (edited by), *Torino in guerra 1940-1945. Catalogo della mostra*, Gribaudo Editore, Torino 1995.
Bollati, G., *L'Italiano. Il carattere nazionale come storia e come invenzione*, Einaudi, Torino 2011.
Bollettino della moda: organo ufficiale di informazione dell'Istituto artistico nazionale per la moda italiana, Soc. an. poligrafica italiana, n. 1, Roma 1928.
Bonadonna, M. F., «Il Fascismo contro i francesismi della moda. Il *Commentario Dizionario* di Cesare Meano», *L'analisi linguistica e letteraria*, anno XXI, n. 2, Educatt, Milano 2014, pp. 191-206.
Boschi, A., *Moda e modestia*, Tip. G. Astesano, Chieri 1943.
Bossaglia, R., *Il giglio, l'iris, la rosa*, Sellerio, Palermo 1984.
Bossaglia, R., Crespi, A., (edited by), *L'ISIA a Monza: una scuola d'arte europea*, Associazione Pro Monza e Amilcare Pizzi Arti Grafiche, Cinisello Balsamo 1986.
Bosworth, Richard J. B., *Mussolini. Un dittatore italiano*, Mondadori, Milano 2004.
Bottai, G., «Stile», *Lo stile nella casa e nell'arredamento*, n. 1, January 1941, p. 9-10.
Bourdieu, P., «Haute culture et haute couture», in *Questions de Sociologie*, Editions de Minuit, Paris 1984.
- *Ragioni pratiche*, Il Mulino, Bologna 1995.
- *La distinzione. Critica sociale del gusto*, Il Mulino, Bologna 2001.
- *Un'arte media. Saggio sugli usi sociali della fotografia*, Meltemi, Milano 2018.
Bourdieu, P., Delsaut, Y., «Le couturier et sa griffe», *Actes de la recherche en sciences sociales*, 1, n. 1, 1975.
Branzi, A., *Introduzione al design italiano. Una modernità incompleta*,

Baldini&Castoldi, Milano 2015.
Braun, E., «Futurist Fashion: Three Manifestoes», *Art Journal*, 54, n. 1, Spring 1995, pp. 34-41.
- *Mario Sironi and Italian Modernism: Art and Politics under Fascism*, Cambridge UP, Cambridge 2000.
Bravo, A., «Donne e seconda guerra mondiale: esperienza, racconto», *Mezzosecolo. Materiali di ricerca storica*, n. 8, 1989.
- (edited by), *Donne e uomini nelle guerre mondiali*, Laterza, Roma-Bari 2008.
Bravo, A., Bruzzone A. M., *In guerra senza armi: storie di donne: 1940-1945*, Laterza, Roma-Bari 2000.
Bravo, A., Jalla, D., (edited by), *Una misura onesta. Gli scritti di memoria della deportazione dall'Italia*, Angeli, Milano 1994.
Braybon, G., Summerfield, P., *Out of the Cage. Women's Experiences in Two World Wars*, Pandora Press, Ontario 1987.
Brayley, M.J., Ingram, R., *WWII British Women Uniforms in Colour Photographs*, Windrow & Greene, London 1995.
Breward, C., *The Culture of Fashion*, Manchester UP, Manchester 1995.
- *Fashion*, Oxford UP, Oxford 2003.
Brin, I., *Usi e costumi 1920-1940*, Donatello De Luigi, Roma 1944.
- «Massima e minima», *Grazia*, n. 4, 1946, pp. 48-50.
- «Come nasce l'alta moda», *Bellezza*, n. 4, 1960, p. 31.
Brockett, L. P., *Woman's work in the Civil War: a record of heroism, patriotism and patience*, 1867.
Brodskij, I., *Fondamenta degli incurabili*, Adelphi, Milano 1991.
Broggini, R., *Terra d'asilo. I rifugiati italiani in Svizzera 1943-45*, Il Mulino, Bologna 1993.
Brunetta, *Il vizio del vestire*, Edizioni delle donne, Roma 1981.
Brunetta, Gian Piero, *Buio in sala: 100 anni di passione dello spettatore cinematografico*, Marsilio, Venezia 1989.
Bruno Guerri, G., *Fascisti. Gli italiani di Mussolini: il regime degli italiani*, Mondadori, Milano 1996.
Buchanan, A., «'Good Morning, Pupil!' American Representations of Italianness and the Occupation of Italy, 1943-1945», *Journal of Contemporary History*, 43, n. 2, pp. 217-240.
Burro o cannoni? Perché i grassi scarseggiano in tempo di guerra, Partito Nazionale Fascista, Ufficio Propaganda, 1940.
Butazzi, G., (edited by), *1922-1943. Vent'anni di moda italiana: proposta per un museo della moda a Milano*, Centro Di, Milano 1980.
- *Moda. Arte, Storia, Società*, Fabbri, Milano 1981.
- «Faschismus und mode», in *Anziehungskräfte: variété de la mode*, Hanser, Monaco 1987, pp. 132-4.
- «Moda, donne e guerra. La moda femminile nella guerra 1940-45», *Il Risorgimento*, n. 1, 1998.
Buzzati, D., *In quel preciso momento*, Mondadori, Milano 2006.
C.M., "Moda e cinema," *Bellezza*, n. 24, 1942, p. 32.

- «Presentazioni di modelli italiani all'estero», *Bellezza*, n. 19, July 1942, pp. 5-7.
Caccia, P., (edited by), *Editori a Milano (1940-1945): Repertorio*, FrancoAngeli, Milano 2013.
Calanca, D., *Storia sociale della moda contemporanea*, Bononia UP, Bologna 2014.
Calzini, R., «Bellezza immortale delle italiane», *Bellezza*, n. 1, January 1941, p. 11.
- (edited by), *La bella italiana: da Botticelli a Tiepolo*, supplemento a *Domus*, 84, December 1934.
Canali, M., Volpini, C., *Mussolini e i ladri di regime. Gli arricchimenti illeciti del regime*, Mondadori, Milano 2019.
Canella, M., Giuntini, S., (edited by), *Sport e fascismo*, Angeli, Milano 2009.
Cannistraro, P.V., *La fabbrica del consenso. Fascismo e mass-media*, Laterza, Roma-Bari 1975.
Capalbo, C., *Storia della moda a Roma. Sarti, culture e stili di una capitale dal 1871 a oggi*, Donzelli, Roma 2012.
Caponetti, G., *Il grande Gualino*, Utet, Milano 2018.
Caramazza, C., Nazzi, L., Macola, N., (edited by), *Citazioni, modelli e tipologie della produzione dell'opera d'arte*, Cleup, Padova 2011.
Carozzi, D., «L'arte decorativa dei tessuti stampati», *Bellezza*, n. 46, 15 October-15 November 1944, pp. 18-21.
Carrarini, R., Giordano, M., (edited by), *Bibliografia dei periodici femminili lombardi 1786-1945*, Editrice Bibliografica, Milano 1993.
Carreri, L., *L'autarchia nella produzione delle fibre tessili vegetali*, Stab. Grafico Fratelli Lega, Faenza 1939.
Carrieri, R., *Immagini di moda 1800-1900*, Domus, Milano 1940.
Casadei, M., *La donna nelle due guerre mondiali: la storia nascosta*, Il Ponte Vecchio, Cesena 2016.
Casati, A., Prezzolini, G., *Carteggio, II, 1911-1944*, Edizioni di Storia e Letteratura, Roma 1990.
Casetti, F., *L'occhio del Novecento. Cinema, esperienza, modernità*, Bompiani, Milano 2005.
Cassamagnaghi, S., *Quando lo zio Sam volle anche loro. Hollywood, le donne e la Seconda guerra mondiale*, Mimesis, Milano-Udine 2011.
Cassirer, E., *Il mito dello Stato*, Longanesi, Milano 1950.
Castiglione, B., *Il Libro del cortegiano*, Garzanti, Milano 1981.
Castiglioni, G., *Nell'Italia di allora*, Peppi Battaglini, Milano 1980.
Castronovo, V., (edited by), *Storia illustrata di Torino, XI. Società e costume*, Mondadori, Milano 1995.
Castronovo, V., Tranfaglia, N., (edited by), *Storia della stampa italiana*, IV, Laterza, Roma 1980.
Catalano, F., *L'economia italiana di guerra 1935-1943*, Istituto Nazionale per la Storia del Movimento di Liberazione, Milano 1969.
Cava, A., *Ineluttabile: moda e mode*, Vita e Pensiero, Milano 1943.
Cavallo, P., Del Bosco, P., Iaccio, P., Messina, R., (edited by), *La guerra*

immaginata. Teatro, canzone e fotografia (1940-1943), Liguori, Napoli 1989.
Cavazza, S., «La folkloristica italiana e il fascismo. Il Comitato per le Arti Popolari», *La ricerca folklorica*, n. 15, April 1987, pp. 109-122.
Cavazza S., Scarpellini E., (edited by), *Storia d'Italia, Annali 27: I consumi*, Einaudi, Torino 2018.
Celani, E., «La moda si muterà in costume?», *Bellezza*, n. 39, March 1944, pp. 43-44.
- «Ritorno alla femminilità», *Bellezza*, n. 1 (nuova serie), November 1945, p. 3.
Celant, G., (edited by), *The Italian Metamorphosis, 1943-1968*, Guggenheim Museums Publications, New York 1995.
Cerio, E., *Guida inutile di Capri*, La Conchiglia, Capri 1946.
Cerruti, E., *Visti da vicino. Memorie di un'ambasciatrice*, Garzanti, Milano 1951.
Cesarani, G. P., *Vetrina del ventennio 1923-1943*, Laterza, Roma-Bari 1981.
Cesari, M., *La censura nel periodo fascista*, Napoli, Liguori Editore, 1978.
Chang, N. V., *The Crisis-Woman: Body Politics and the Modern Woman in Fascist Italy*, University of Toronto Press, Toronto 2015.
Chevallard, C., *Diario 1942-1945. Cronache del tempo di guerra*, Blu edizioni, Torino 2005.
Chiarelli, C., (edited by), *Moda femminile tra le due guerre*, Sillabe, Firenze 2000.
Chiostrini Mannini, A., (edited by), *Il bello dell'utile: ceramiche Richard e Ginori dal 1750 al 1950*, Polistampa, Firenze 2001.
- *Le arti a Vienna: dalla Secessione alla caduta dell'Impero Asburgico*, Mazzotta, Milano 1984.
Ciano, E., *La mia vita. Intervista di Domenico Olivieri*, Mondadori, Milano 2001.
Ciano, G., *1937-1938 Diario*, Cappelli Editore, Bologna 1948.
- *Diario. Volume Primo 1941-1943*, Rizzoli, Milano-Roma 1946.
Cicogna, A., *Per l'autarchia: manuale del consumatore italiano*, Edizione di Saggi e Commenti, Roma 1938.
Coarelli, R., *Da "Bertoldo" a "Settebello". Donne e morale di regime: l'autarchia e la guerra*, La scuola, Brescia 2010.
Coarelli, R., Imperioso, A.M., *Giuseppa, Genoveffa e le altre: donne nell'occhio della satira durante gli anni del fascismo (1923-1944)*, Barbieri, Manduria 2008.
Cole, D.J., Deihl, N., *Storia della moda dal 1850 a oggi*, Einaudi, Torino 2016.
Condell, D., Liddiard, J., *Working for Victory?*, Rouledge & Kegan, London 1987.
Confederazione Generale Fascista dell'Industria Italiana, *L'industria italiana a metà del XX secolo*, Castaldi, Roma 1929.
Congresso Nazionale Abbigliamento e Autarchia: relazioni e riassunti di comunicazioni presentate (bozze di stampa), Ente nazionale della moda, Torino, 8-9 June 1940.

Conti, E., *Dal taccuino di un borghese*, Il Mulino, Bologna 1986.
Contorbia, F., (edited by), *Giornalismo italiano*, III, *1939-1968*, Mondadori, Milano 2009.
Corgnati, M., Majno, G., (edited by), *Mario Buccellati: storie di uomini e di gioielli*, Milano 1998.
Corsi, Mario, "I tre volti di Rosetta Tofano," *Bellezza*, n. 13, 1942, pp. 44-47.
Costa, D., *Corso di merceologia: con particolare riguardo alla produzione autarchica nazionale* (appunti presi alle lezioni del prof. Domenico Costa), La Grafolito, Bologna 1943.
Costantino, M., *Fashion of a decade. The 30s*, Chelsea House, London 1991.
Cowling, E., Jennifer Mundy, J., *On Classic Ground: Picasso, Léger, de Chirico and the New Classicism* 1910-1930, Tate Gallery, London 1990.
Crane, D., *Fashion and Its Social Agendas: Class, Gender and Identity in Clothing*, Chicago UP, Chicago 2001.
Crispolti, E., *Il Futurismo e la moda: Balla e gli altri*, Marsilio, Venezia 1986.
- (edited by), *Il Futurismo e la moda*, Marsilio, Venezia 1988.
- (edited by), *Futurismo moda design: la ricostruzione futurista dell'universo quotidiano*, Musei provinciali di Gorizia, Gorizia 2009.
Cuffaro, R., Vasselli, L., Anita Pittoni, in Finessi, B., (edited by), *Autarchia Austerità Autoproduzione*, Corraini, Mantova 2015.
Cutrufelli, M.R., (edited by), *Piccole italiane: un raggiro durato vent'anni*, Anabasi, Milano 1994.
D'Annunzio, G., *Prose di romanzi vol. 2: Romanzi e novelle*, Mondadori, Milano 1968.
D'Aquino, D., «Poche chiacchiere», *La donna fascista*, n. 11, 5 May 1940, p. 5.
Dal Falco, F., «Materiali e tipi autarchici. La cultura del prodotto tra industria e artigianato nell'Italia dei primi anni Quaranta», *AIS/Design. Storia e ricerche*, n. 4, 2014.
- *Prodotti autarchici 1930-1944: architettura, design, moda*, Designpress, Roma 2014.
Davanzo Poli, D., *Il genio della tradizione: otto secoli di velluti a Venezia*, Cicero, Venezia 2004.
Davidov, C., Dawes, R.G., *The Bakelite Jewelry Book*, Abbeville, New York 1988.
De Andreis, M.L., *Capri 1939*, Inedita, Roma 2002.
De Benedetti, P. E., *Fata autarchia*, La Sorgente, Milano 1942.
De Berti, R., Piazzoni, I., *Forme e modelli del rotocalco italiano tra fascismo e guerra*, Monduzzi, Milano 2009.
De Felice, R., *Mussolini*, Einaudi, Torino 2005.
- *Il fascismo: le interpretazioni dei contemporanei e degli storici*, Laterza, Roma 2008.
De Francesco, A., *L'antichità della nazione. Il mito delle origini del popolo italiano dal Risorgimento al fascismo*, FrancoAngeli, Milano 2020.
De Fusco, R., *Made in Italy. Storia del design italiano*, Altralinea, Bari 2014.
De Giorgio, M., *Le italiane dall'Unità a oggi. Modelli culturali e comportamenti*

sociali, Laterza, Roma-Bari 1992.
De Grand, A., «Women Under Italian Fascism», *The Historical Journal*, 19, n. 4, 1976, pp. 947-968.
De Grazia, V., *Consenso e cultura di massa nell'Italia fascista*, Laterza Roma-Bari 1981.
- *Le donne nel regime fascista*, Marsilio, Venezia 2007.
- De Grazia, V., Furlough, E., (edited by), *The Sex of Things: Gender and Consumption in Historical Perspective*, University of California Press, Berkley 1996.
De Grazia, V., Luzzato, S., (edited by), *Dizionario del fascismo*, Torino, Einaudi 2002.
De La Haye, A., (edited by), *The Cutting Edge: 50 Years of British Fashion 1947-1997*, V&A, London 1997.
De Liguoro, L., «Verso una moda italiana», *Il Popolo d'Italia*, 19 November 1932, p. 3.
- *Le battaglie della moda 1929-33*, Tip. Luzzatti, Roma 1934.
De Luna, G., Torcellan, N., Murialdi, P., (edited by), *La stampa italiana dalla Resistenza agli anni Sessanta*, Laterza, Roma-Bari 1980.
De Marinis, F., Fiorentini Capitani, A., (edited by), *Velluto: fortune, tecniche, mode*, Idea books, Milano 1993.
De Marly, D., *The History of Haute Couture, 1850-1950*, Holmes & Meier, New York 1986.
De Martino, E., *La fine del mondo. Contributo alle analisi sulle apocalissi culturali*, Einaudi, Torino 2002.
De Pisis, F., *Adamo o dell'eleganza. Per una estetica del vestire*, Abscondita, Milano 2019.
De Vincentis, L., *Io son te*, UTAC, Milano 1947.
Deihl, N., *The Hidden History of American Fashion. Rediscovering 20th Century Women Designers*, Bloomsbury, London-New York 2018.
Del Puppo, A., *Modernità e nazione: Temi di ideologia visiva nell'arte italiana del primo Novecento*, Quodlibet, Macerata 2013.
- *Egemonia e consenso: ideologie visive nell'arte italiana del Novecento*, Quodlibet, Macerata 2020.
Del Zanna, P., *Gallomania e parigismo negl'italiani: per l'autarchia spirituale*, Il Quadrante Europeo, Roma 1940.
Di Castro, F, (edited by), *1900-1960 L'alta moda capitale. Torino e le sartorie torinesi*, Fabbri, Milano 1991.
Di Giardinelli, G., *Una gran bella vita*, Mondadori, Milano 1988.
Di Robilant, G., «Perché ho creato la gonna da sci», *Grazia*, n. 2, January 1940, p. 6.
Di Robilant, O., *Sangue blu*, Mondadori, Milano 1991.
Dittrich-Johansen, H., «Dal privato al pubblico: maternità e lavoro nelle riviste femminili dell'epoca fascista», *Studi Storici*, anno 35, n. 1, January-March 1994, pp. 207-243.
- «La "Donna nuova" di Mussolini tra evasione e consumismo», *Studi Storici*, anno 36, n. 3, July-September 1995, pp. 811-843.

- «Le professioniste del Pnf. Un'aristocrazia del comando agli ordini del duce», Studi Storici, 42, n. 1, Jan-Mar 2001, pp. 181-201.
- *Le militi dell'idea. Storia delle organizzazioni femminili del Partito Nazionale Fascista*, Olshki, Firenze 2002.

Doctor, M., «Le realizzazioni della SNIA-Viscosa e il miracolo di Torviscosa», *L'industria nazionale. Rivista mensile dell'autarchia*, n. 4, April 1941, pp. 19-21.

1. Domini, C., Ghergo, C., *Arturo Ghergo. Fotografie 1930-1959*, Silvana Editoriale, Cinisello Balsamo 2012.

Donà Dalle Rose, A., *Autarchia delle fibre tessili vegetali*, Tipografia Paolo Cuppini, Bologna 1941.

Drake, R., *A Political History of National Citizenship and Identity in Italy, 1861-1950*, Stanford UP, Stanford, CA 2013.

Duby, G., *Storia delle donne. Il Novecento*, Laterza, Bari-Roma 2011.

Dulio, R., *Un ritratto mondano. Fotografie di Ghitta Carell*, Johan & Levi, Monza 2014.

During, S., (edited by), *The Cultural Studies Reader*, Routledge, London-New York 1993.

Durkheim, É., *Le forme elementari della vita religiosa*, Edizioni di Comunità, Milano 1982.

Elena (Celani), «Bilancio delle attività della moda», *Bellezza*, n. 36, December 1943, pp. 7-9.
- «Cortina 1941», *Bellezza*, n.1, January 1941, p. 13-4.
- «Senso di proprietà nel vestire», *Bellezza*, n. 35, November 1943, p. 5.
- «Valore del presente», *Bellezza*, n. 44, August 1944, p. 3.

Elias, N., *La società di corte*, Il Mulino, Bologna 1981.

Elleci, «Camerate interrogateci», *La donna fascista*, n. 10, 21 April 1940, p. 3.

Elshtain, J. B., *Donne e guerra*, Il Mulino, Bologna 1991.

Ente autonomo per la mostra permanente nazionale della moda, *II Mostra nazionale della moda*, October, Roggero e Tortia, Torino 1933.

Ente nazionale della moda, *Regolamento per l'istituzione dell'albo delle case di alta moda e della 'marca d'oro'*, Accame, Torino s.d.
- Relazione del presidente sull'attività svolta nel 1940, Stamperia Nazionale Artistica, Torino 1941.

Entwistle, J., *Fashioned Body. Fashion, Dress, and Modern Social Theory*, Polity Press, Cambridge 2015.

Ercolano, M., «I giocattoli dei figli della borghesia fascista. Uno spaccato sulla Napoli di inizio Novecento», *Rivista italiana di educazione familiare*, n. 1, 2017, pp. 201-219.

Evans. M., Lee, E., (edited by), *Real Bodies. A Sociological Introduction*, Palgrave, Hampshire 2002.

Evers, G., «Der Niedergang der Pariser Mode», *Der deutsche Volkswirt*, n. 10, 6 December 1940, pp. 378-380.

Faengyong, W., *Liala. Compagna d'ali e d'insolenze*, Tesi di dottorato, Università di Salerno, 2012-13.

Falasca Zamponi, S., *Lo spettacolo del fascismo*, Rubbettino, Soveria Mannelli

2003.
Fanelli, G., Fanelli, R., *Il tessuto Art Deco e anni Trenta. Disegno. Moda. Architettura*, Cantini, Firenze 1986.
Federico, G., Natoli, S., Tattara. G., Vasta, M., *Il commercio estero italiano (1862-1950)*, IV, Laterza, Roma-Bari 2011.
Felice, E., *Storia economica d'Italia. Ascesa e declino*, Il Mulino, Bologna 2018.
Ferrari, A. F., *Autarchia spirituale*, Arti Grafiche Saturnia, Trento 1940.
Ferrario, R., *Margherita Sarfatti. La regina dell'arte nell'Italia fascista*, Mondadori, Milano 2015.
Field, G.L., *The Syndical and Corporative Institutions of Italian Fascism*, Columbia UP, New York 1938.
Finessi, B., *Il design italiano oltre le crisi: autarchia, austerità, autoproduzione*, Corraini, Mantova 2014.
Fiorella, *Eleganza del freddo*, s.e., s.l., 1942.
Fitzpatrick, Sheila, *Tear Off the Masks! Identity and Imposture in Twentieth-Century Russia*, Princeton UP, Princeton and Oxford 2005.
Flécheux, C., *L'orizzonte. Un saggio in cinquanta questioni*, Mucchi, Modena 2017.
Flora, F., *Ritratto di un ventennio. La stampa dell'era fascista*, Bologna, Edizioni Alfa, 1965.
Flügel, J. C., *The Psychology of Clothing*, Hogarth, London 1930.
Fogu, C., *The Historic Imaginary: Politics of History in Fascist Italy*, University of Toronto Press, Toronto 2003.
- «The Fascist Stylisation of Time», *Journal of Modern European History*, XIII, n. 1, 2015, pp. 98-114.
Fonti, D., (edited by), *Thayaht. Futurista irregolare*, Skira, Milano 2005.
Fonzi, P., «Nazionalsocialismo e Nuovo ordine europeo: La discussione sulla "Großraumwirtschaft"», *Studi Storici*, n. 2, April-June 2004, pp. 313-365.
Forgacs, D., *A Gramsci Reader*, Lawrence & Wishart, London 1988.
Fox, G.P., *Fashion: The Power That Influences the World*, Lange & Hillman, New York 1871.
Fraddosio, M., «The Fallen Hero: The Myth of Mussolini and Fascist Women in the Italian Social Republic (1943-5), *Journal of Contemporary History*, 31, n. 1, 1996, pp. 99-124.
- «La militanza femminile nella Repubblica sociale italiana. Miti e organizzazione», in *Storia e problemi contemporanei*, n. 24, December 1999, pp. 75-88.
Franceschini, C., «Il primo radio-rapporto dei fasci femminili», *La donna fascista*, 30 March 1941, p. 4.
Franck, Louis R., *Il corporativismo e l'economia dell'Italia fascista*, Bollati Boringhieri, Torino 1990.
Frank, G., Podewski, M., «Kultur – Zeit – Schrift. Literatur- und Kulturzeitschriften als ›kleine Archive‹», in *Internationales Archiv für Sozialgeschichte der deutschen Literatur*, 34, n. 2, 2010, pp. 1-45.
Frescobaldi Malenchini, L., Rucellai, O., (edited by), *Gio Ponti e la Richard-*

Ginori: una corrispondenza inedita, Corraini, Mantova 2015.
Freud, L., *Psicologia delle masse e analisi dell'Io*, Bollati Boringhieri, Torino 1975.
Friedland, R., Mohr, J., (edited by), *Matters of Culture. Cultural Sociology in Practice*, Cambridge UP, Cambridge 2004.
Friedmann, G., pubblica *La crise du progrès. Esquisse d'une histoire des idées (1895-1935)*, Gallimard, Paris 1936.
Frisa, M.L., Mattirolo, A., Tonchi, S., (edited by), *Bellissima. L'Italia dell'alta moda 1945-68*, Electa, Milano 2014.
Fusco, G., *Mussolini e le donne*, Sellerio, Palermo 2006.
G. P., «L'industria dell'abbigliamento e la moda. Presentazione dei modelli alla clientela straniera», *Torino. Rassegna mensile della città*, n. 8, August 1941, pp. 43-5.
Gagliani, D., «Microstoria e guerra. Intorno a una ricerca in corso», in *Guerra vissuta guerra subita*, Clueb, Bologna 1991.
Gagliardi, A., *L'impossibile autarchia*, Rubbettino, Soveria Mannelli 2006.
Gagliardini, G., «Autarchia dell'abbigliamento nella mostra del tessile a Venezia», *La donna fascista*, n. 44, 30 September 1941, p. 12.
Gambardella, C., *Il sogno bianco: architettura e mito mediterraneo nell'Italia degli anni Trenta*, Clean, Napoli 1989.
Garavaglia, L.F., *Il Futurismo e la moda*, Excelsior, Milano 2009.
Garnier., G., *Paris Couture Années Trente*, Musée de la Mode & du Costume, Parigi 1987.
Garofoli, (edited by), *Le fibre intelligenti. Un secolo di storia e cinquant'anni di moda*, Electa, Milano 1991.
Gasco, A., *La guerra alla guerra: storie di donne a Torino e in Piemonte tra il 1940 e il 1945*, SEB 27, Torino 2007.
Gaudenzi, V., «La moda femminile in tempo di guerra», *La donna fascista*, 15 July 1942, p. 9.
Gaulme, D., Gaulme, F., *Power and Style. A World History of Politics and Dress*, Flammarion, Paris 2016.
Gazzetta, L., *Orizzonti nuovi. Storia del primo femminismo in Italia (1865-1925)*, Viella, Roma 2018.
Gennaioli, R., (edited by), *I tesori della Fondazione Buccellati: da Mario a Gianmaria, 100 anni di storia dell'arte orafa*, Skira, Milano 2015.
Genoni, R., «Arte e storia del costume. Rivendicazioni femminili nella moda», *Vita d'arte: rivista mensile illustrata d'arte antica e moderna*, II, 1908, fasc. 11, pp. 202-207.
Gentile, E., *Il culto del littorio*, Laterza, Roma-Bari 1993.
- *Le religioni della politica. Fra democrazia e totalitarismi*, Laterza, Roma-Bari 2001.
- *The Struggle for Modernity. Nationalism, Futurism and Fascism*, Preger, Westport-London 2003.
- *Fascismo di pietra*, Laterza, Roma-Bari 2008.
- *Fascismo. Storia e interpretazione*, Laterza, Roma, 2008.
- *Il culto del littorio. La sacralizzazione della politica nell'Italia fascista*,

Laterza, Bari 2003.
- (edited by), *Modernità totalitaria. Il fascismo italiano*, Laterza, Roma-Bari 2008.
- *La Grande Italia. Il mito della nazione nel XX secolo*, Laterza, Roma-Bari 2011.
- *Le origini dell'ideologia fascista 1918-1925*, Il Mulino, Bologna 2011.
- *Le religioni della politica*, Laterza, Bari 2007.
- *Né Stato né Nazione. Italiani senza meta*, Laterza, Bari 2013.
- *25 luglio 1943*, Laterza, Roma-Bari 2018.

Gentile, G., *La donna e il fanciullo. Due conferenze*, Firenze, Sansoni 1934.
- *Politica e cultura*, Libero, Roma 2004.

Giani, P., *Autarchia e guerra: lineamenti, realizzazioni e sviluppi dell'autarchia*, Editrice Libraria Italiana, Torino 1942.

Gianni Mazzocchi editore, Domus, Rozzano 1994.

Gilbert, M., *La grande storia della Seconda guerra mondiale*, Mondadori, Milano 2017.

Ginzburg, N., *Lessico famigliare*, Einaudi, Torino 1972.

Gioannini, M., Massobrio, G., *Bombardate l'Italia: storia di guerra di distruzione aerea 1940-1945*, Rizzoli, Milano 2007.

Gioia, A., *Donne senza qualità. Immagini femminili nell'Archivio storico dell'Istituto Luce*, FrancoAngeli, Milano 2010.

Giorgetti, C., (edited by), *Uberto Bonetti. Opere dell'autarchia e del lusso: l'aerofuturismo, la moda, la cartellonistica, il costume*, Bandecchi & Vivaldi, Pontedera 1998.

Gnoli, S., *Un secolo di moda italiana 1900-2000*, Meltemi, Roma 2005.
- *The Origins of Italian Fashion: 1900-1945*, V&A Publishing, London 2014.
- *Eleganza fascista. La moda dagli anni venti alla fine della guerra*, Carocci, Roma 2017.
- *Eleganza fascista*, Carocci, Roma 2020.
- *Moda, dalla nascita della haute couture a oggi*, Carocci, Roma 2020.

Gramsci, A., *Passato e presente*, Einaudi, Torino 1951.
- *Letteratura e vita nazionale*, Editori Riuniti, Roma 1996.

Grandi, S., Vaccari, A., *Vestire il ventennio: moda e cultura artistica in Italia tra le due guerre*, Bononia UP, Bologna 2004.

Gravagnuolo, B., *Il mito mediterraneo nell'architettura contemporanea*, Electa, Napoli 1994.
- «From Schinkel to Le Corbusier: The Myth of the Mediterranean in Modern Architecture», in Lejeune, J., Sabatino, M., (edited by), *Modern Architecture and the Mediterranean*, Routledge, New York-London 2010.

Gregorio, O., «Limite alla rinuncia», *Per voi signora*, October 1943, p. 12.

Gregotti, L., Berni, V., Farina, P., Grimoldi, A., «Per una storia del design italiano, 1918-1940: Novecento, Razionalismo e la produzione industriale», *Ottagono*, n. 36, March 1975, p. 77-82.

Griffin, R., *Modernism and Fascism. The Sense of a Beginning under Mussolini and Hitler*, Palgrave Macmillan, London 2007.

Grimaldi, U.A., Addis Saba, M., (edited by), *Cultura a passo romano, Storia e strategie dei littoriali della cultura e dell'arte*, Feltrinelli, Milano 1983.
Gualerni, G., *Storia dell'industria italiana*, II, Vita e pensiero, Milano 1981.
Guardigli. S., «Orientamenti. Il lavoro della donna nelle industrie», *La donna fascista*, n. 11, 5 May 1940, p. 5.
Guenther, I., *Nazi Chic? Fashioning Women in the Third Reich*, Berg, Oxford-New York 2004.
Guerra vissuta guerra subita, Seminar proceedings, "Società e guerra", University of Bologna, 16-17 May 1990.
Guerrieri, O., *Curzio*, Neri Pozza, Vicenza 2015.
Guidetti Serra, B., *Compagne*, I, Einaudi, Torino 1977.
Guiglia, G., *La sostituzione dei consumi e la sua propaganda come strumento di autarchia: 2. Convegno Nazionale di studi autarchici*, I.S.C.A., Milano 1940.
Gundle, S., *Figure del desiderio: storia della bellezza femminile italiana dall'Ottocento a oggi*, Laterza, Roma-Bari 2009.
Hall, C., *The Forties in Vogue*, Harmony Books, New York 1985.
Hancock, W.K., Gowing, M.M., (edited by), *British War Economy*, H. M. Stationary Office, 1949.
Harari, G., (edited by), *Fernanda Pivano. The beat goes on*, Mondadori, Milano 2004.
Hargreaves, E.L., Gowing, M., *Civil Industry and Trade*, XII, 37, n. 6, H.M. Stationery Office & Longmans, Green & Co., London 1952.
Harris, C., *Women at War in Uniform 1939-45*, Sutton, Stroud 2003.
Harrison, M., (edited by), *The Economics of World War II. Six Great Powers in International Comparison*, Cambridge UP, Cambridge 1998.
Hartley, J., *Hearts Undefeated. Women's Writing of the Second World War*, Virago, London 1995.
Hartnell, N., *Silver and Gold. The Autobiography of Norman Hartnell*, V&A Publishing, London 2019.
Heymann, D., *Poor Little Rich Girl*, Lyle Stuart, New York 1984.
Hobsbawm, E., *Il secolo breve. 1914-1991*, Rizzoli, Milano 1994.
Hollander, A., *Seeing Through Clothes*, University of California Press, Berkley 1993.
- *Sex and Suits. The Evolution of Modern Dress*, Knopf, New York 1994.
Horkeimer, M., Adorno, Theodor W., *Dialettica dell'Illuminismo*, Einaudi, Torino 2010.
Howell, G., *Wartime Fashion. From Haute Couture to Homemade, 1939-45*, Berg, London-New York 2012.
- *Women in Wartime. Dress Studies from Picture Post 1938-45*, Bloomsbury, London-New York 2019.
I documenti diplomatici italiani 9. serie: 1939-1943, Libreria dello Stato, Roma 1988.
I Fasci femminili, Libreria d'Italia, Milano 1929.
Innocenti, M., *L'Italia del 1943: come eravamo nell'anno in cui crollò il fascismo*, Mursia, Milano 1993.

Invernizio, C., *I sette capelli d'oro della fata Gusmara*, Moizzi, Milano 1975.
Irace, F., *Gio Ponti. La casa all'italiana*, Electa, Milano 1988.
Isnenghi, M., *Le guerre degli italiani 1848-1945*, Mondadori, Milano 1989.
Jenson, J., Michel, S., Collins Weitz, M., (edited by), *Behind the Lines. Gender and the Two World Wars*, Yale UP, New Haven-London 1987.
Jocteau, G.C., «I nobili del Fascismo», *Studi Storici*, n. 3, 2004.
Kawamura, Y., *La moda*, Il Mulino, Bologna 2006.
Keesing-Tonkinson, «Reinventing traditional culture: the politics of custom in Melanesia», *Mankind* (special issue), XIII, n. 4, 1982.
Kermode, F., *The Sense of an Ending. Studies in the Theory of Fiction*, Oxford UP, New York 1967.
Keynes, J.M., *La fine del lasciar fare: autarchia economica*, Utet, Torino 1936.
Koselleck, R., *The Practice of Conceptual History. Timing History, Spacing Concepts*, Stanford UP, Stanford 2002.
Kunnas, T., *Il fascino del fascismo. L'adesione degli intellettuali europei*, Settimo Sigillo-Europa Lib. Ed, 2017.
La Rinascente-Upim durante la Seconda guerra mondiale 1940-1945, Rizzoli, Milano 1946.
La Pietra, U., *Gio Ponti: l'arte s'innamora dell'industria*, Rizzoli, Milano 2009.
La Rosa, F., «Il "nuovo" nella Mediterraneità, tra la fuga in avanti e l'arresto attonito», *L'ombra: tracce e percorsi a partire da Jung*, n. 4, 2014.
Labroca, M., «Valore delle stoffe stampate», *Bellezza*, n. 16, 1942, p. 5, 61.
Laver, J., «Where is Fashion Going», *Vogue* UK, n. 9, September 1944, pp. 31-33.
- *Costume and Fashion: A Concise History*, Thames & Hudson, London 2012.
Lazzarini, L., «Documento-Moda dell'E.N.M.», *Torino. Rassegna mensile della città*, n. 7, July 1941, pp. 33-8.
Le Bon, G., *Psicologia delle folle*, Tea, Milano 2004.
Le Goff, J., *Storia e memoria*, Einaudi, Torino 1977.
Lees-Maffei, G., Fallan, K., (edited by), *Made in Italy: Rethinking a Century of Italian Design*, Bloomsbury, London-New York 2014.
Lenti, L., Bergesio, M.C., (edited by), *Dizionario del gioiello italiano del XIX e XX secolo*, Bergesio, Allemandi, Torino 2005.
Leone De Andreis, M., *Capri 1939*, Inedita, Roma 2002.
Lepre, A., *L'occhio del Duce. Gli italiani e la censura di guerra 1940-1943*, Mondadori, Milano 1992.
Les noblesses européennes au XIXe siècle, Actes du colloque de Rome, 21-23 November 1985, École Française de Rome, Roma 1988.
Levi Pisetzky, R., *Il costume e la moda nella società italiana*, Einaudi, Torino 1978.
Liguori, G., Voza, P., *Dizionario Gramsciano 1926-37*, Carocci, Roma 2011.
Lipovetsky, G., *L'impero dell'effimero*, Garzanti, Milano 1989.
Lista, G., Sheridan, S., «The Activist Model; or the Avant-Garde as Italian Invention», *South Central Review*, 13, n. 2/3, pp. 13-34.

References

Lo Biundo, E., «Radio London 1943-1945: Italian Society at the Microphones of the BBC», *Modern Italy*, 23, n. 1, 2018, pp. 35-50.
Loffredo, F., *Politica della famiglia*, Bompiani, Milano 1938.
Lombardo, E., «'Durare' verbo dell'industria della moda e della produzione di lusso», *Vita femminile*, December 1941, p. 21.
- «Consuntivo di una polemica», *Vita Femminile*, March 1938, pp. 9-10.
Ludwig, E., *Colloqui con Mussolini*, Mondadori, Milano 1965.
Lupano, M., Vaccari, A., *Una giornata moderna. Moda e stili nell'Italia fascista 1922-43*, Damiani, Bologna 2009.
Lynam, R., *Paris Fashion: The Great Designers and Their Creations*, M. Joseph, London 1972.
Mafai, M., *Pane nero. Donne e vita quotidiana nella seconda guerra mondiale*, Mondadori, Milano 1987.
Maher, V., *Tenere le fila. Sarte, sartine e cambiamento sociale 1860-1960*, Rosenberg & Sellier, Torino 2007.
Malinowski, B., *Argonauts of the Western Pacific. An account of native enterprise and adventures in the archipelagoes of Melanesian New Guinea*, London, Routledge, 1922.
Malossi, G., (edited by), *La Sala Bianca: nascita della moda italiana*, Electa, Milano 1992.
Malvano, L., *Fascismo e politica dell'immagine*, Bollati Boringhieri, Torino 1988.
Mancini, U., *1939-40 La vigilia della seconda guerra mondiale*, Armando Editore, Roma 2004.
Mannucci, E., *Il marchese rampante. Emilio Pucci: avventure, illusioni, successi di un inventore della moda italiana*, Baldin&Castoldi, Milano 1998.
Marchetti, M. C., *Moda e politica. La rappresentazione simbolica del potere*, Meltemi, Roma 2020.
Marcucci, R., *Anibo e made in Italy. Storia dei buying offices in Italia*, Vallecchi, Firenze 2004.
Marini, A. G., «Verso la vittoria», *La donna fascista*, N. 22, 3 November 1940, p. 6.
Marino, N., Marino, E.V., *L'Ovra a Cinecittà. Polizia politica e spie in camicia nera*, Bollati Boringhieri, Torino 2005.
Marra, C., *Nelle ombre di un sogno. Storia e idee della fotografia di moda*, Mondadori, Milano 2010.
Marrani, P., *L'autarchia nel presente periodo bellico*, Eugenio Jovene, Napoli 1941.
Martignoni, M., *Gio Ponti. Gli anni di Stile 1941-47*, Abitare Segesta, Milano 2002.
Marucelli, G., *Le favole del ferro da stiro*, East 128, Milano 1964.
Marx, K., Engels, F., *Manifesto of the Communist Party*, translated by Samuel Moore, Marx/Engels Selected Works, I, Progress Publishers, Mosca 1969.
Masina, L, (edited by), *Vedere l'Italia nelle esposizioni universali del XX secolo*, Educatt, Milano 2016.

Masino, P., *Album di vestiti*, Lit Edizioni, Roma 2015.
Matard-Bonucci, M., *L'Italia fascista e la persecuzione degli ebrei*, Il Mulino, Bologna 2016.
Matteini, C., *Ordini alla stampa*, Roma, Editrice Polilibraria Italiana, 1945.
Mauss, M., *Teoria generale della magia e altri saggi*, Torino, Einaudi, 1965.
Maxwell, A., *Patriots Against Fashion: Clothing and Nationalism in Europe's Age of Revolutions*, Palgrave Macmillan, New York 2014.
Mazower, M., «Violence and the State in the Twentieth Century», *The American Historical Review*, 107, No. 4 (October 2002), pp. 1158-1178.
Mazzatosta, T.M., *Il regime fascista tra educazione e propaganda*, Cappelli, Bologna 1978.
Mazzei, J., *Autarchia e tenor di vita*, Cya, Firenze 1941.
McCullog Thew, L., *From Store to War*, Pluto Press, London 1987.
McDowell, C., *Forties Fashion and the New Look*, Bloomsbury, London 1997.
McFeaters, A. P., «The Past is How We Present It: Nationalism and Archaeology in Italy from Unification to WWII», *Nebraska Anthropologist*, n. 33, 2007, pp. 49-62.
Meano, C., *Commentario dizionario italiano della moda*, Ente Nazionale della Moda, Torino 1936.
Meldini, P., *Sposa e madre esemplare: ideologia e politica della donna e della famiglia durante il fascismo*, Guaraldi, Rimini 1975.
Merjan, A. H., «A Future by Design: Giacomo Balla and the Domestication of Trascendence», *Oxford Art Journal*, 35, n. 2, 2012, pp. 121-146.
Merlo, E., *Moda italiana. Storia di un'industria dell'Ottocento a oggi*, Marsilio, Venezia, 2008.
Messina, A., (edited by), *L'economia nello Stato totalitario fascista*, Aracne, Roma 2017.
Mezzo secolo di SNIA Viscosa, Pan editrice, Milano 1970.
Miccoli, G., «L'Italia cattolica e il fascismo», *La rassegna mensile di Israel*, 69, n. 1, January-April 2003, pp. 163-186.
Milward, A. S., «Towards a Political Economy of Fascism», in Hagtvet, B., Reinhard, K., (edited by), *Who Were The Fascists?*, Stockholm University Press, Stockholm 1980.
Mondello, E., *La nuova italiana. La donna nella stampa e nella cultura del Ventennio*, Editori Riuniti, Roma 1987.
Monelli, P., *Roma 1943*, Einaudi, Torino 2012.
Mori, M. T., Pescarolo, A., Scattigno, A., Soldani., S., (edited by), *Di generazione in generazione. Le italiane dall'Unità a oggi*, Viella, Roma 2014.
Morini, E., *Maria Pezzi, giornalista di moda. L'Europeo 1947-58*, Società per l'Enciclopedia delle donne, Milano 2017.
Mormorio, D., *Vestiti. Lo stile degli italiani in un secolo di fotografie*, Laterza, Bari 1999.
Mortara, G., *Curiosità indiscrete della statistica matrimoniale*, Tip. Leonardo da Vinci, Città di Castello 1936.
Moseley, R., *Mussolini's Shadow. The Double Life of Count Galeazzo Ciano*,

Yale UP, New Haven 2000.
Mosse, G., *Le guerre mondiali. Dalla tragedia al mito dei caduti*, Laterza, Roma-Bari 2005.
- *Sessualità e nazionalismo*, Laterza, Roma-Bari 2011.
Motta, G., *La moda si fa storia. Borghesi, rivoluzionari, ruoli e identità nazionali*, Nuova Cultura, Roma 2017.
Motta, G., Biagini, A., *Fashion Through History. Costumes, Simbols, Communication*, Cambridge Scholars Publishing 2017.
Mrazek, W., *Die Wiener Werkstätte. Modernes Kunsthandwerk von 1903-1932*, Vienna 1967.
Mulvagh, J., *Vogue History of Twentieth Century Fashion*, Viking, London-New York 1988.
Munich, A., (edited by), *Fashion in Film*, Indiana UP, Bloomington 2011.
Munoz, A., *Echi della mostra del tessile*, Palombi, Roma 1938.
Mussolini, B., «Dopo due anni», *Il Popolo d'Italia*, 23 March 1921, p. 1.
- *Scritti e discorsi di Benito Mussolini. Dal gennaio 1934 al 4 novembre 1935*, IX, Hoepli, Milano 1935.
- «Il capestro di Démos», *Il popolo d'Italia*, 3 December 1937, p. 1.
- «Il discorso del Duce all'assemblea delle corporazioni», *Assistenza fascista*, n. 1-2, 1942, pp. 137-142.
Muzzarelli, M. G., *Breve storia della moda in Italia*, Il Mulino, Bologna 2011.
Muzzarelli, M. G., Riello, G., Brandi, E. T., (edited by), *Moda. Storia e storie*, Bruno Mondadori, Milano 2010.
Nelis, J., «Constructing Fascist Identity: Benito Mussolini and the Myth of "Romanità"», *The Classical Journal*, 100, n. 4, estate 2007, pp. 391-415.
- *From ancient to modern: the myth of romanità during the ventennio fascista. The written imprint of Mussolini's cult of the 'Third Rome'*, Belgisch Historisch Instituut te Roma-Bruxelles, Brepols 2011.
Nichil, R. L., «La retorica del regime attraverso i *Fogli di disposizioni* di Achille Starace: la questione della razza», in Caffarelli, E., Fanfani, M., *Lo spettacolo delle parole. Studi di storia linguistica e di onomastica*, Società Editrice Romana, Roma 2011, pp. 237-254.
Nicoletto, M., *Donne nel cinema di regime fra tradizione e modernità*, Falsopiano, Alessandria 2014.
Nodolini, A., Bernasconi, S., (edited by), *Brunetta. Moda, critica, storia*, CSAC, Parma 1981.
Notari, U., «Nostra intervista», *Gazzetta del Popolo*, 9 March 1932, p. 6.
- «La grande industria e la crisi», *Gazzetta del Popolo*, 13 March 1932, p. 7.
- «Della prosperità di Torino», *Gazzetta del popolo*, 26 March 1932, p. 7.
Novus: La Chaussure Nouvelle, le Cuir, le Sac et les Accessoires pour la Saison d'Hiver, n. 16, primavera 1939-40, Typographie G. Avenel, Paris 1939.
Odon Por, *Dall'autarchia di guerra all'autarchia di pace*, Arti Grafiche A. Chicca, Tivoli 1940.
Olds, L., «World War II and Fashion», *Constructing the Past*, 2, n. 1, 2001, URL: http://digitalcommons.iwu.edu/constructing/vol2/iss1/6.
Olivari, O., *Memorie d'un "travett,"* Pagano, Genova 1951.

Olschki, M., *Terza Liceo 1939*, Sellerio, Palermo 1993.
Omero Gallo, G., «La rassegna autarchica della moda e dell'abbigliamento a Venezia», *L'Illustrazione italiana*, n. 37, 14 September 1941, p. 354-6.
Orano, P., (edited by), *L'autarchia*, Casa editrice Pinciana, Roma 1940.
Origine e sviluppo dei velluti a Venezia: il velluto allucciolato d'oro, Università internazionale dell'arte, Venezia 1986.
Orsi Landini, R., *La Galleria del costume*, V, Centro Di, Firenze 1993.
- *I velluti nella collezione della Galleria del Costume di Firenze*, Mauro Pagliai, Firenze 2017.
Osborne, P., *The Politics of Time. Modernity and the Avant-Garde*, Verso, London-New York 1995.
Ottaviani, G., *Il controllo del Minculpop sulla pubblicità, il cinema, la moda, la cucina, la salute e la stampa*, Todariana Editrice, Milano 2005.
Pagano, G., Daniel, G., (edited by), *Architettura rurale italiana*, Hoepli, Milano 1936.
Paris, I., *Oggetti cuciti. L'abbigliamento pronto in Italia dal primo dopoguerra agli anni Settanta*, FrancoAngeli, Milano 2006.
Passamonti, L.S., «La Nobiltà della Stirpe: il sogno di un'Italia aristocratica e fascista», Diacronie, 27, n.3, 2016.
URL: http://journals.openedition.org/diacronie/4235.
Patriarca, S., *Italianità. La costruzione del carattere nazionale*, Laterza, Bari 2010.
Paulicelli, E., *Fashion Under Fascism. Beyond the Black Shirt*, Berg, New York 2004.
- «Italian Fashion: Yesterday, Today and Tomorrow», *Journal of Modern Italian Studies*, 20, n. 1, 2014, pp. 1-9.
- «Fashion: The Cultural Economy of Made in Italy», *Fashion Practice*, 6, n. 2, 2015, pp. 155-174.
- *Rosa Genoni: la moda è una cosa seria. Milano Expo 1906 e la Grande Guerra*, Deleyva, Monza 2015.
- *Italian Style: Fashion and Film from Early Cinema to the Digital Age*, Bloomsbury, 2016.
- Paulicelli, E., *Writing Fashion in Early Modern Italy. From Sprezzatura to Satire*, Routledge, London-New York 2016.
Payne, S. G., *A History of Fascism 1914-45*, Routledge, London 1996.
Penrose, A., (edited by), *Lee Miller's War*, Thames & Hudson, London 2005.
Pericoli, U., *Le divise del Duce. Tutte le divise e i distintivi del fascismo dalle origini alla caduta*, Albertelli, Parma 2010.
Persico, E., (edited by), *Arte romana. La scultura romana e quattro affreschi della Villa dei Misteri*, Domus, Milano 1935.
Petacco, A., *Il superfascista, Vita e morte di Alessandro Pavolini*, Mondadori, Milano 2016.
- *Come eravamo negli anni di guerra. La vita quotidiana degli italiani tra il 1940 e il 1945*, Utet, Milano 2020.
Pintor, G., *Doppio diario 1936-1943*, Einaudi, Torino 1978.
Pio XII, *Discorsi e radiomessaggi di sua santità Pio XII*, III, Tip. Poliglotta

Vaticana, Città del Vaticano 1960.
Pisetzky, R.L., *Il costume e la moda nella società italiana*, Einaudi, Torino 1978.
Poe, E. A., *Racconti*, I, Adelphi, Milano 2004.
Pompei, M., «Donne e culle», *Critica fascista*, n. 6, 15 March 1930.
Ponti, G., «La casa all'italiana», *Domus*, n.1, January 1928, p. 7.
- «La casa di moda», *Domus*, n. 8, August 1928, p. 11.
- «Le industrie femminili alla VII Triennale di Milano», *Fili*, July 1939, p. 11.
- «Sotto l'egida d'una parola altamente impegnativa», *Stile*, n. 1, January 1941, p. 11.
- «Costume e civiltà», *Bellezza*, n.1, January 1941, p. 1.
- «Oroscopi sulla moda», *Bellezza*, n. 1., January 1941, p. 32.
- «La moda nella nuova Europa», *Stile*, n. 3, March 1941, p. 99.
- «L'Antico e noi», *Stile*, n. 3, March 1941, p. 57.
- «Scelta di bellezza», *Bellezza*, n. 16, April 1942, p. 2.
- «Abbigliamento ed arredamento», *Bellezza*, n. 36, December 1943, pp. 47-51.
- «I punti della ricostruzione», in *Stile*, 49, n. 1, 1945, p. VII.
- «È superfluo il superfluo?», *Bellezza*, n. 1 (new series), November 1945, p. 45-46.
Pontiggia, E., (edited by), *Il ritorno all'ordine*, Abscondita, Milano 2005.
- Pontiggia, E., *Modernità e classicità: il ritorno all'ordine in Europa dal primo dopoguerra agli anni trenta*, Bruno Mondadori, Milano 2008.
- Pontiggia, E., Quesada, M., (edited by), *L'idea del classico 1916-1932: temi classici nell'arte italiana degli anni Venti*, Fabbri, Milano 1992.
Pope, V., «The Fashion Capital Moves Across Seas», *New York Times*, 18 August 1940, p. 2.
Portaccio, S., «La donna nella stampa popolare cattolica. "Famiglia Cristiana" 1931-1945», *Italia contemporanea*, n. 143, 1981, pp. 45-68.
Pozzilli, G., (edited by), *Cento anni di pubblicità nello sviluppo economico e nel costume italiano*, Sipra, Torino 1974.
Primo Concorso nazionale di modelli per l'abbigliamento maschile e femminile, Edizioni Tiber, Roma 1929.
Pratesi, M., *Vita e percorso artistico di un protagonista del ventesimo secolo*, Pisa UP, Pisa 2016.
Pryce-Jones, D., *Paris in the Third Reich: A History of the German Occupation, 1940-44*, Holt, Rhinehart, and Winston, New York 1981.
Puppo, G., «Mostra dell'abbigliamento autarchico al Palazzo della Moda», *Torino. Rassegna mensile della città*, n. 5, May 1940, pp. 2-13.
Quasimodo, S., *Giorno dopo giorno*, Mondadori, Milano 1947.
Quercia, A., (edited by), *Donne d'Europa. Quali prospettive*, Luigi Pellegrini Editore, Roma 1999.
Raggi, M., *L'economia domestica nella battaglia per l'autarchia*, s.e, s.l., 1939.
Raimondi, E., «Dal simbolo al segno: il D'Annunzio e il simbolismo»,

Strumenti Critici, n. 28, 1975.
Rassegna del tessile e dell'abbigliamento autarchico, C. Ferrari, Venezia 1941.
Reutern Aloisi, L., «Le carte dicono che...», *Bellezza*, n. 11, November 1941, pp. 18-9.
Revelli, N., *L'ultimo fronte. Lettere di soldati caduti o dispersi nella seconda guerra mondiale*, Einaudi, Torino 1971.
Ribeiro, A., «Re-fashioning Art: Some Visual Approaches to the Study of the History of Dress», *Fashion Theory*, II, n. 4, December 1998, pp. 315-325.
Ridenti, L., *Cappello*, S.E.T., Torino 1944.
Riello, G., *La moda: Una storia dal medioevo a oggi*, Laterza, Roma-Bari 2012.
- Riello, G., «Per una storia della moda. Concetti, oggetti e cultura materiale», *Venezia arti*, XXV, December 2016.
Riello, G., McNeil, P., *The Fashion History Reader. Global Perspectives*, Routledge, London & New York 2010.
Ristuccia, C.A., «The 1935 Sanctions against Italy: Would coal and oil have made a difference?», *European Review of Economic History*, 4, n. 1, 2000, pp. 85-110.
Rizzi, L., *Lo sguardo del potere. La censura militare in Italia nella seconda guerra mondiale*, Rizzoli, Milano 1984.
Robiola, E., «Moda a Torino», *Bellezza*, n. 1, January 1941, p. 70.
- «Plasmare e proteggere la bellezza», Bellezza, n.1, January 1941, pp. 98-9.
- «In questa primavera una linea più semplice, più sciolta?», *Bellezza*, n. 2, febbraio 1941, p. 3.
- «20 chili di bagaglio», *Bellezza*, n. 19, July 1942, pp. 46-47.
- «Moda Autunno Inverno 1942-1943. Orientamento», *Bellezza*, n. 21, September 1942, p. 5.
- «Donne che lavorano», *Bellezza*, n. 23, November 1942, p. 56.
- «Nascita di modelli senza cerimonia», n. 35, November 1943, p. 12.
- «Malgrado tutto», *Bellezza*, n. 46, 15 October-15 November 1944, pp. 3-4.
- «Carattere e ripresa delle attività torinesi», *Bellezza*, n. 47, November-December 1944.
- «Dall'album di Brunetta: atto di fede», *Bellezza*, n. 1 (new series), November 1945, pp. 4-13.
- «Dopo vent'anni», *Bellezza*, n. 4, 1960, p. 26.
Rocamora, A., «Field of fashion: critical insights into Bourdieu Sociology of Culture», *Journal of Consumer Culture*, II, n. 3, 2002, pp. 349-370.
Rocamora, A., Smelik, A., *Thinking Through Fashion*, I.B. Tauris, London 2015.
Roche, D., *La culture des apparences: une histoire du vetement XVII-XVIII siècle*, Fayard, Paris 1989.
Roche, H., Kyriakos N. D., *Brill's Companion to the Classics, Fascist Italy and Nazi Germany. Brill's Companions to Classical Reception, 12*. Brill, Leiden 2017.
Rodogno, D., *Il nuovo ordine mediterraneo. Le politiche di occupazione*

dell'Italia fascista in Europa (1940-43), Bollati Boringhieri, Torino 2003.
Romani, G., «Fashioning the Italian Nation: Risorgimento and its *costume all'italiana*», *Journal of Modern Italian Studies*, 20, n. 1, pp. 10-23.
Rossi Lodomez, V., «Le signore hanno visto...», *Bellezza*, n. 10, October 1941, p. 5.
Rostagni, C., (edited by), *Gio Ponti, Stile di*, Electa, Milano 2016.
Roth, J., *Al bistrot dopo mezzanotte. Un'antologia francese*, Adelphi, Milano 2013.
- *La quarta Italia*, Castelvecchi, Roma 2013.
Rubetti, V., *Fascismo al femminile*, Armando Editore, Roma 2019.
Rubeo, U., «Tra alienazione e mercato: la città moderna secondo Edgar Allan Poe», *Fictions. Studi sulla narratività*, V, June 2007.
Rudofsky, B., «La moda: abito disumano», *Domus*, n. 124, April 1938, pp. 10-3.
- *Are clothes modern? An Essay on Contemporary Apparel*, P. Theobold, Chicago 1947.
Russo, G., (edited by), *L'avvenire industriale di Napoli negli scritti del primo '900*, Guida, Napoli 2004.
Salvati, M., «Tra pubblico e privato: gli spazi delle donne negli anni Trenta», *Studi Storici*, anno 38, n. 3, July-September 1997, pp. 669-692.
Sansovino, F., *Venetia città nobilissima et singolare*, appresso Iacomo Sansouino, 1581.
Santoianni, V., *Il Razionalismo nelle colonie italiane. La "nuova architettura" delle Terre d'Oltremare*, Università di Napoli Federico II, 2008, PhD thesis.
Santomassimo, G., «Antifascismo popolare», *Italia Contemporanea*, n. 140, September 1980, pp. 39-69.
Sarfatti, M., *My Fault. Mussolini as I Knew Him*, Enigma Books, New York 2014.
Scarpellini, E., *L'Italia dei consumi. Dalla Belle époque al nuovo millennio*, Laterza, Roma-Bari 2016.
- *La stoffa dell'Italia. Storia e cultura della moda dal 1945 a oggi*, Laterza, Roma-Bari 2017.
Schiaparelli, E., «Needles and Guns», *Vogue*, 1 September 1940, p. 57.
- *Shocking life: autobiografia di un genio della moda*, Alet, Padova 2008.
Schnapp, J., «The Fabric of Modern Times», *Critical Inquiry*, 24, n. 1, 1997.
Sciola, G., «Il Novecento degli Istituti. L'Italia nella Seconda guerra mondiale», *Italia contemporanea*, n. 190, 1993, pp. 199-203.
Sciolla, G.C., (edited by), *Riviste d'arte tra Ottocento ed età contemporanea. Forme, modelli e funzioni*, Skira, Milano 2003.
Segre, S., (edited by), «La cultura della moda italiana-Made in Italy», *Zone/moda Journal*, n. 2, 2011.
Sheridan, D., *Wartime Women, a Mass Observation Anthology*, Heinemann, London 1990.
Schnapp, J., «The Fabric of Modern Times», *Critical Inquiry*, 24, n. 1, 1997.
Shrimpton, J., *Fashion in the 40s*, Shire, Oxford-New York 2014.
Silvestrini, E., «L'abito popolare in Italia», *La ricerca folklorica*, n. 14,

October 1986, pp. 5-44.
Silvia, «Rimettiamo a nuovo i vestiti a maglia», *La donna fascista*, 30 October 1941, p. 15.
Simmel, G., *La moda*, Mondadori, Milano 2009.
Simonetta, R., «Eleganza e semplicità nel vestire», *La Famiglia Rinascente-Upim*, n. 1, febbraio 1941, pp. 25-27.
- «Presentazione dei modelli primavera-estate», *La Famiglia Rinascente-Upim*, n. 2, April 1941, pp. 40-42.
- «La moda e i prodotti tipo», *La Famiglia Rinascente-Upim*, n. 1, January-March 1942, pp. 21-22.
Sladen, C., *The Conscription of Fashion. Utility Cloth, Clothing, and Footwear, 1941-1952*, Ashgate, Brooksfield 1995.
Smith, M., *Britain and 1940. History, Myth and Popular Memory*, Routledge, Oxon-New York 2000.
Sombart, W., *Dal lusso al capitalismo*, Armando, Roma 2003.
Sottochiesa, G., *Che cosa è l'autarchia: la lotta contro gli sprechi*, Paravia, Torino 1939.
Spadoni, M., *Il gruppo SNIA dal 1917 al 1951*, Giappichelli, Torino 2003.
Spampinato, F., «Macchina, monumento, manichino: l'uomo nuovo italiano», in Celanti, G., (edited by), *Post Zang Tumb Tuuum. Art, Life, Politics, Italia 1918-1943*, Progetto Prada Arte, Milano 2018, pp. 584-587.
Spring Rice, M., *Working Class Wives: Their Health and Conditions*, Penguin, London 1939.
Stagnitti, B., «Dal "vestito antineutrale" all'"abito della vittoria". Futurismo e moda», *Studi Novecenteschi*, 34, n. 74, July-December 2007, pp. 397-408.
Stanfill, S., (edited by), *The Glamour of Italian Fashion Since 1945*, V&A Publishing, London 2014.
Steele, V., «The F-Word», *Lingua Franca*, April 1991, pp. 17-20.
- «Letter from the Editor», *Fashion Theory*, 1, n. 1, March 1997, p. 1.
- *Fashion, Italian Style*, Yale UP, New Haven 2003.
- (edited by), *Paris, Capital of Fashion*, Bloomsbury, London-New York 2019.
Storchi, S., «Margherita Sarfatti and Il Popolo d'Italia. National Classicism between Tradition and Modernity», *The Modern Language Review*, CVIII, n. 4, pp. 1135-1155.
Styles, J., «Dress History: Reflections on a Contested Terrain», *Fashion Theory*, 2, n. 4, December 1998, pp. 337-358.
Summerfield, P., «Mass-Observation on Women at Work in the Second World War», *Feminist Praxis Monographs*, n. 37-38, 1992.
Summers, J., *Fashion on the Ration. Style in the Second World War*, Profile Books, London 2015.
Susmel, E. e D., (edited by), *Opera omnia*, La Fenice, Firenze 1951-1961.
Tarde, G., *Le leggi dell'imitazione*, Rosenberg-Seller, Torino 2012.
Tarquini, A., *Storia della cultura fascista*, Il Mulino, Bologna 2016.
- «Il mito di Roma nella cultura e nella politica del regime fascista: dalla diffusione del fascio littorio alla costruzione di una nuova città (1922-

1943)», *Cahiers de la Méditerranée*, 2017, URL: http:// journals. openedition.org/cdlm/9153.
Taylor, F., (edited by), *The Goebbels Diaries: 1939-1941*, Putnam's Sons, New York 1983.
Taylor, L., «Doing the Laundry? A Reassessment of Object-Based Dress History», *Fashion Theory*, 2, n. 4, December 1998, pp. 337-58.
Taylor, L., McLoughlin, M., (edited by), *Paris Fashion and World War Two*, Bloomsbury, London 2020.
Thébaud, T., (edited by), *Il Novecento*, Laterza, Roma-Bari 2007.
Tognato, L., *Il Veneto e l'economia di guerra fascista 1935-46*, Marsilio, Venezia 2013.
Tonelli Michail, M.C., *Il design in Italia 1925-1943*, Laterza, Roma 1987.
Tongiorigi, F., Torricelli, G., Principalli. M., (edited by), *Per una storia della moda pronta: problemi e ricerche*, Firenze, Edifir 1991.
Toniolo, G., *L'economia dell'Italia fascista*, Laterza, Roma 1980.
Toniolo, G., Bastiasin, C., *La strada smarrita. Breve storia dell'economia italiana*, Laterza, Roma-Bari 2020.
Torino e l'abbigliamento, Ente nazionale della moda, Torino 1966.
Torino 1938-45. Una guida per la memoria, Città di Torino – Istituto Piemontese per la Storia della Resistenza e della società contemporanea "Giorgio Agosti," Torino 2000.
Train, S., Braun-Munk, C., (edited by), *Théâtre de la Mode*, Rizzoli, New York 1991.
Tranfaglia, N., (edited by), *Storia di Torino VIII. Dalla Grande Guerra alla liberazione (1915-1945)*, Einaudi, Torino 1998.
Tranfaglia, N., *La stampa del regime 1932-1943. Le veline del Minculpop per orientare l'informazione*, Bompiani, Milano 2005.
Traverso, E., *Paperino: 1072 paperinate in tempi di autarchia*, Mondadori, Milano 1994.
Turroni, G., *Luxardo: l'italica bellezza*, Mazzotta, Milano 1980.
V. g., «Donne fasciste in linea», *La donna fascista*, n. 15, 30 June 1940, p. 4.
Vallorani, N., *Introduzione ai Cultural Studies. UK, USA e paesi anglofoni*, Carocci, Roma 2016.
Veblen, T., *La teoria della classe agiata. Studio economico sulle istituzioni*, Einaudi, Torino 1949.
Veillon, D., *La mode sous l'Occupation*, Éditions Payot, Paris 1990.
Vera, «Moda e bellezza», *Bellezza*, n. 1, January 1941, p. 5.
- , «Necessità di domani: le confezioni in serie», *Bellezza*, n. 46, 15 October-15 November 1944, p. 42-43.
Vergani, G., Malossi, G., (edited by), *The Sala Bianca: The Birth of Italian Fashion*, Electa, Milano 1992.
Veronesi, G., *Stile 1925. Ascesa e caduta delle Arts Déco*, Vallecchi, Firenze 1978.
Villari, L., *Capitalismo italiano del Novecento*, Laterza, Bari 1972.
Vincent, G., *La vita privata. Il Novecento*, Laterza, Roma-Bari 1988.
Vitrotto, G., (edited by), *Documento Moda*, anno II, Grafitalia, Milano 1942.

Von Mises, L., *Omnipotent Government. The Rise of the Total State and Total War*, Yale UP, New Haven 1974.
Wagener, A. P., «A Classical Background for Fascism», *The Classical Journal*, XXIII, n. 9, June 1928, pp. 668-677.
Walford, J., *Forties Fashion. From Sirens Suits to the New Look*, Thames & Hudson, London 2011.
Walters, J. E., «Women in Industry», *Annals of the American Academy of Political Science and Social Science*, 229, September 1943, pp. 56-62.
Welk, W.G., *Fascist Economic Policy: An Analysis of Italy's Economic Experiment*, Harvard UP, Cambridge 1938.
White, N., *Reconstructing Italian Fashion. America and the Development of the Italian Fashion Industry*, Berg, Oxford-New York 2000.
White, P., *Elsa Schiaparelli: Empress of Paris Fashion*, Aurum, London 1986.
Willson, P., «The Fairytale Witch: Laura Marani Argnani and the Fasci Femminili of Reggio Emilia, 1929-1940», *Contemporary European History*, 15, n. 1, febbraio 2006, pp. 23-42.
- «Empire, Gender and the 'Home Front' in Fascist Italy», *Women's History Review*, 16, n. 4, 2007, pp. 487-500.
- *Italiane. Biografia del Novecento*, Laterza, Bari 2011.
- «Italian Fascism and the Political Mobilisation of Working-Class Women 1937-43», *Contemporary European History*, 22, n. 1, febbraio 2013, pp. 65-86.
- «The Nation in Uniform? Fascist Italy, 1919-43», *Past & Present*, n. 221, 2013, pp. 239-272.
Wilson, E., *Adorned in Dreams*, Virago Press, London 1985.
Wilson, E., Taylor, L., (edited by), *Through the Looking Glass*, Bbc, London 1995.
Wolbert, K., *Massimo Campigli. Mediterraneità e modernità*, Mazzotta, 2003.
Wolcott, C., «Adolf Hitler: Grand Couturier», *The Living Age*, 1 June 1941, p. 325-6.
Zacchè, G., *Lo stile su misura. La sartoria Piccinini: creatività e maestria nella città del Premio*, Editoriale Sometti, Mantova 2013.
Zani, L., *Fascismo, autarchia, commercio estero: Felice Guarnieri un tecnocrate al servizio dello «Stato nuovo»*, Il Mulino, Bologna 1996.
Zanoni, E., «"Per Voi, Signore": Gendered Representations of Fashion, Food, and Fascism in Il Progresso Italo-Americano during the 1930's», *Journal of American Ethnic History*, 31, n. 3, 2012, pp. 33-71.

INDEX

Adani, Laura: 170
Ajazzi & Fantechi: 49
Agnelli, Virginia: 159
Alda: 182
Alessandrini, Renato: 148
Altara, Edina: 101, 104, 182
Alvino, Rodolfo: 103
Anna, Madame: 43, 116, 117, 188
Aprato: 161, 162

Bacci, Lina: 182
Balla, Giacomo: 147
Banti, Anna: 104
Barbieri: 147
Barzini, Luigi: 101, 104
Battaglia, Maria: 138
Bellini, Emilia: 143
Bellom: 25
Belmoda: 156, 157
Benjamin, Walter: 19
Benois, Nicola: 176
Bergman, Vera: 174
Berman, Marshall: 21
Bevilacqua, Giuseppe: 182
Bianchi, Vittorina: 103
Bianchi-Mina, Ivan: 26, 27
Biki: 20, 49, 108, 138, 143, 153, 159, 170, 176
Bilinsky: 174
Binello, Maria Rosa: 147, 162
Blasetti, Alessandro: 168

Bo, Lina: 68, 104, 123, 126
Boetto, Giulio: 57
Bonnard, Mario: 174
Bontempelli, Massimo: 104
Borgialli: 25
Borletti, Ida Pozzi: 142
Borsalino: 163
Botti, Sisters: 147
Branchini, Luigi: 67
Breward, Cristopher: 21
Bricarelli: 103
Brignone, Guido: 178, 185
Brin, Irene: 101, 104, 123, 167
Bronzini, Gegia: 46, 145
Bronzini, Marisa: 46
Bronzo, Maria: 25
Bruschi, Dora: 159
Buscaroli: 49
Butazzi, Graziella: 29

Cagossi, Ida: 13
Calamai, Clara: 178, 180, 181, 188
Calzini, Raffaele: 17
Camerini, Mario: 175, 186
Capponi, Giuseppe: 185
Caracciolo, Giovanna: 124
Carboni, Erberto: 100
Carboni, Giacomo: 114
Carocci, Eva: 103
Carolina, Donna: 117

Carosa: 124
Carosio, Margherita: 182
Castellani, Mario: 24
Castellani, Renato: 178
Cattadori, Germana: 144
Cecchi, Emilio: 101, 104
Cederna, Camilla: 13-15
Cegani, Elena: 168
Celani, Beatrice: 103
Celani, Elena: 8, 101, 104, 108, 109, 134, 135, 142, 143, 163-65
Cerri: 164
Ciano, Costanzo: 117
Ciano, Edda: 48, 116-19, 188
Ciano, Galeazzo: 116-18, 120
Ciano, Maria: 117
Cicogna, Annamaria: 142, 143
Ciuti, Enrico: 103, 126
Colasanti, Veniero: 178
Colonna, Simonetta: 124
Colonna, Stefanella: 124
Comolli: 143
Contex: 163
Conti, Ettore: 41
Coronedi, P. H.: 19
Crawford, Joan: 168
Cromwell, John: 174

D'Annunzio, Gabriele: 182
D'Elys, Flora: 43
Dafmi: 157
Dal Forno, Gian Giacomo: 126
Dal Pozzo, Barbara: 118
De Angeli-Frua: 144, 157
De Gasperi-Zezza: 25, 49, 147
De Grazia, Victoria: 9, 10, 12, 13
De Liguoro, Lydia: 29
De Pisis, Filippo: 126
De Reutern, Luciana: 103, 124, 151
De Rossi: 25
De Vincentis, Luigi: 115
Dea, Marie: 174
Della Sciarra, Stefanella: 103
Dessalles, Barbara Rota: 124
Di Fenizio: 49
Di Robilant, Gabriella Bosdari: 103, 123
Dietrich, Marlene: 168
Dolci, Carlo: 158
Dompè, Giovanna: 51
Dragoni: 49, 174
Duranti, Doris: 180, 181

Evangelisti, Anna: 104
Evans, Caroline: 21

Fantechi, Augusta: 43
Farinacci, Roberto: 36
Fercioni: 49, 139, 178, 181
Ferracini, Silvio: 29
Ferragamo, Salvatore: 156
Ferrario: 157, 163
Ferrati, Sara: 182
Fields, Gracie: 120
Fiorini, Guido: 185
Filippini, Piera: 181
Fontaine, Joan: 178
Fontana Sisters: 20
Francini, Alberto: 103
Fratti, Giuliano: 151
Freddi, Luigi: 168
Freud, Sigmund: 16
Frigerio, Mario: 48
Fulchignoni, Enrico: 102

Gabriellasport: 49, 123, 143, 144, 147
Galdieri, Michele: 176
Galleani, Lea: 143

Index

Gallone, Carmine: 187
Gambino: 138, 147, 162
Gandini: 147
Garbo, Greta: 168
Garretto, Paolo: 104
Gentile, Emilio: 17, 19, 183
Giobergia: 25
Gioi, Vivi: 171, 188
Giorgini, Giovanni Battista: 123
Giovannelli, Aurora: 124
Giovannetti, Eugenio: 170-75, 178, 180, 185
Giuriati, Giovanni: 26
Giusta Manca di Villahermosa: 137
Gomez, Pier Filippo: 103, 105, 106
Gori, Beppina: 49, 125, 138, 188
Gray, Ezio Maria: 102
Guareschi, Giovannino: 74
Guarini, Alfredo: 174
Guarnati, Daria: 130
Guido, Carla: 103
Guillermaz: 164
Gundle, Stephen: 11, 183-88

Haake, Lina: 103
Hay, James: 186
Hitchcock, Alfred: 178
Hollander, Anne: 22
Hunt, Lynn: 113
Hutton, Barbara: 120

Irene di Savoia: 48

Keller, Dr.: 64

Lamma, Fernanda: 46, 47
Landis Nadoolman, Deborah: 172
Lazzaro, Claudia: 9

Le Bon, Gustav: 16
Leumann, Roberto: 112
Levi, Carlo: 185
Levi-Montalcini, Gino: 24
Ley, Robert: 64
Lilly Mode: 164
Lionella: 164, 182
Lodomez, Vera Rossi: 104, 153
Lojacono, Vincenzo: 117
Lombard, Carole: 174
Lombardo, Ester: 36
Lotti, Mariella: 178

Magistrati, Massimo: 117
Malossi, Giannino: 184
Maltagliati, Evi: 170
Mancini, Beatrice: 171
Manthey, Dr: 64
Marchiò, Fanni: 182
Margherita: 151
Maria Cristina: 161
Marinucci, Vinicio: 180, 181
Marucelli, Germana: 20, 43
Masino, Paola: 121
Massel, Teresa: 124
Matarazzo, Raffaello: 178
Mateldi, Brunetta: 101, 104, 107, 124, 126, 127, 159, 165-67, 180, 186
Matrigali: 144
Mattè: 49, 138, 168
McDowell, Colin: 71
Meano, Cesare: 40, 41, 100, 128, 154
Medin, Gastone: 185
Merlini, Marisa: 188
Michaelles, Ernesto: 103
Miranda, Isa: 174, 188
Mo, Francesco Ilorini: 123
Modelia: 147

Mola, Norberto: 48
Montano, Vittorio: 24
Montenegro, Conchita: 174
Moretti: 147
Moschini: 147
Mossotti: 58
Musacchio, Jacqueline: 9
Mussolini, Benito: 9-11, 16, 18, 19, 22, 24, 26, 29, 39, 47, 49, 51, 68, 74, 106, 113-19, 128, 138, 175, 183
Myricae: 124

Noberasko, Vita: 20, 139, 147, 158, 187
Noble, Andrew: 119
Noris, Assia: 178
Notari, Umberto: 27
Novarese, Nino: 187

Oberon, Merle: 171
Oppo, Cipriano Efisio: 103, 105, 107
Osiri, Wanda: 182

Pacces, Attilio: 102
Pagano, Giuseppe: 123
Pagnani, Andreina: 178
Pallavicini, Federico: 101, 104, 108, 109, 125, 127, 144, 180
Panissera, Giriodi di Monastero: 70, 102
Paolucci, Enrico: 185
Parolari, Gabriele: 70
Pascali: 164
Paulicelli, Eugenia: 12, 19, 22, 169
Pavanello: 103
Pederzini, Gianna: 138
Pende, Nicola: 17

Petacci, Claretta: 114, 115
Pezzi, Maria: 101, 104
Pirandello, Luigi: 180
Pittoni, Anita: 46, 47
Pius XII: 61
Poe, Edgar Allan: 16
Poli, Nives: 48
Polverelli, Gaetano: 171
Ponti, Gio: 8, 17, 18, 68, 101-112, 123, 125, 127, 129-37, 155, 156, 158, 170, 173
Prampolini, Enrico: 126
Primalba: 163, 164
Proietti: 163
Pucci, Emilio: 117
Puccini, Giacomo: 48

Ricci, Umberto: 24
Ridenti, Lucio: 48, 100, 101, 103, 108, 110, 111, 123, 125, 152, 174-76
Riesla: 151
Righelli, Gennaro: 185
Rina: 164
Rissone, Giuditta: 178
Robiola, Elsa: 17, 101, 103, 107-10, 123, 129, 138, 139, 141, 142, 158, 159, 161, 164, 166
Robiolio: 138
Rovescalli: 182
Rudofsky, Bernard: 129, 173
Ruffo di Bagnara, Marinetta: 151

Sacerdote: 25
San Lorenzo: 161
Sanfelice di Monteforte, Marita: 159
Saporiti, Maria Teresa: 137
Sarfatti, Margherita: 118.
Savinio, Alberto: 104.

Schettini: 181.
Schiaparelli, Elsa: 53, 153.
Sciarra, Stefanella: 103
Seiter, William: 175
Sensani, Gino: 175, 186
Serafin, Tullio: 48
Sheridan, Richard B.: 178
Simmel, Georg: 12
Siodmak, Robert: 174
Soldati, Mario: 174
Starace, Achille: 47, 173
Steele, Valerie: 148, 183, 184

Tancredi, Tancredo: 103
Targiani Giunti, Irene: 13
Tenyelmann, Dr: 64
Tessital: 156
Testa, Michelangelo: 112, 165
Tizzoni: 124, 147, 163, 164
Tofanelli, Arturo: 123
Tofano, Rosetta: 176, 177
Tofano, Sergio: 176, 177
Toninelli: 157
Torrieri, Diana: 181
Traglia: 151
Trinelli: 49, 138, 147

Valente, Manette: 163
Valla, Ondina: 141
Valli, Alida: 174, 180
Valstar: 163
Vanna: 20, 142, 144, 147, 158, 163, 164
Vazsari: 182
Veneziani: 20
Ventura: 24, 43, 49, 124, 125, 137, 147, 170
Villa: 49, 147, 163
Viora: 151
Visconti, Luchino: 188
Visconti, Nicoletta: 143
Voga: 161

Williams, Mona: 120
Wilson, Elizabeth: 171
Wilson, Perry: 15
Wyler, William: 171

Zanollo: 153
Zecca: 49, 174
Zoppelli, Lia: 181

ACKNOWLEDGEMENTS

This book would not have been possible without the kind cooperation of many individuals. Among them, Marco di Maggio, Paolo Acanfora, Alessio Gagliardi and Professor Emeritus Emilio Gentile.

Further thanks go to Viviana Damiano and Claudia Pracanica of the historic Library *Fiamma Lanzara* of the Accademia di Costume e Moda in Rome who, with care and professionalism, assisted me during the consultation of *Bellezza Mensile dell'alta moda e della vita italiana* and help obtain permission to reproduce images of the fashion items discussed in this book.

This project started as a thesis in the very special department of History Anthropology Religions Performing Arts (SARAS) of Sapienza University, Rome. An infinite thank you to my supervisor Romana Andò, who helped me navigate tough times, to my committee members, Gianluca Fiocco, Maria Cristina Marchetti and Valerij Ljubin, to Eugenia Paulicelli – whose work inspired this book – and Patrizia Calefato, who were thoughtful and precious voices, and to Alessandro Saggioro, who believed in me since day one. I am deeply grateful for the friendship and support offered by Sapienza University and my PhD colleagues.

During a postdoctoral fellowship at the University of Udine, the Department of Humanities and Cultural Heritage warmly welcomed me and helped me to negotiate the transitions from PhD student to faculty member and from dissertation to book. Thank you in particular to Francesco Pitassio and the students of my seminar "*Lo spettacolo della moda*" (The Spectacle of Fashion).

This project would not have been possible without financial support received from Sapienza University.

Most of all, thank you to Alberto, and Beatrice, Aurelio and Vito.

MIMESIS GROUP
www.mimesis-group.com

MIMESIS INTERNATIONAL
www.mimesisinternational.com
info@mimesisinternational.com

MIMESIS EDIZIONI
www.mimesisedizioni.it
mimesis@mimesisedizioni.it

ÉDITIONS MIMÉSIS
www.editionsmimesis.fr
info@editionsmimesis.fr

MIMESIS COMMUNICATION
www.mim-c.net

MIMESIS EU
www.mim-eu.com

Printed by
Rotomail Italia S.p.A.
April 2023

www.ingramcontent.com/pod-product-compliance
Lightning Source LLC
Chambersburg PA
CBHW031426150426
43191CB00006B/413